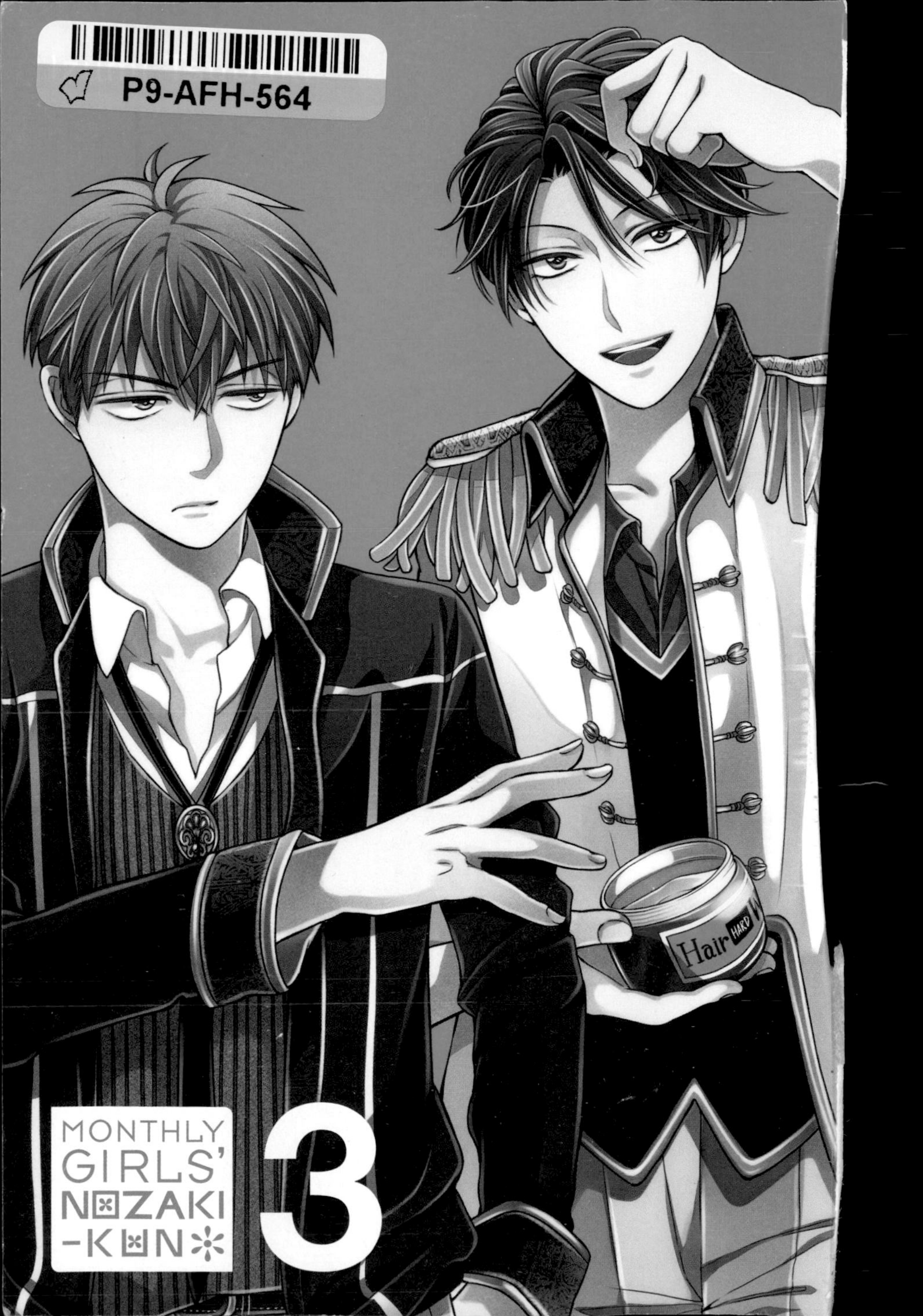
MONTHLY
GIRLS'
NOZAKI
-KUN
3
Hair HARD

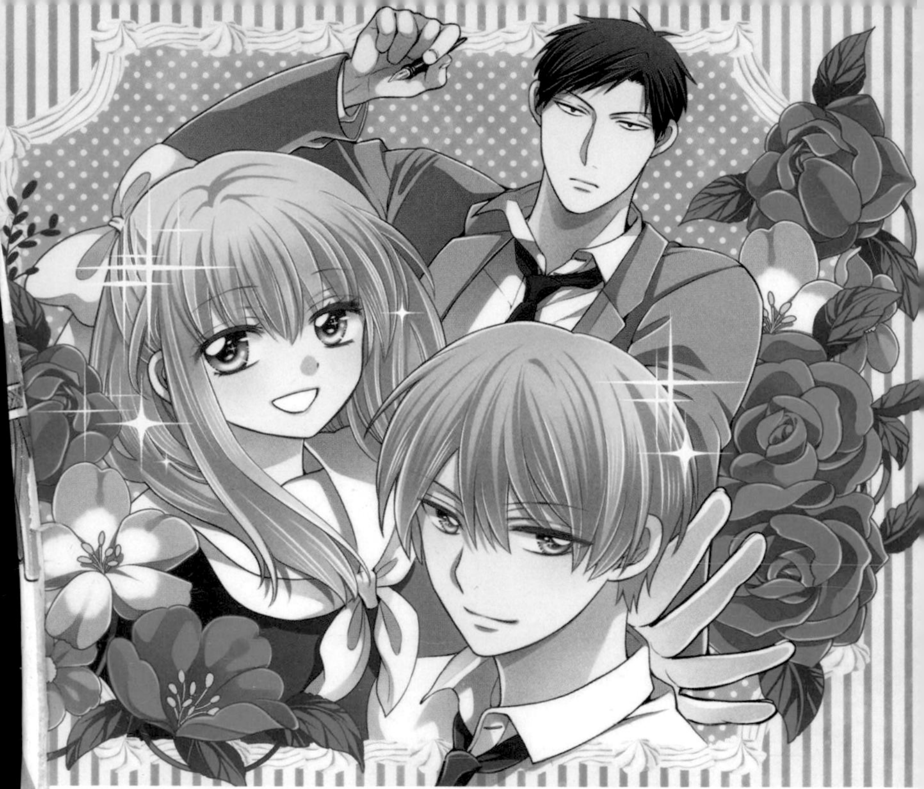

MONTHLY GIRLS' NOZAKI-KUN 3

contents

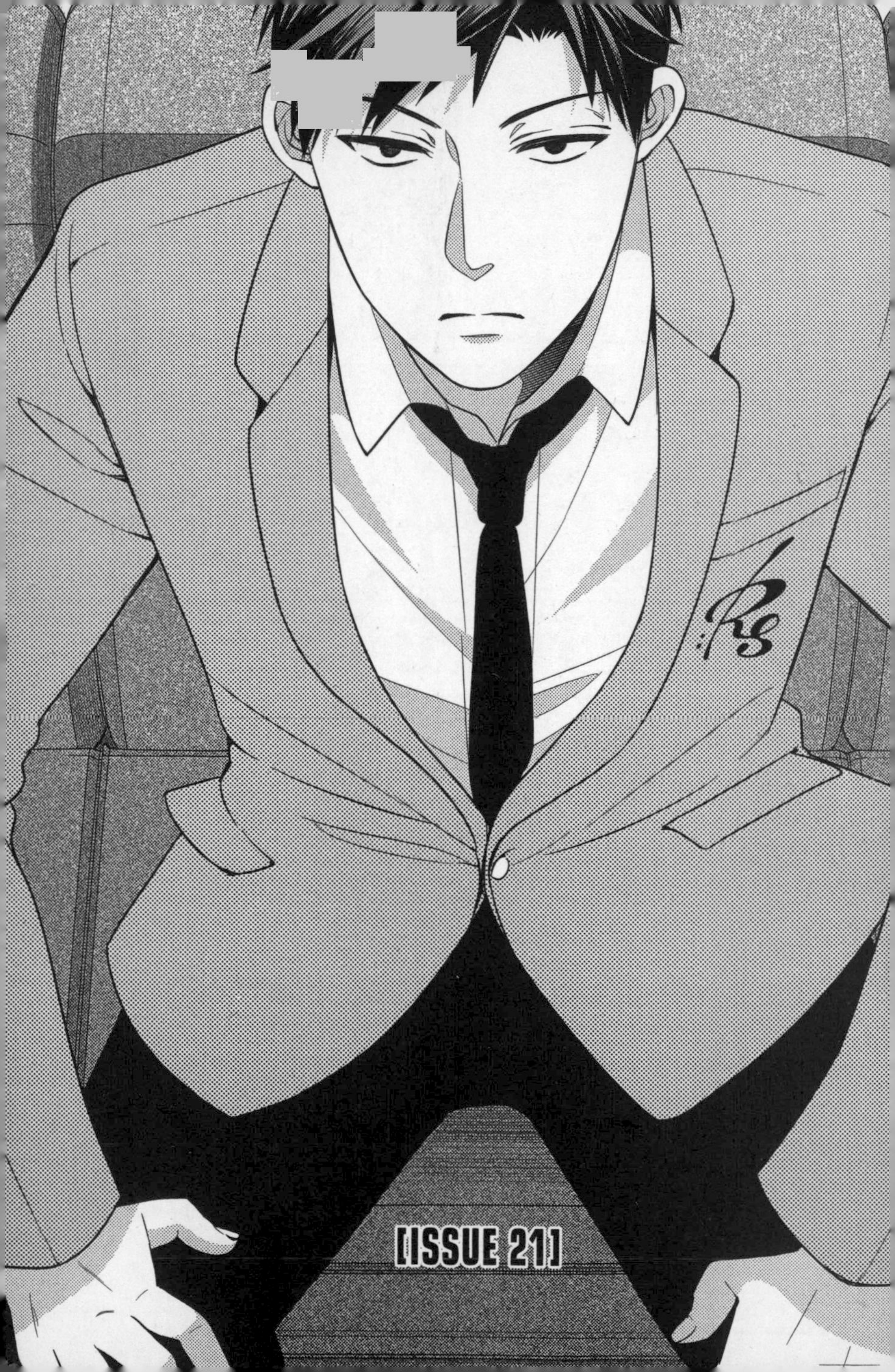
[ISSUE 21]

DON'T YOU REGRET IT

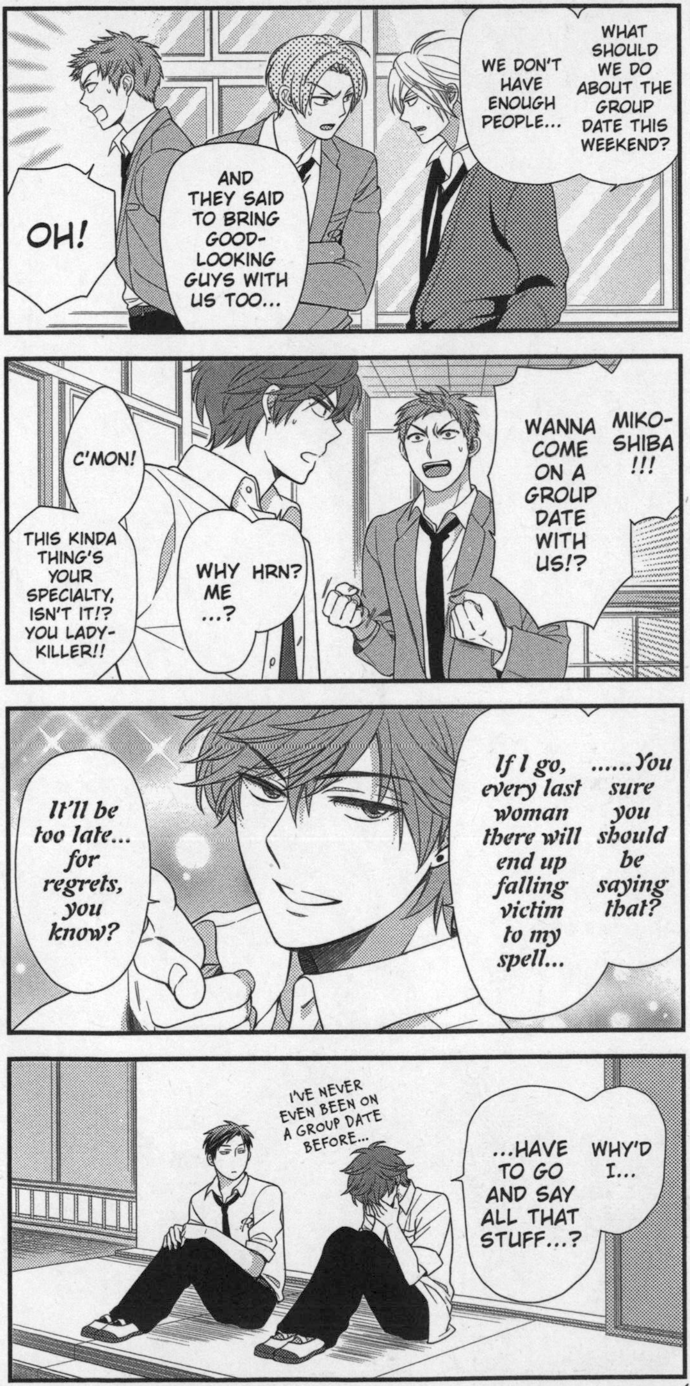
WHAT SHOULD WE DO ABOUT THE GROUP DATE THIS WEEKEND?
WE DON'T HAVE ENOUGH PEOPLE...
AND THEY SAID TO BRING GOOD-LOOKING GUYS WITH US TOO...
OH!
MIKO-SHIBA!!!
WANNA COME ON A GROUP DATE WITH US!?
HRN?
WHY ME...?
C'MON!
THIS KINDA THING'S YOUR SPECIALTY, ISN'T IT!? YOU LADY-KILLER!!
......You sure you should be saying that?
If I go, every last woman there will end up falling victim to my spell...
It'll be too late... for regrets, you know?
WHY'D I...
...HAVE TO GO AND SAY ALL THAT STUFF...?
I'VE NEVER EVEN BEEN ON A GROUP DATE BEFORE...

FIRST REHEARSAL

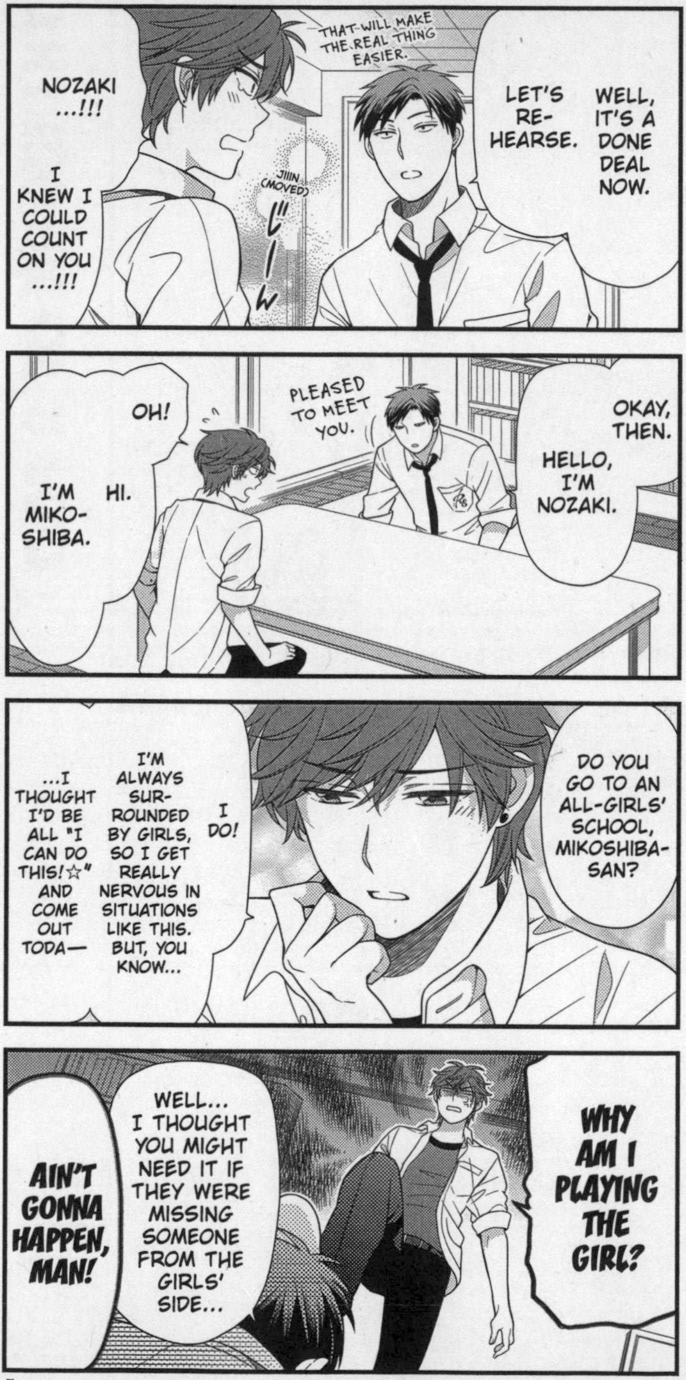

WELL, IT'S A DONE DEAL NOW.
LET'S RE-HEARSE.
THAT WILL MAKE THE REAL THING EASIER.
JIIIN (MOVED)
NOZAKI ...!!!
I KNEW I COULD COUNT ON YOU ...!!!
OKAY, THEN.
HELLO, I'M NOZAKI.
PLEASED TO MEET YOU.
OH!
HI.
I'M MIKO-SHIBA.
DO YOU GO TO AN ALL-GIRLS' SCHOOL, MIKOSHIBA-SAN?
I DO!
I'M ALWAYS SUR-ROUNDED BY GIRLS, SO I GET REALLY NERVOUS IN SITUATIONS LIKE THIS. BUT, YOU KNOW...
...I THOUGHT I'D BE ALL "I CAN DO THIS!☆" AND COME OUT TODA—
WHY AM I PLAYING THE GIRL?
WELL... I THOUGHT YOU MIGHT NEED IT IF THEY WERE MISSING SOMEONE FROM THE GIRLS' SIDE...
AIN'T GONNA HAPPEN, MAN!

THE WORK OF A PRO

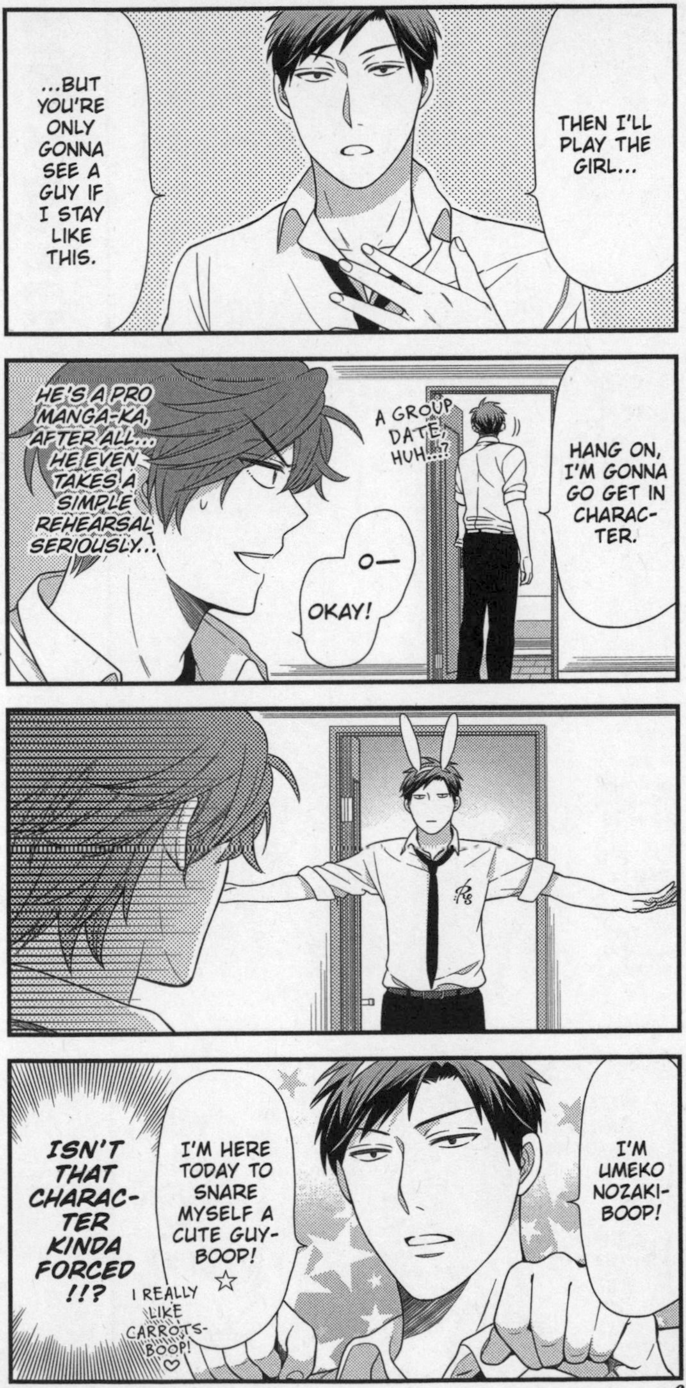
THEN I'LL PLAY THE GIRL...
...BUT YOU'RE ONLY GONNA SEE A GUY IF I STAY LIKE THIS.
HANG ON, I'M GONNA GO GET IN CHARACTER.
A GROUP DATE, HUH...?
O— OKAY!
HE'S A PRO MANGA-KA, AFTER ALL... HE EVEN TAKES A SIMPLE REHEARSAL SERIOUSLY...
I'M UMEKO NOZAKI-BOOP!
I'M HERE TODAY TO SNARE MYSELF A CUTE GUY-BOOP! ☆
I REALLY LIKE CARROTS-BOOP! ♡
ISN'T THAT CHARACTER KINDA FORCED!!?

※IN THE ORIGINAL, NOZAKI ADDS -PYON TO THE ENDS OF UMEKO'S SENTENCES. THIS IS BOTH A CUTESY VERBAL TIC THAT WAS POPULAR IN 1980s JAPAN AND AN ONOMATOPOEIC WORD ASSOCIATED WITH BUNNIES AND HOPPING.

NOZAKI'S BUDDY

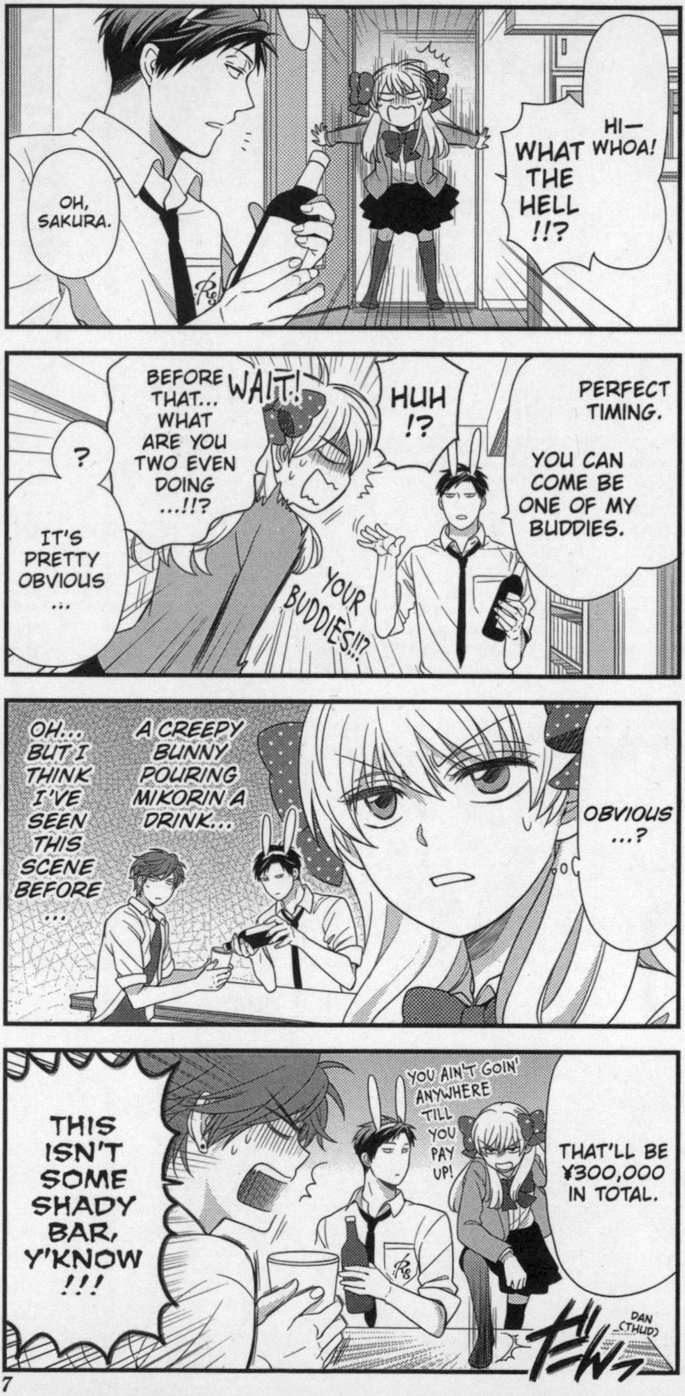
HI— WHOA! WHAT THE HELL!!?
OH, SAKURA.
PERFECT TIMING.
YOU CAN COME BE ONE OF MY BUDDIES.
HUH!?
YOUR BUDDIES!!?
WAIT!
BEFORE THAT... WHAT ARE YOU TWO EVEN DOING...!!?
?
IT'S PRETTY OBVIOUS...
OBVIOUS...?
A CREEPY BUNNY POURING MIKORIN A DRINK...
OH... BUT I THINK I'VE SEEN THIS SCENE BEFORE...
THAT'LL BE ¥300,000 IN TOTAL.
YOU AIN'T GOIN' ANYWHERE TILL YOU PAY UP!
DAN (THUD)
THIS ISN'T SOME SHADY BAR, Y'KNOW!!!

GIRL POWER

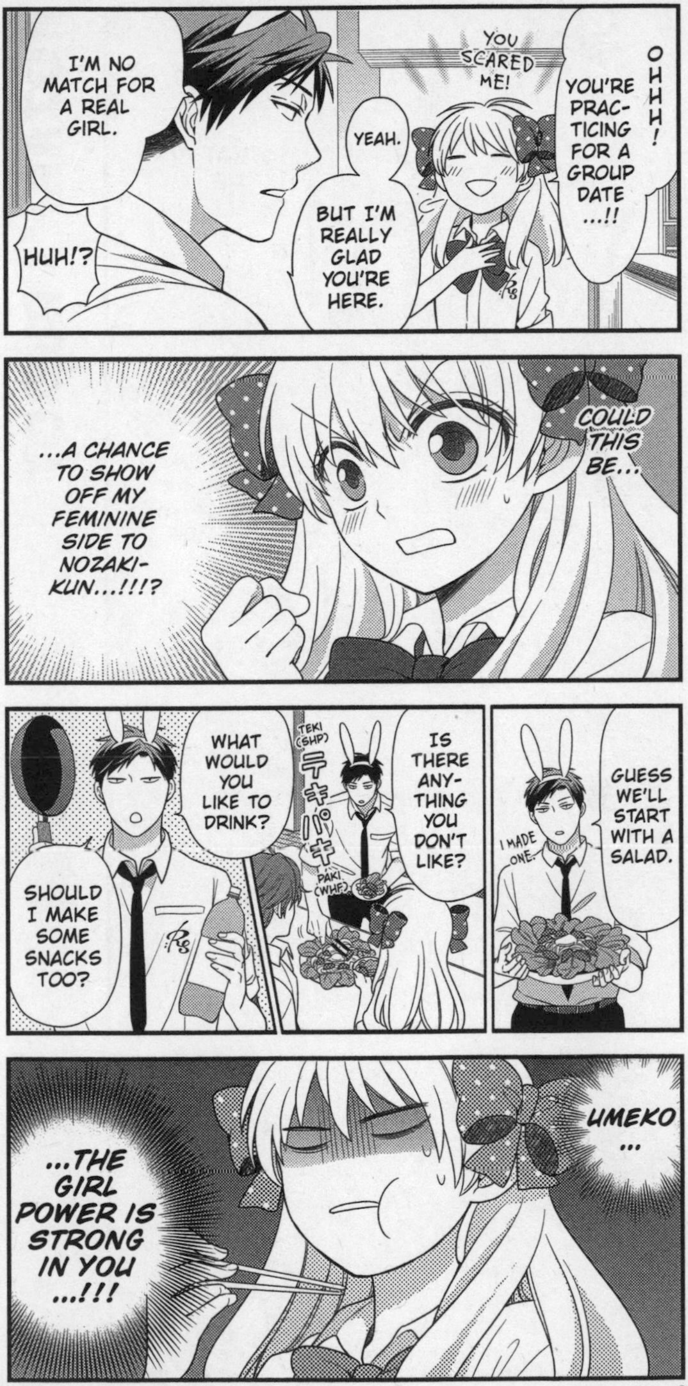
OHHH!
YOU'RE PRAC-TICING FOR A GROUP DATE ...!!
YOU SCARED ME!
YEAH.
BUT I'M REALLY GLAD YOU'RE HERE.
I'M NO MATCH FOR A REAL GIRL.
HUH!?
COULD THIS BE...
...A CHANCE TO SHOW OFF MY FEMININE SIDE TO NOZAKI-KUN...!!!?
GUESS WE'LL START WITH A SALAD.
I MADE ONE.
IS THERE ANY-THING YOU DON'T LIKE?
TEKI (SHP)
テキパキ
PAKI (WHF)
WHAT WOULD YOU LIKE TO DRINK?
SHOULD I MAKE SOME SNACKS TOO?
UMEKO ...
...THE GIRL POWER IS STRONG IN YOU ...!!!

NOZAKI-KUN'S GROUP DATE WISDOM ①

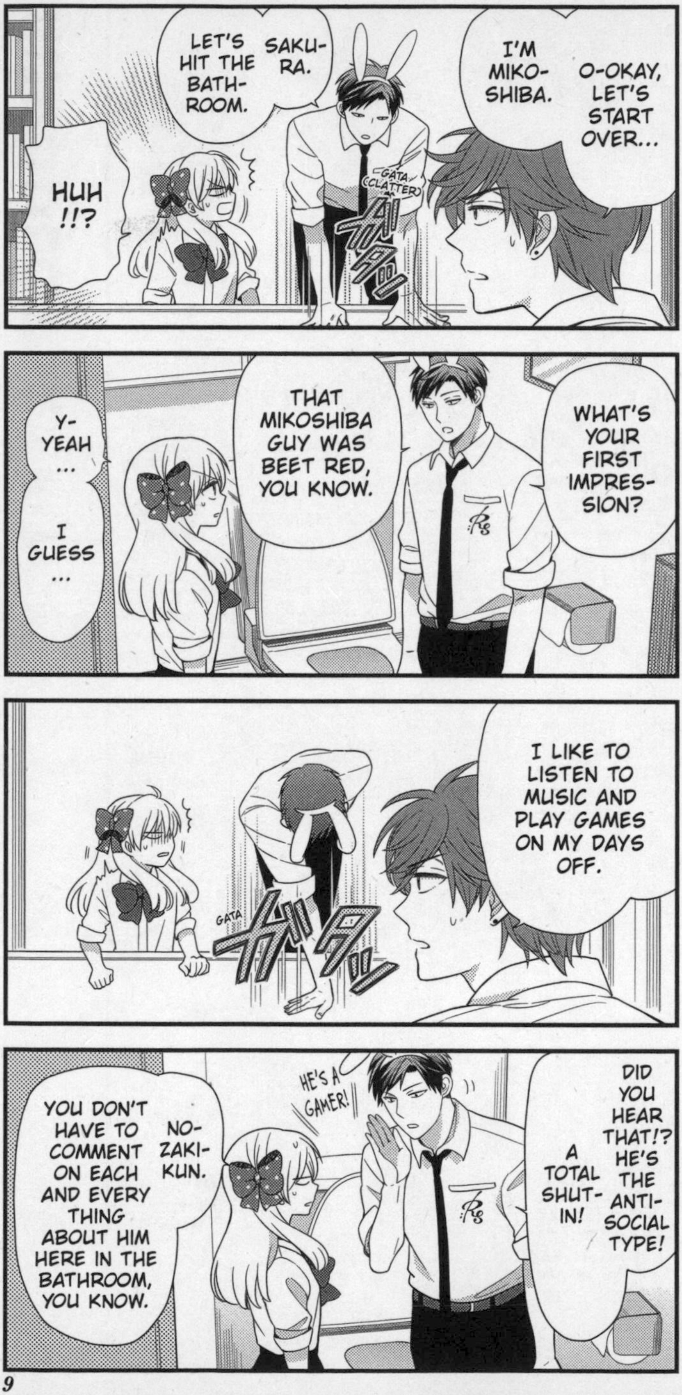
O-OKAY, LET'S START OVER...
I'M MIKO-SHIBA.
SAKU-RA.
LET'S HIT THE BATH-ROOM.
GATA (CLATTER)
HUH!!?
WHAT'S YOUR FIRST IMPRESSION?
THAT MIKOSHIBA GUY WAS BEET RED, YOU KNOW.
Y-YEAH... I GUESS...
I LIKE TO LISTEN TO MUSIC AND PLAY GAMES ON MY DAYS OFF.
GATA
DID YOU HEAR THAT!? HE'S THE ANTI-SOCIAL TYPE!
A TOTAL SHUT-IN!
HE'S A GAMER!
NO-ZAKI-KUN.
YOU DON'T HAVE TO COMMENT ON EACH AND EVERY THING ABOUT HIM HERE IN THE BATHROOM, YOU KNOW.

INTRODUCTORY PITCH

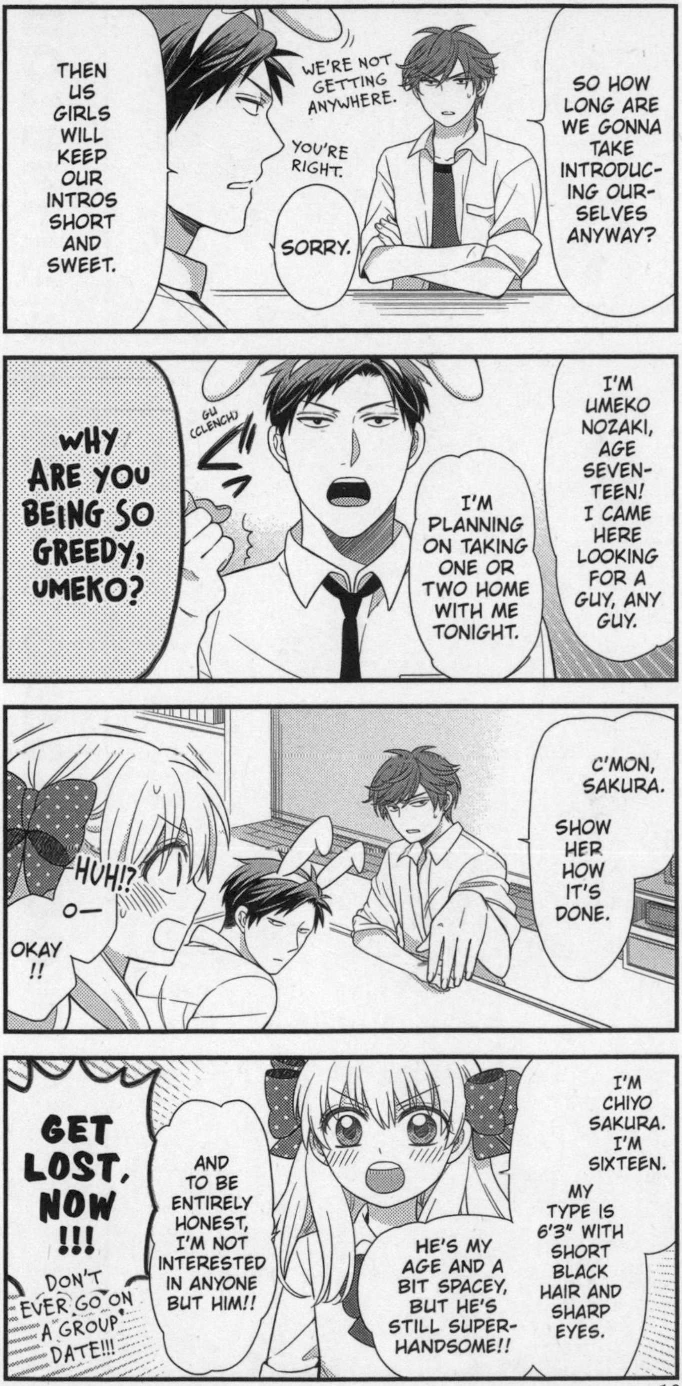

SO HOW LONG ARE WE GONNA TAKE INTRODUCING OURSELVES ANYWAY?
WE'RE NOT GETTING ANYWHERE.
YOU'RE RIGHT.
SORRY.
THEN US GIRLS WILL KEEP OUR INTROS SHORT AND SWEET.
I'M UMEKO NOZAKI, AGE SEVENTEEN! I CAME HERE LOOKING FOR A GUY, ANY GUY.
I'M PLANNING ON TAKING ONE OR TWO HOME WITH ME TONIGHT.
GU (CLENCH)
WHY ARE YOU BEING SO GREEDY, UMEKO?
C'MON, SAKURA.
SHOW HER HOW IT'S DONE.
HUH!?
O—
OKAY !!
I'M CHIYO SAKURA. I'M SIXTEEN.
MY TYPE IS 6'3" WITH SHORT BLACK HAIR AND SHARP EYES.
HE'S MY AGE AND A BIT SPACEY, BUT HE'S STILL SUPER-HANDSOME!!
AND TO BE ENTIRELY HONEST, I'M NOT INTERESTED IN ANYONE BUT HIM!!
GET LOST, NOW !!!
DON'T EVER GO ON A GROUP DATE!!!

NOZAKI-KUN'S GROUP DATE WISDOM ②

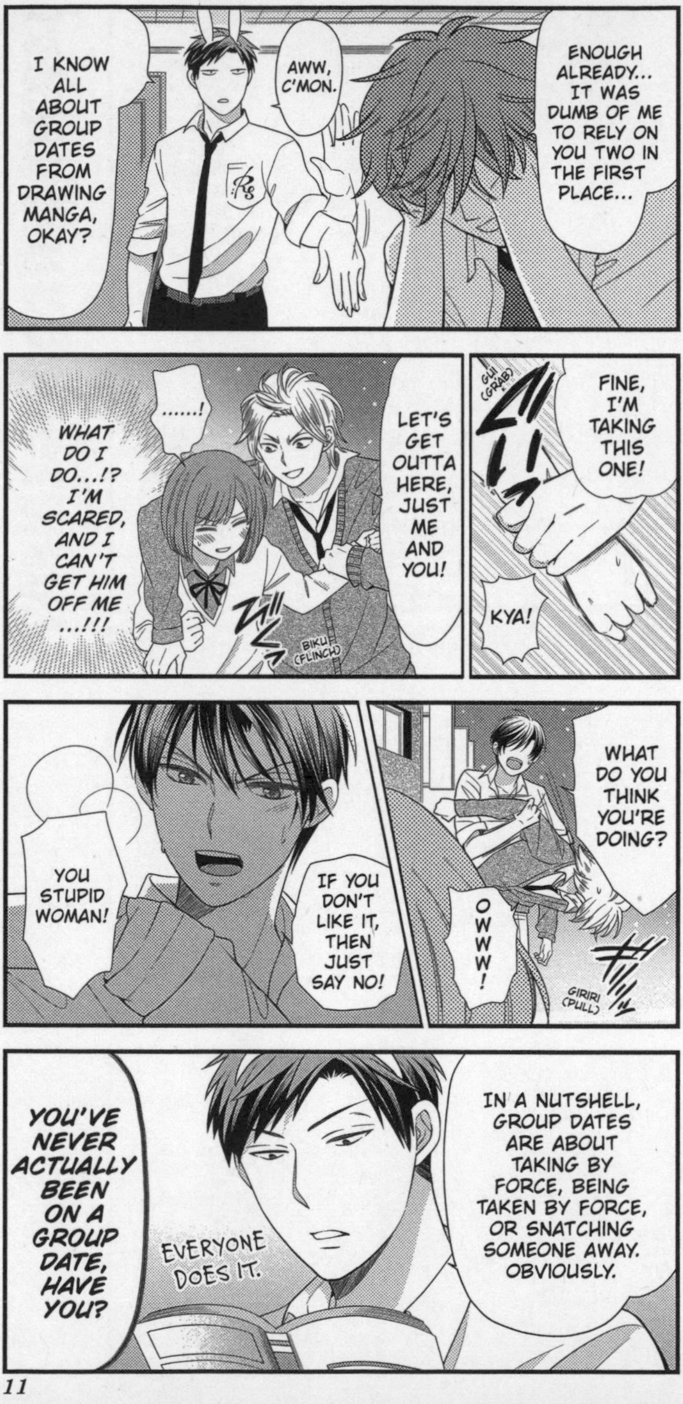

ENOUGH ALREADY... IT WAS DUMB OF ME TO RELY ON YOU TWO IN THE FIRST PLACE...
AWW, C'MON.
I KNOW ALL ABOUT GROUP DATES FROM DRAWING MANGA, OKAY?
GUI (GRAB)
FINE, I'M TAKING THIS ONE!
KYA!
LET'S GET OUTTA HERE, JUST ME AND YOU!
......!
WHAT DO I DO...!? I'M SCARED, AND I CAN'T GET HIM OFF ME ...!!!
BIKU (FLINCH)
WHAT DO YOU THINK YOU'RE DOING?
OWWW!
GIRIRI (PULL)
IF YOU DON'T LIKE IT, THEN JUST SAY NO!
YOU STUPID WOMAN!
IN A NUTSHELL, GROUP DATES ARE ABOUT TAKING BY FORCE, BEING TAKEN BY FORCE, OR SNATCHING SOMEONE AWAY. OBVIOUSLY.
EVERYONE DOES IT.
YOU'VE NEVER ACTUALLY BEEN ON A GROUP DATE, HAVE YOU?

SEATING ARRANGEMENTS

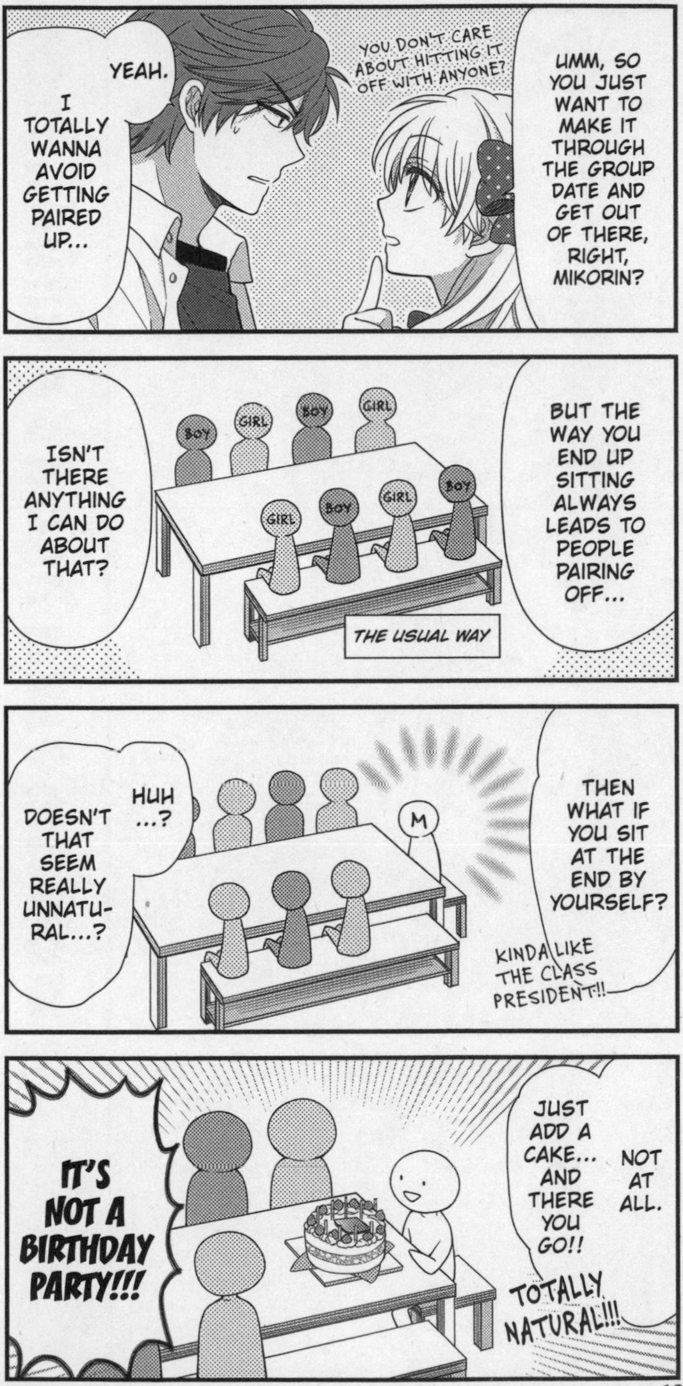
UMM, SO YOU JUST WANT TO MAKE IT THROUGH THE GROUP DATE AND GET OUT OF THERE, RIGHT, MIKORIN?
YOU DON'T CARE ABOUT HITTING IT OFF WITH ANYONE?
YEAH.
I TOTALLY WANNA AVOID GETTING PAIRED UP...
BUT THE WAY YOU END UP SITTING ALWAYS LEADS TO PEOPLE PAIRING OFF...
GIRL
BOY
GIRL
BOY
BOY
GIRL
BOY
GIRL
THE USUAL WAY
ISN'T THERE ANYTHING I CAN DO ABOUT THAT?
THEN WHAT IF YOU SIT AT THE END BY YOURSELF?
KINDA LIKE THE CLASS PRESIDENT!!
M
HUH ...?
DOESN'T THAT SEEM REALLY UNNATU-RAL...?
JUST ADD A CAKE... AND THERE YOU GO!!
NOT AT ALL.
TOTALLY NATURAL!!!
IT'S NOT A BIRTHDAY PARTY!!!

CONVERSATION SKILLS

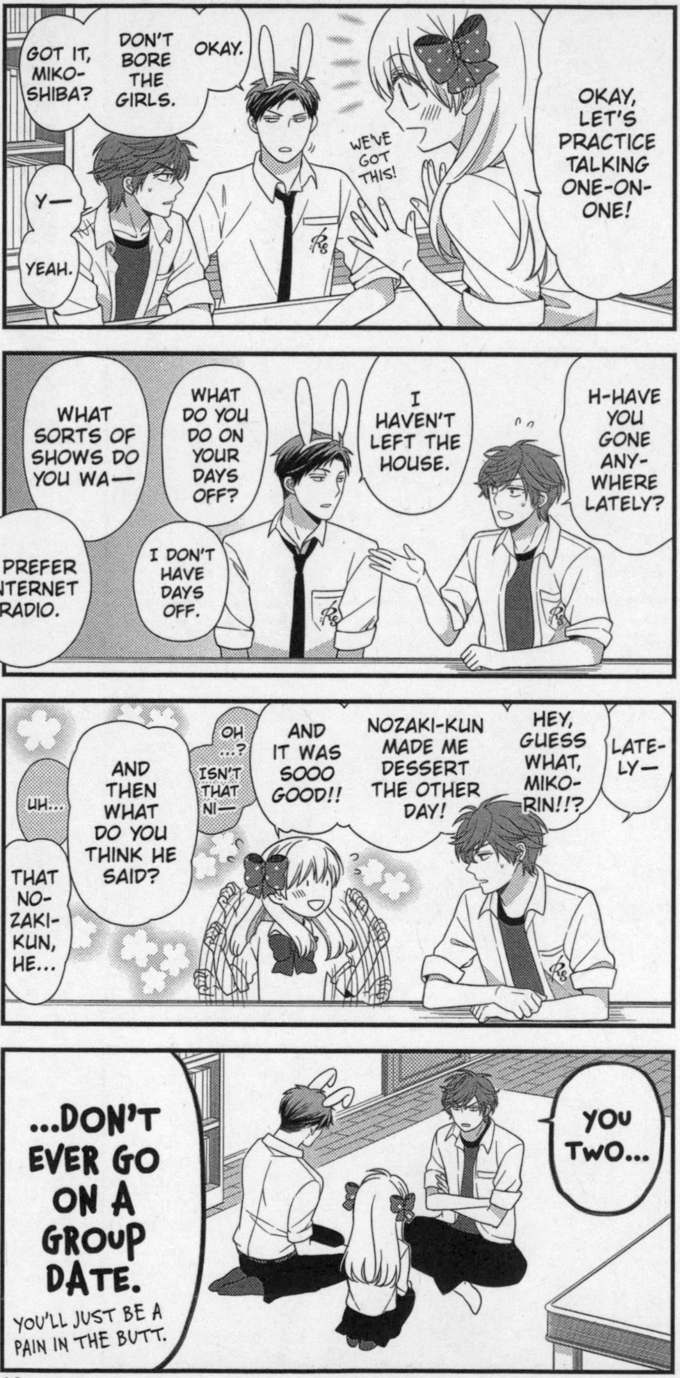
OKAY, LET'S PRACTICE TALKING ONE-ON-ONE!
WE'VE GOT THIS!
OKAY.
DON'T BORE THE GIRLS.
GOT IT, MIKO-SHIBA?
Y—
YEAH.
H-HAVE YOU GONE ANYWHERE LATELY?
I HAVEN'T LEFT THE HOUSE.
WHAT DO YOU DO ON YOUR DAYS OFF?
I DON'T HAVE DAYS OFF.
WHAT SORTS OF SHOWS DO YOU WA—
I PREFER INTERNET RADIO.
LATELY—
HEY, GUESS WHAT, MIKO-RIN!!?
NOZAKI-KUN MADE ME DESSERT THE OTHER DAY!
AND IT WAS SOOO GOOD!!
OH ...? ISN'T THAT NI—
AND THEN WHAT DO YOU THINK HE SAID?
UH...
THAT NOZAKI-KUN, HE...
YOU TWO...
...DON'T EVER GO ON A GROUP DATE.
YOU'LL JUST BE A PAIN IN THE BUTT.

ANGRY MIKORIN

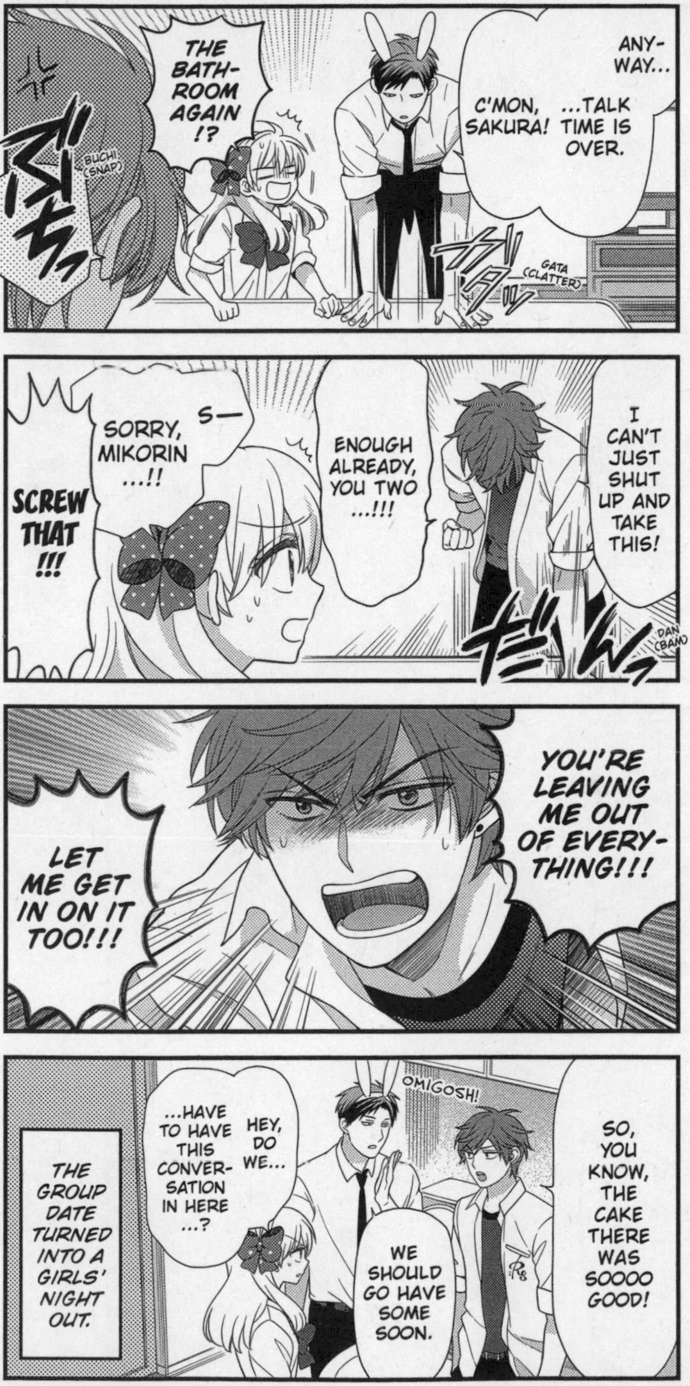
ANY-WAY...
...TALK TIME IS OVER.
C'MON, SAKURA!
GATA (CLATTER)
THE BATH-ROOM AGAIN!?
BUCHI (SNAP)
I CAN'T JUST SHUT UP AND TAKE THIS!
DAN (BAM)
ENOUGH ALREADY, YOU TWO ...!!!
S— SORRY, MIKORIN ...!!
SCREW THAT!!!
YOU'RE LEAVING ME OUT OF EVERY-THING!!!
LET ME GET IN ON IT TOO!!!
SO, YOU KNOW, THE CAKE THERE WAS SOOOO GOOD!
OMIGOSH!
HEY, DO WE...
...HAVE TO HAVE THIS CONVER-SATION IN HERE ...?
WE SHOULD GO HAVE SOME SOON.
THE GROUP DATE TURNED INTO A GIRLS' NIGHT OUT.

AS ONE OF THEM

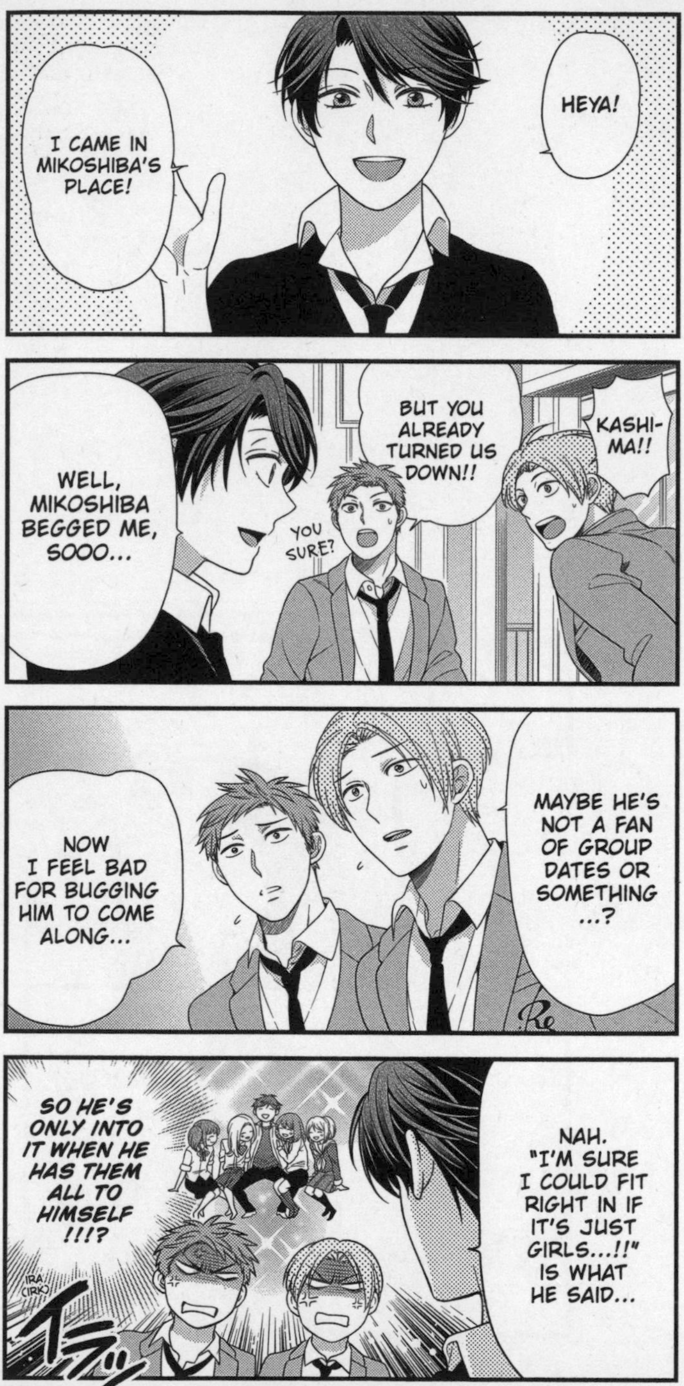

HEYA!
I CAME IN MIKOSHIBA'S PLACE!
KASHI-MA!!
BUT YOU ALREADY TURNED US DOWN!!
YOU SURE?
WELL, MIKOSHIBA BEGGED ME, SOOO...
MAYBE HE'S NOT A FAN OF GROUP DATES OR SOMETHING ...?
NOW I FEEL BAD FOR BUGGING HIM TO COME ALONG...
NAH. "I'M SURE I COULD FIT RIGHT IN IF IT'S JUST GIRLS...!!" IS WHAT HE SAID...
SO HE'S ONLY INTO IT WHEN HE HAS THEM ALL TO HIMSELF !!!?
IRA (IRK)
イラッ

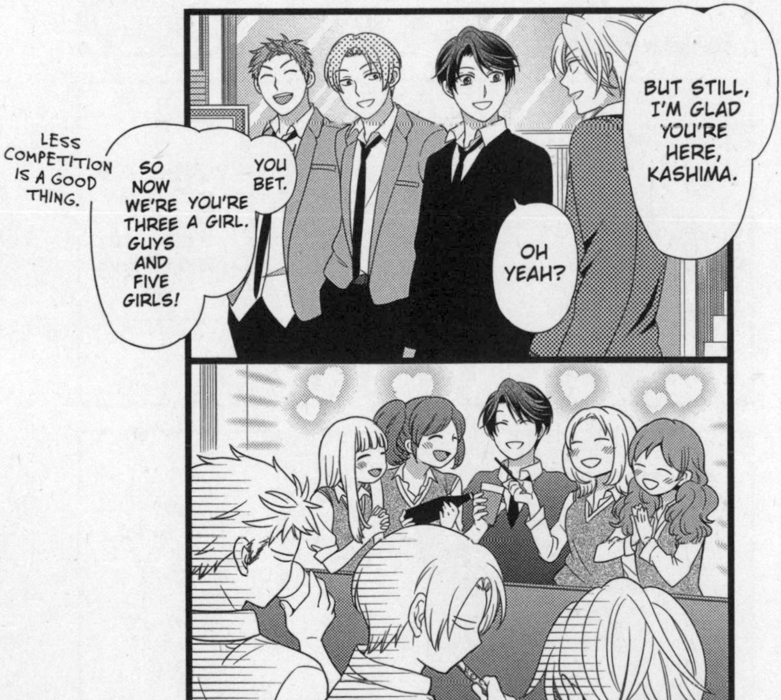
BUT STILL, I'M GLAD YOU'RE HERE, KASHIMA.
OH YEAH?
YOU BET.
YOU'RE A GIRL.
SO NOW WE'RE THREE GUYS AND FIVE GIRLS!
LESS COMPETITION IS A GOOD THING.

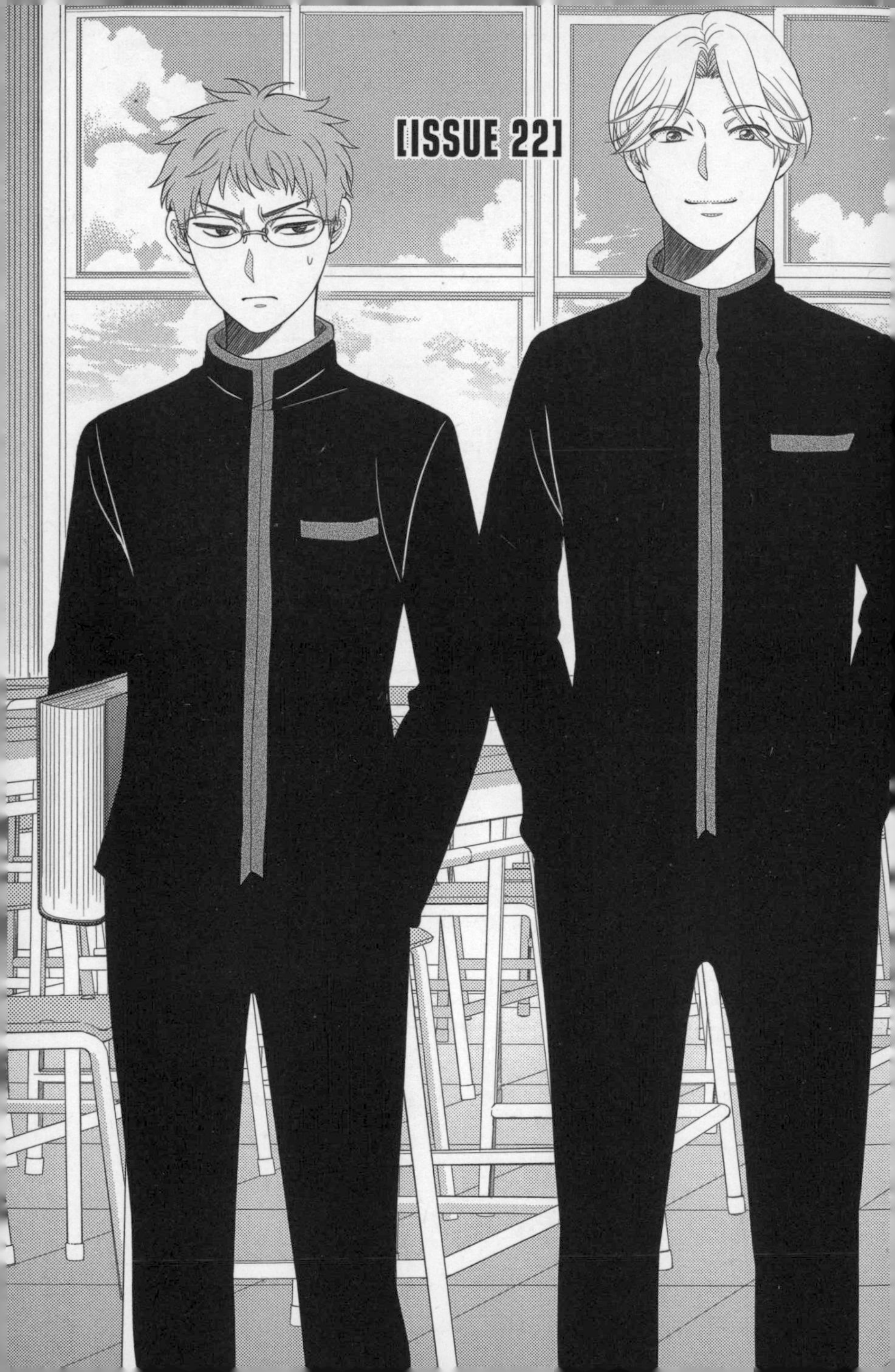
[ISSUE 22]

PRIVATE INFORMATION ①

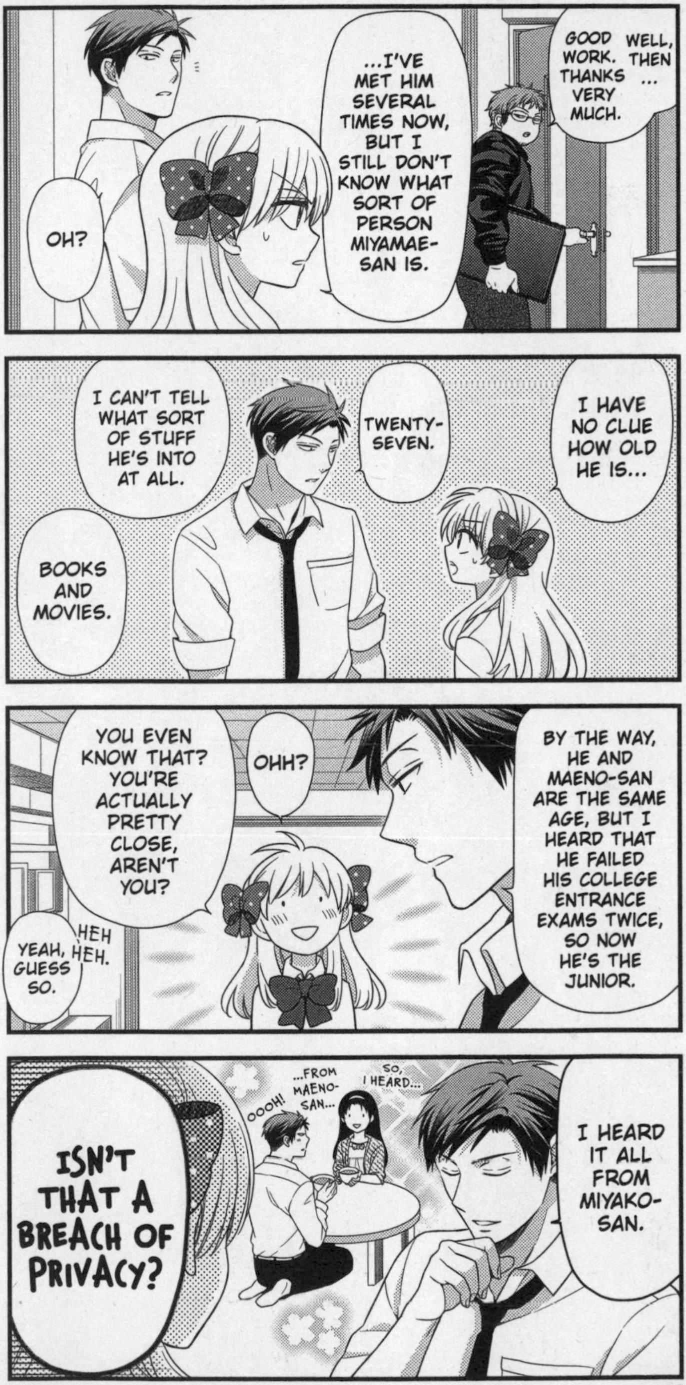
WELL, THEN ...
GOOD WORK. THANKS VERY MUCH.
...I'VE MET HIM SEVERAL TIMES NOW, BUT I STILL DON'T KNOW WHAT SORT OF PERSON MIYAMAE-SAN IS.
OH?
I HAVE NO CLUE HOW OLD HE IS...
TWENTY-SEVEN.
I CAN'T TELL WHAT SORT OF STUFF HE'S INTO AT ALL.
BOOKS AND MOVIES.
BY THE WAY, HE AND MAENO-SAN ARE THE SAME AGE, BUT I HEARD THAT HE FAILED HIS COLLEGE ENTRANCE EXAMS TWICE, SO NOW HE'S THE JUNIOR.
OHH?
YOU EVEN KNOW THAT? YOU'RE ACTUALLY PRETTY CLOSE, AREN'T YOU?
HEH HEH.
YEAH, GUESS SO.
I HEARD IT ALL FROM MIYAKO-SAN.
SO, I HEARD...
...FROM MAENO-SAN...
OOOH!
ISN'T THAT A BREACH OF PRIVACY?

MAENO-SAN AND KEN-SAN

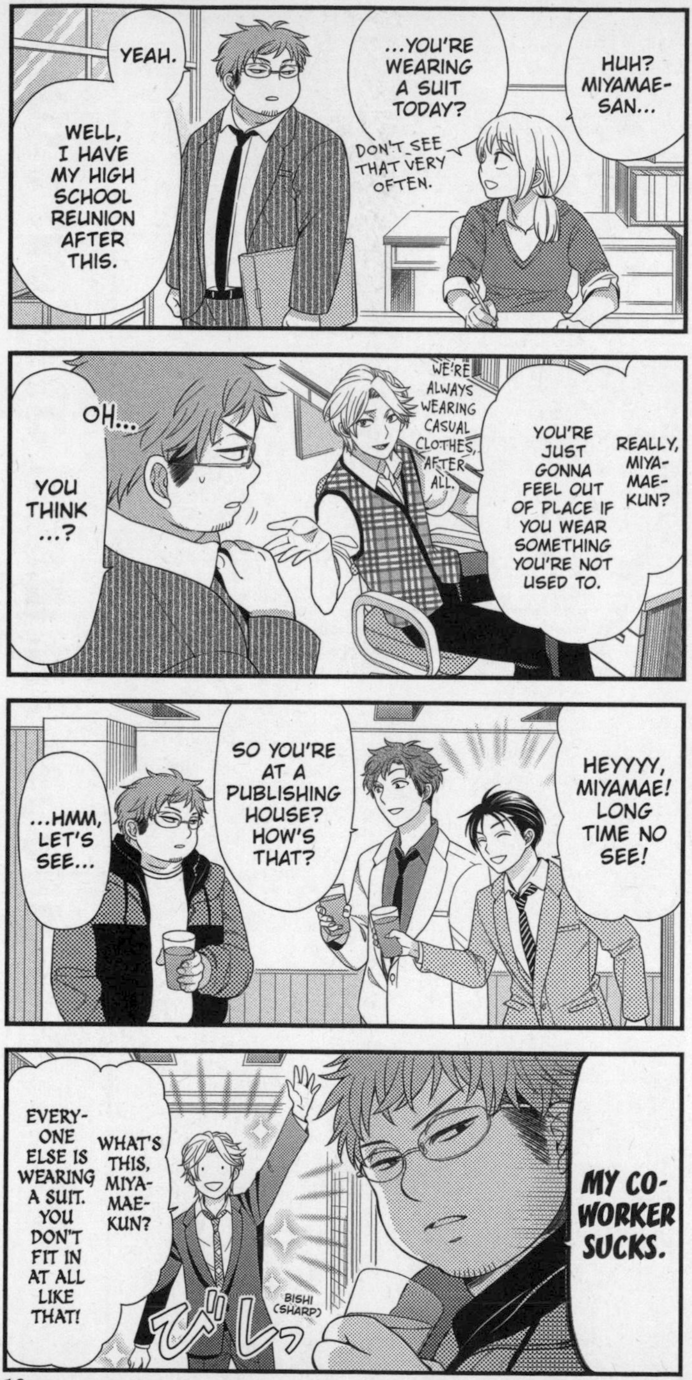
HUH? MIYAMAE-SAN...
...YOU'RE WEARING A SUIT TODAY?
DON'T SEE THAT VERY OFTEN.
YEAH.
WELL, I HAVE MY HIGH SCHOOL REUNION AFTER THIS.
REALLY, MIYAMAE-KUN?
YOU'RE JUST GONNA FEEL OUT OF PLACE IF YOU WEAR SOMETHING YOU'RE NOT USED TO.
WE'RE ALWAYS WEARING CASUAL CLOTHES, AFTER ALL.
OH...
YOU THINK...?
HEYYYY, MIYAMAE! LONG TIME NO SEE!
SO YOU'RE AT A PUBLISHING HOUSE? HOW'S THAT?
...HMM, LET'S SEE...
MY CO-WORKER SUCKS.
BISHI (SHARP)
びしっ
WHAT'S THIS, MIYA-MAE-KUN?
EVERY-ONE ELSE IS WEARING A SUIT. YOU DON'T FIT IN AT ALL LIKE THAT!

WHAT I LEARNED FROM MY SENPAI

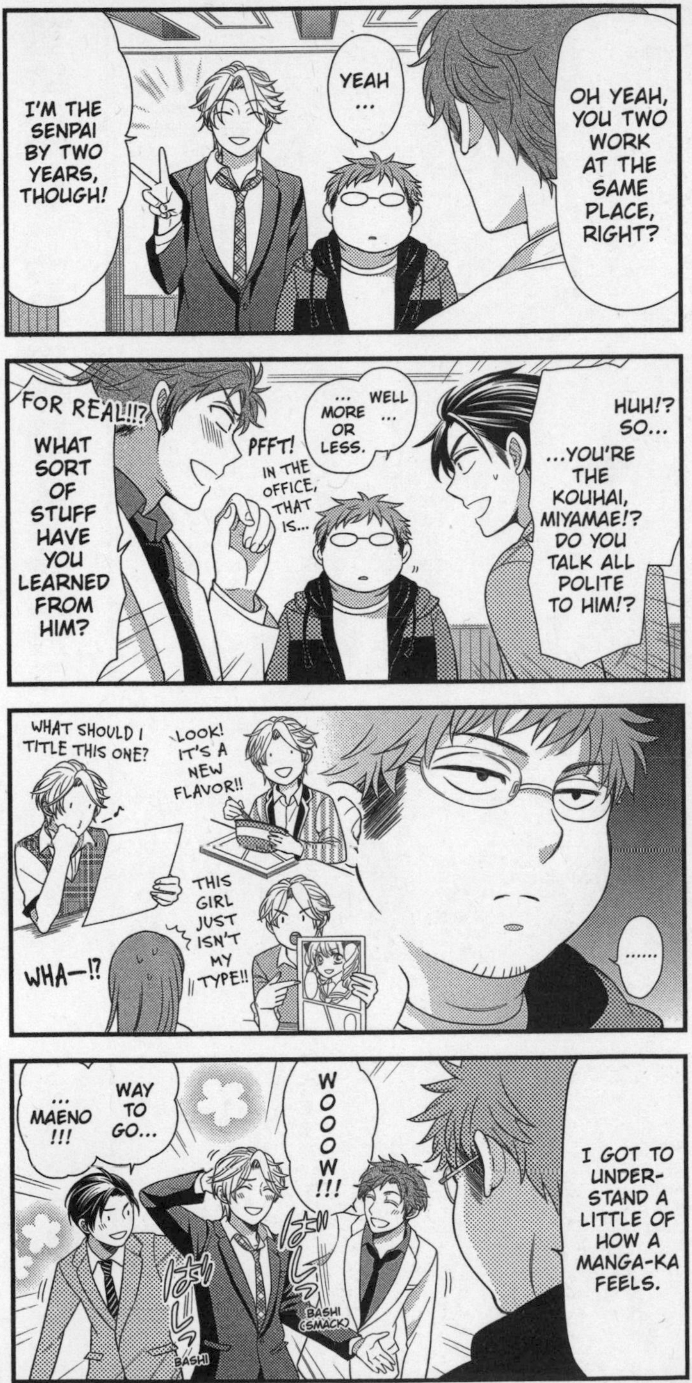

OH YEAH, YOU TWO WORK AT THE SAME PLACE, RIGHT?
YEAH ...
I'M THE SENPAI BY TWO YEARS, THOUGH!
HUH!? SO...
...YOU'RE THE KOUHAI, MIYAMAE!? DO YOU TALK ALL POLITE TO HIM!?
WELL ...
... MORE OR LESS.
IN THE OFFICE, THAT IS...
PFFT!
FOR REAL!!?
WHAT SORT OF STUFF HAVE YOU LEARNED FROM HIM?
......
LOOK! IT'S A NEW FLAVOR!!
WHAT SHOULD I TITLE THIS ONE?
THIS GIRL JUST ISN'T MY TYPE!!
WHA—!?
I GOT TO UNDER-STAND A LITTLE OF HOW A MANGA-KA FEELS.
WOOOOW!!!
BASHI (SMACK)
WAY TO GO...
... MAENO !!!
BASHI

NO ONE UNDERSTANDS

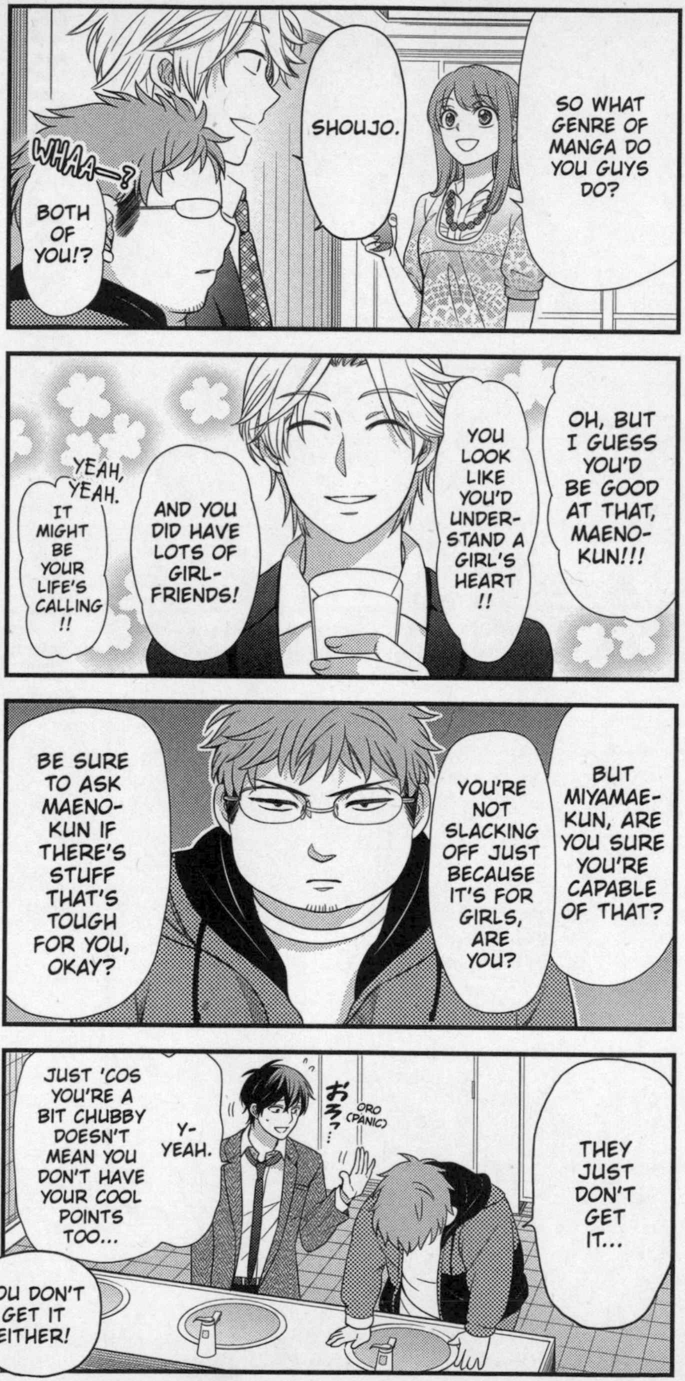

SO WHAT GENRE OF MANGA DO YOU GUYS DO?
SHOUJO.
WHAAA—?
BOTH OF YOU!?
OH, BUT I GUESS YOU'D BE GOOD AT THAT, MAENO-KUN!!!
YOU LOOK LIKE YOU'D UNDER-STAND A GIRL'S HEART!!
AND YOU DID HAVE LOTS OF GIRL-FRIENDS!
YEAH, YEAH.
IT MIGHT BE YOUR LIFE'S CALLING!!
BUT MIYAMAE-KUN, ARE YOU SURE YOU'RE CAPABLE OF THAT?
YOU'RE NOT SLACKING OFF JUST BECAUSE IT'S FOR GIRLS, ARE YOU?
BE SURE TO ASK MAENO-KUN IF THERE'S STUFF THAT'S TOUGH FOR YOU, OKAY?
THEY JUST DON'T GET IT...
おろ…
ORO (PANIC)
Y-YEAH.
JUST 'COS YOU'RE A BIT CHUBBY DOESN'T MEAN YOU DON'T HAVE YOUR COOL POINTS TOO...
YOU DON'T GET IT EITHER!

CAUSE UNKNOWN

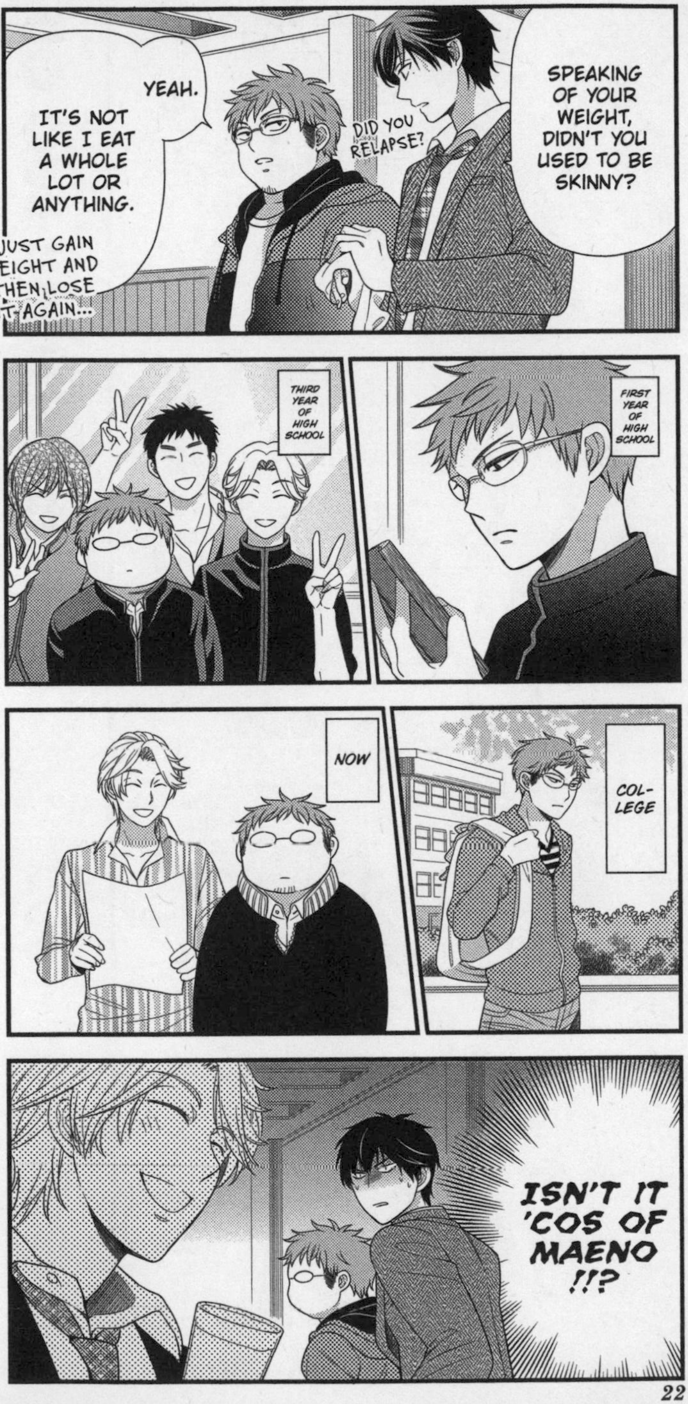
SPEAKING OF YOUR WEIGHT, DIDN'T YOU USED TO BE SKINNY?
DID YOU RELAPSE?
YEAH.
IT'S NOT LIKE I EAT A WHOLE LOT OR ANYTHING.
I JUST GAIN WEIGHT AND THEN LOSE IT AGAIN...
FIRST YEAR OF HIGH SCHOOL
THIRD YEAR OF HIGH SCHOOL
COL-LEGE
NOW
ISN'T IT 'COS OF MAENO!!?

A ROUGH JOB

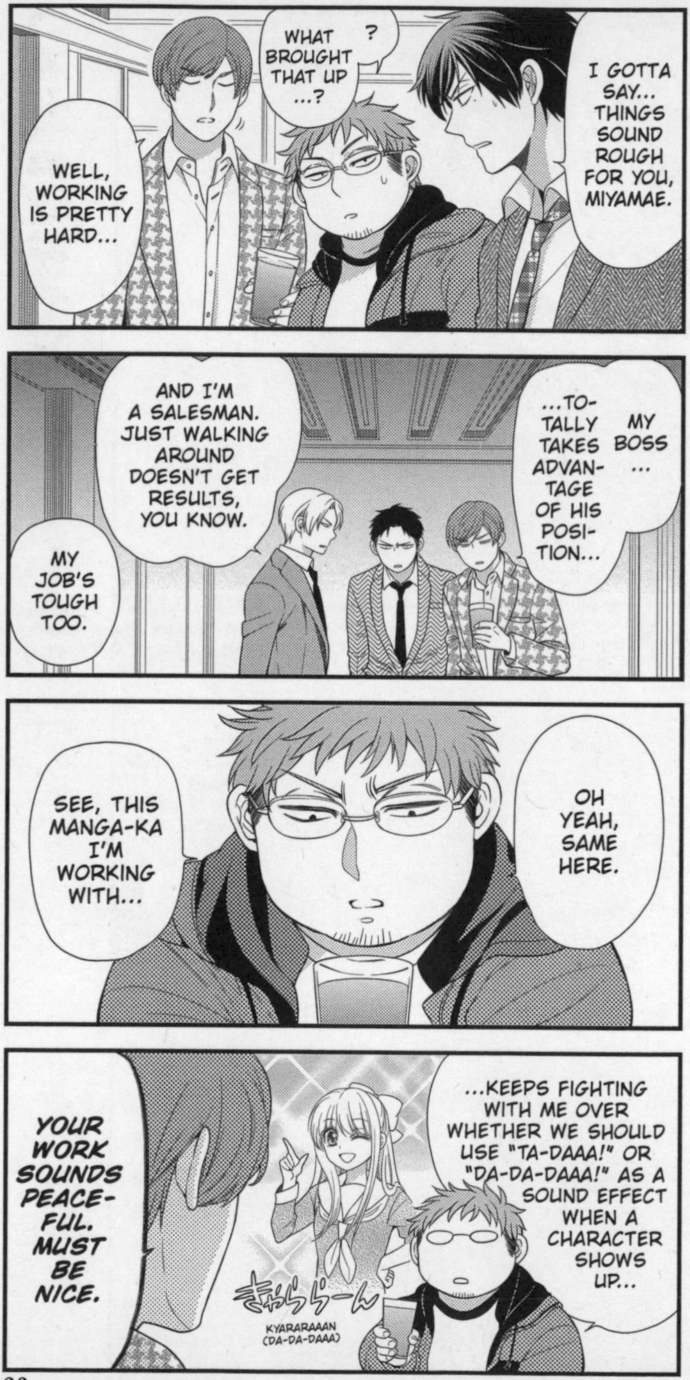
I GOTTA SAY... THINGS SOUND ROUGH FOR YOU, MIYAMAE.
WHAT BROUGHT THAT UP ...?
WELL, WORKING IS PRETTY HARD...
MY BOSS ...
...TO-TALLY TAKES ADVAN-TAGE OF HIS POSI-TION...
AND I'M A SALESMAN. JUST WALKING AROUND DOESN'T GET RESULTS, YOU KNOW.
MY JOB'S TOUGH TOO.
OH YEAH, SAME HERE.
SEE, THIS MANGA-KA I'M WORKING WITH...
...KEEPS FIGHTING WITH ME OVER WHETHER WE SHOULD USE "TA-DAAA!" OR "DA-DA-DAAA!" AS A SOUND EFFECT WHEN A CHARACTER SHOWS UP...
きゃららーん
KYARARAAAN (DA-DA-DAAA)
YOUR WORK SOUNDS PEACE-FUL. MUST BE NICE.

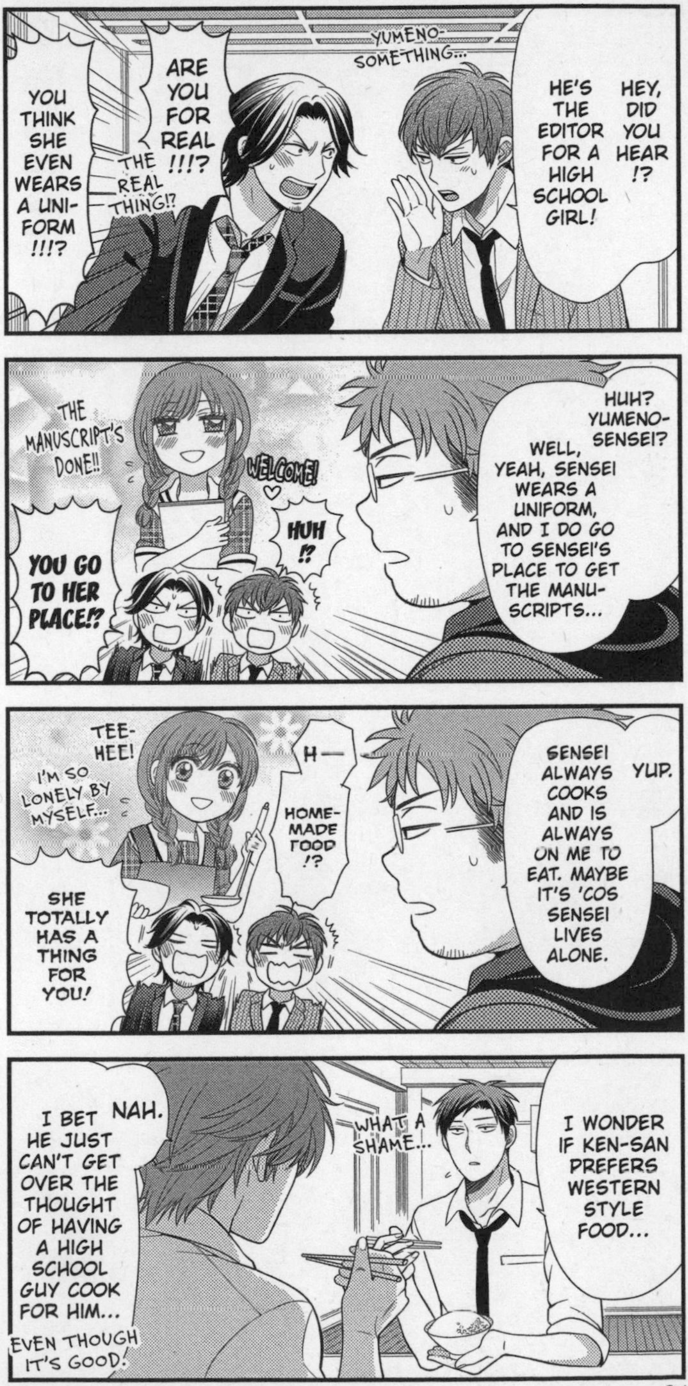
HEY, DID YOU HEAR!?
HE'S THE EDITOR FOR A HIGH SCHOOL GIRL!
YUMENO-SOMETHING...
ARE YOU FOR REAL!!!?
THE REAL THING!?
YOU THINK SHE EVEN WEARS A UNIFORM!!!?
HUH? YUMENO-SENSEI?
WELL, YEAH, SENSEI WEARS A UNIFORM, AND I DO GO TO SENSEI'S PLACE TO GET THE MANU-SCRIPTS...
HUH!?
WELCOME! ♡
THE MANUSCRIPT'S DONE!!
YOU GO TO HER PLACE!?
YUP.
SENSEI ALWAYS COOKS AND IS ALWAYS ON ME TO EAT. MAYBE IT'S 'COS SENSEI LIVES ALONE.
H—
HOME-MADE FOOD!?
TEE-HEE!
I'M SO LONELY BY MYSELF...
SHE TOTALLY HAS A THING FOR YOU!
I WONDER IF KEN-SAN PREFERS WESTERN STYLE FOOD...
WHAT A SHAME...
NAH.
I BET HE JUST CAN'T GET OVER THE THOUGHT OF HAVING A HIGH SCHOOL GUY COOK FOR HIM...
EVEN THOUGH IT'S GOOD!

HIGH SCHOOL MANGA-KA ②

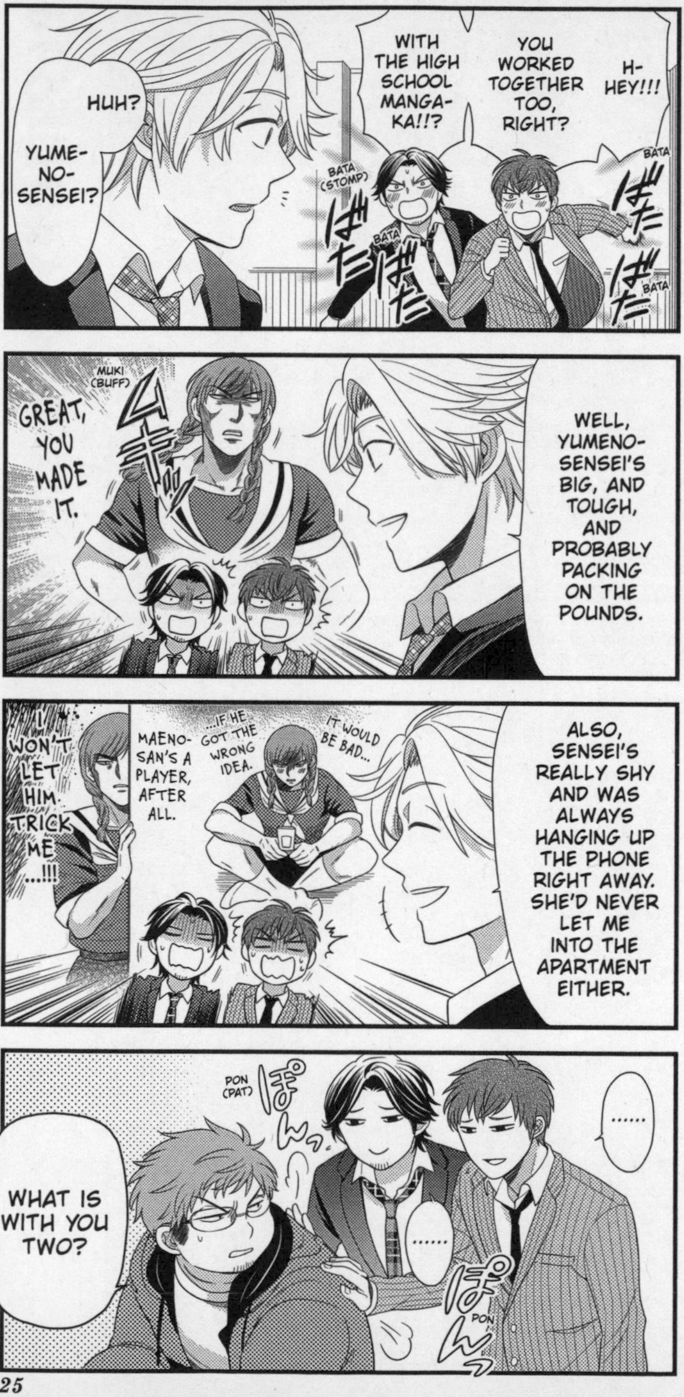
H-HEY!!!
BATA
BATA
YOU WORKED TOGETHER TOO, RIGHT?
WITH THE HIGH SCHOOL MANGA-KA!!?
BATA (STOMP)
BATA
HUH?
YUME-NO-SENSEI?
WELL, YUMENO-SENSEI'S BIG, AND TOUGH, AND PROBABLY PACKING ON THE POUNDS.
MUKI (BUFF)
GREAT, YOU MADE IT.
ALSO, SENSEI'S REALLY SHY AND WAS ALWAYS HANGING UP THE PHONE RIGHT AWAY. SHE'D NEVER LET ME INTO THE APARTMENT EITHER.
IT WOULD BE BAD...
...IF HE GOT THE WRONG IDEA.
MAENO-SAN'S A PLAYER, AFTER ALL.
I WON'T LET HIM TRICK ME ...!!!
......
PON (PAT)
......
PON
WHAT IS WITH YOU TWO?

PERSONAL BLOG

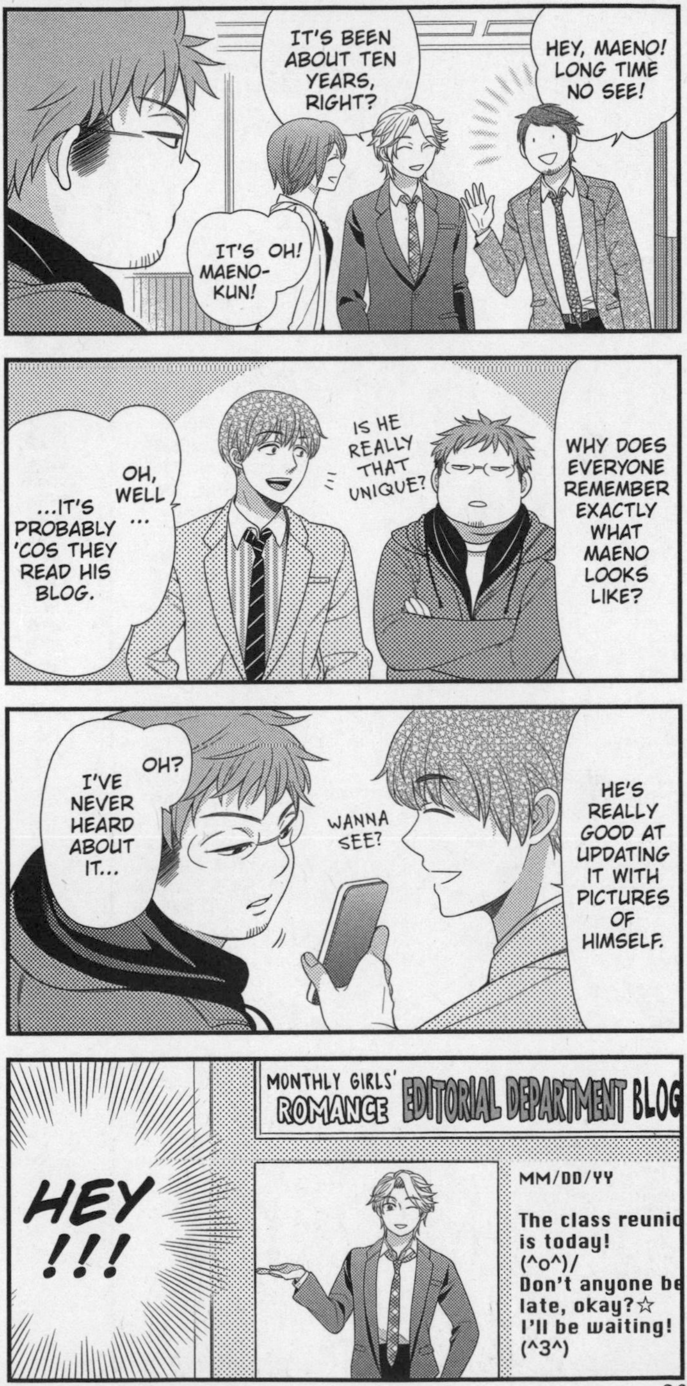

HEY, MAENO! LONG TIME NO SEE!
IT'S BEEN ABOUT TEN YEARS, RIGHT?
OH! IT'S MAENO-KUN!
WHY DOES EVERYONE REMEMBER EXACTLY WHAT MAENO LOOKS LIKE?
IS HE REALLY THAT UNIQUE?
OH, WELL ...
...IT'S PROBABLY 'COS THEY READ HIS BLOG.
HE'S REALLY GOOD AT UPDATING IT WITH PICTURES OF HIMSELF.
WANNA SEE?
OH?
I'VE NEVER HEARD ABOUT IT...
MONTHLY GIRLS' ROMANCE EDITORIAL DEPARTMENT BLOG
MM/DD/YY
The class reunio
is today!
(^o^)/
Don't anyone be
late, okay?☆
I'll be waiting!
(^3^)
HEY!!!

FLOATY, FLOATY MAENO

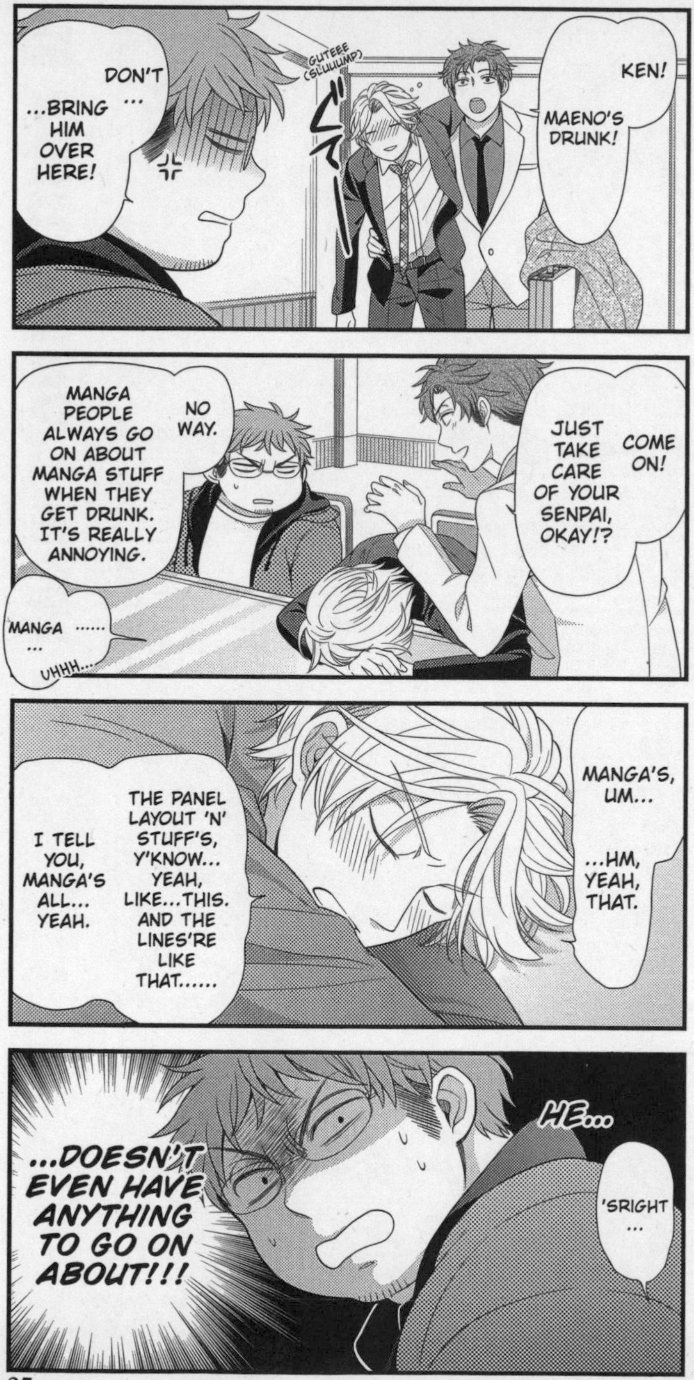

KEN!
MAENO'S DRUNK!
GUTEEE (SLUUUMP)
DON'T ...
...BRING HIM OVER HERE!
COME ON!
JUST TAKE CARE OF YOUR SENPAI, OKAY!?
NO WAY.
MANGA PEOPLE ALWAYS GO ON ABOUT MANGA STUFF WHEN THEY GET DRUNK. IT'S REALLY ANNOYING.
MANGA ....
UHHH...
MANGA'S, UM...
...HM, YEAH, THAT.
THE PANEL LAYOUT 'N' STUFF'S, Y'KNOW... YEAH, LIKE...THIS. AND THE LINES'RE LIKE THAT......
I TELL YOU, MANGA'S ALL... YEAH.
HE...
'SRIGHT ...
...DOESN'T EVEN HAVE ANYTHING TO GO ON ABOUT!!!

HE REALLY DIDN'T WANT TO

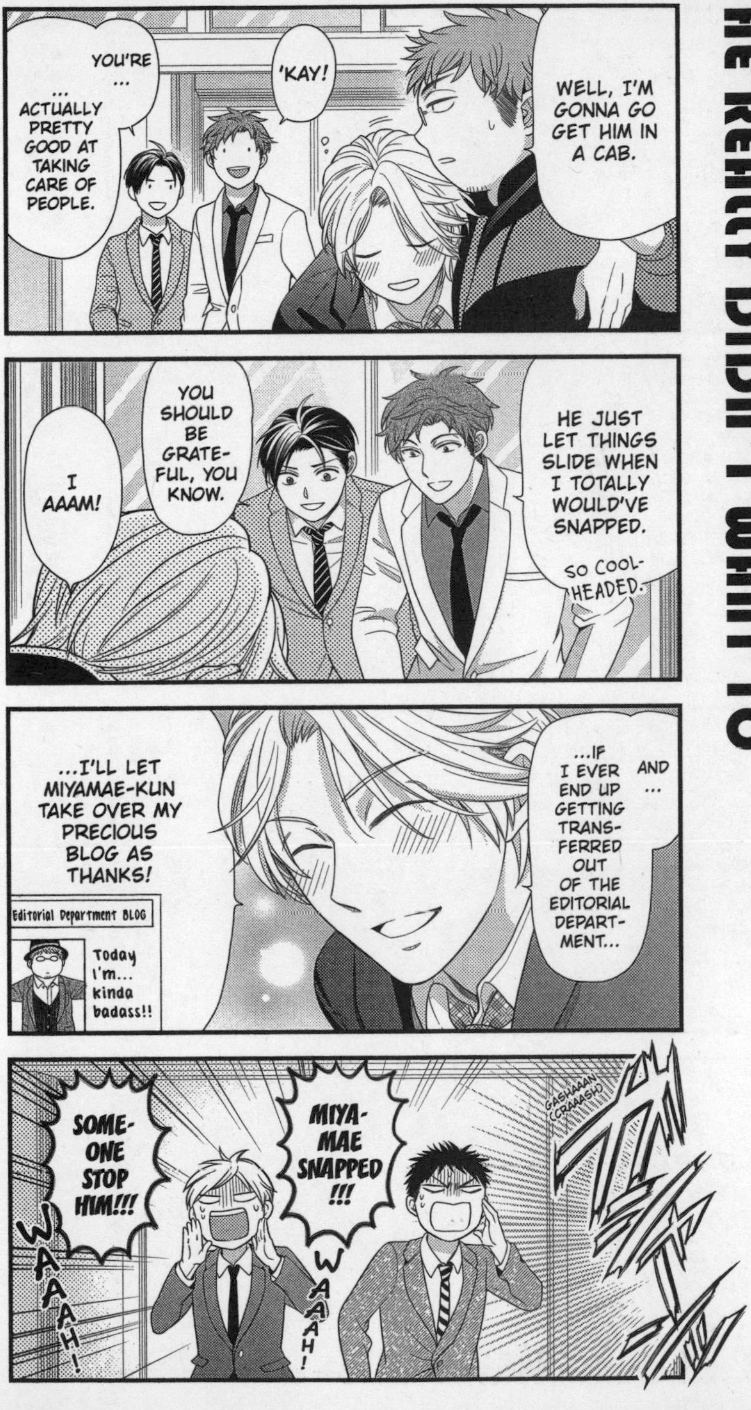
WELL, I'M GONNA GO GET HIM IN A CAB.
'KAY!
YOU'RE ... ... ACTUALLY PRETTY GOOD AT TAKING CARE OF PEOPLE.
HE JUST LET THINGS SLIDE WHEN I TOTALLY WOULD'VE SNAPPED.
SO COOL-HEADED.
YOU SHOULD BE GRATE-FUL, YOU KNOW.
I AAAM!
AND ...
...IF I EVER END UP GETTING TRANS-FERRED OUT OF THE EDITORIAL DEPART-MENT...
...I'LL LET MIYAMAE-KUN TAKE OVER MY PRECIOUS BLOG AS THANKS!
Editorial Department BLOG
Today I'm... kinda badass!!
GASHAAAN (CRAAASH)
MIYA-MAE SNAPPED!!!
WAAAH!
SOME-ONE STOP HIM!!!
WAAAH!

PRIVATE INFORMATION ②

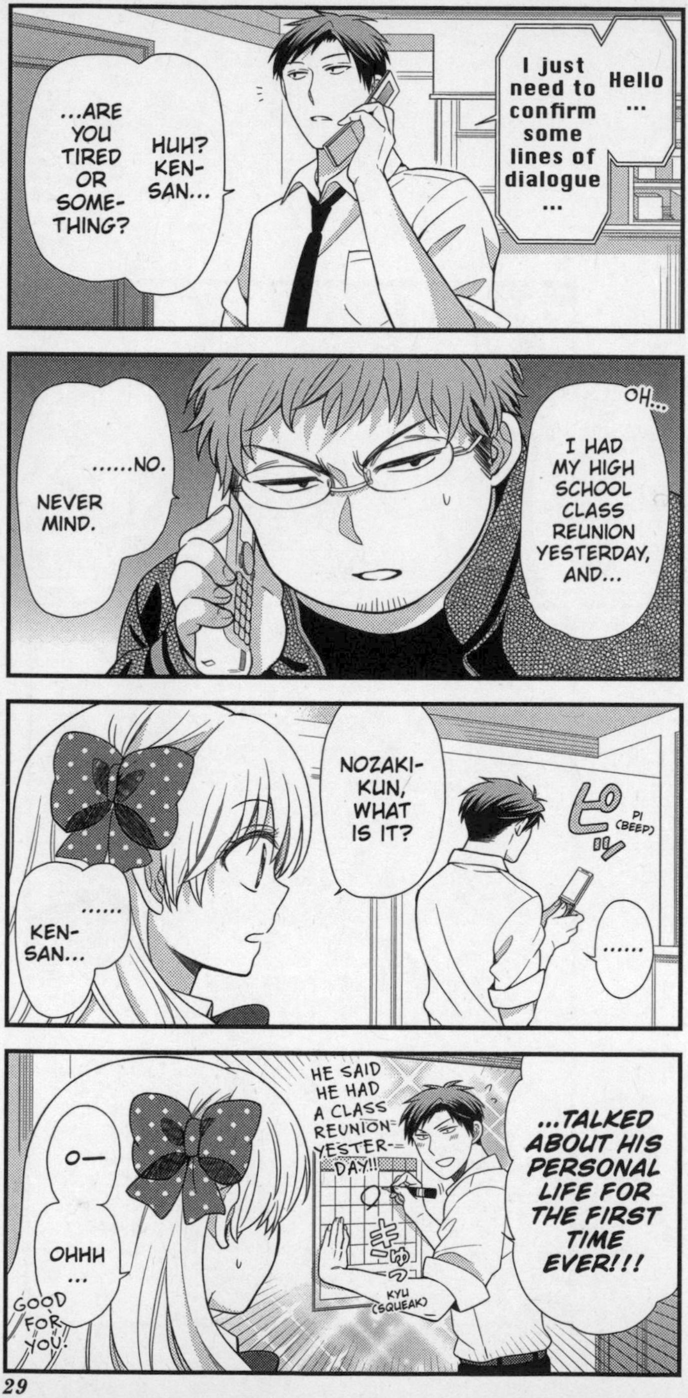

Hello ...
I just need to confirm some lines of dialogue ...
HUH? KEN-SAN...
...ARE YOU TIRED OR SOME-THING?
OH...
I HAD MY HIGH SCHOOL CLASS REUNION YESTERDAY, AND...
......NO.
NEVER MIND.
ピッ
PI (BEEP)
......
NOZAKI-KUN, WHAT IS IT?
...... KEN-SAN...
...TALKED ABOUT HIS PERSONAL LIFE FOR THE FIRST TIME EVER!!!
HE SAID HE HAD A CLASS REUNION YESTER-DAY!!
キゅっ
KYU (SQUEAK)
O—
OHHH ...
GOOD FOR YOU.

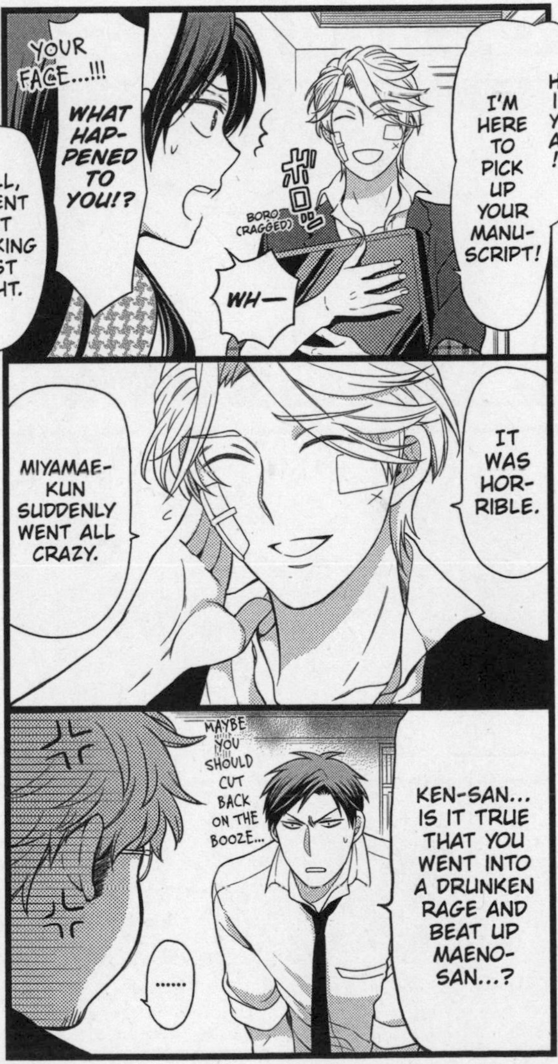
HIYA! I'M HERE TO PICK UP YOUR MANUSCRIPT!
ボロッ
BORO (RAGGED)
WH—
YOUR FACE...!!!
WHAT HAPPENED TO YOU!?
WELL, I WENT OUT DRINKING LAST NIGHT.
IT WAS HORRIBLE.
MIYAMAE-KUN SUDDENLY WENT ALL CRAZY.
KEN-SAN... IS IT TRUE THAT YOU WENT INTO A DRUNKEN RAGE AND BEAT UP MAENO-SAN...?
MAYBE YOU SHOULD CUT BACK ON THE BOOZE...
......

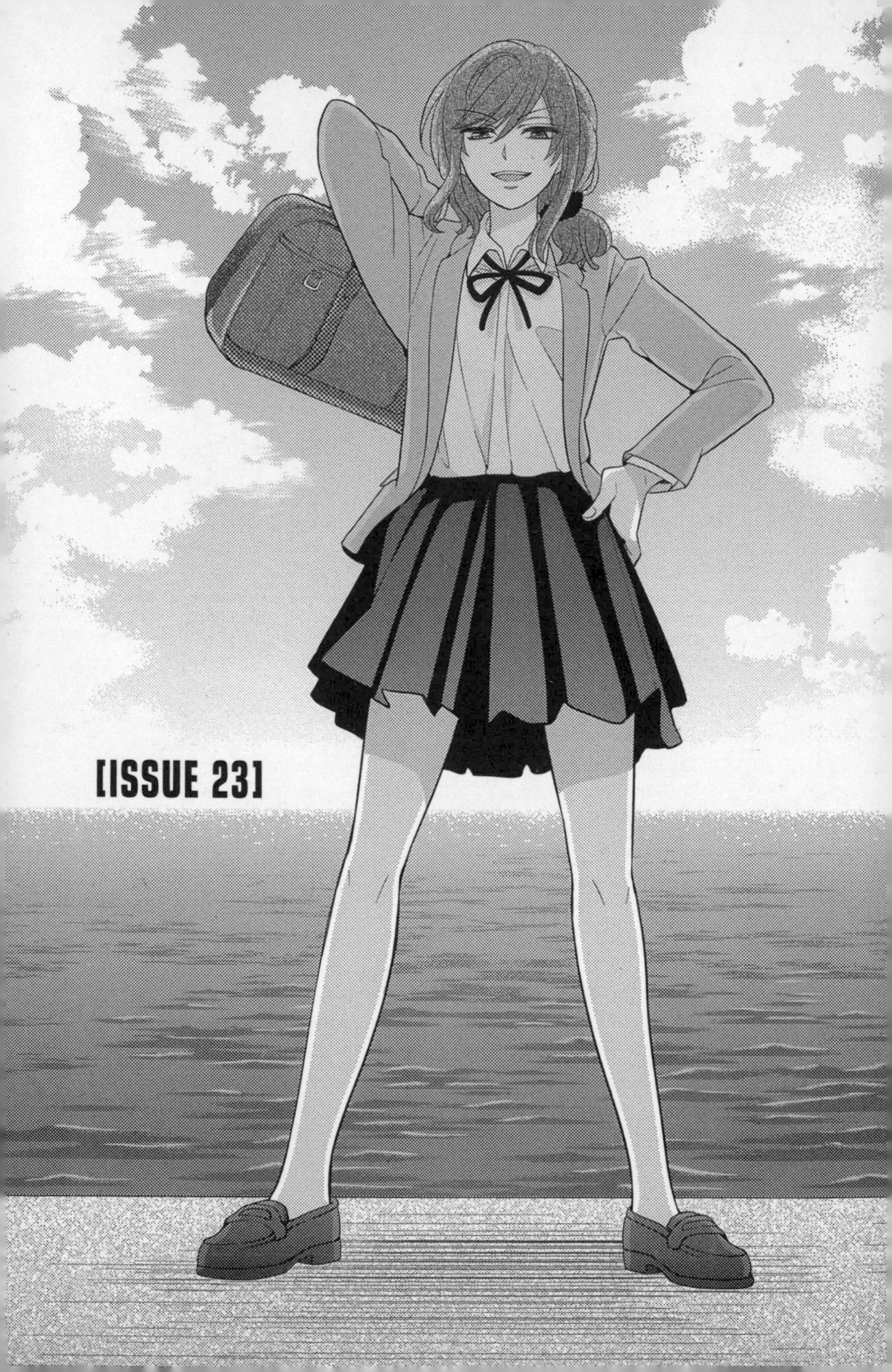
[ISSUE 23]

WORRIES

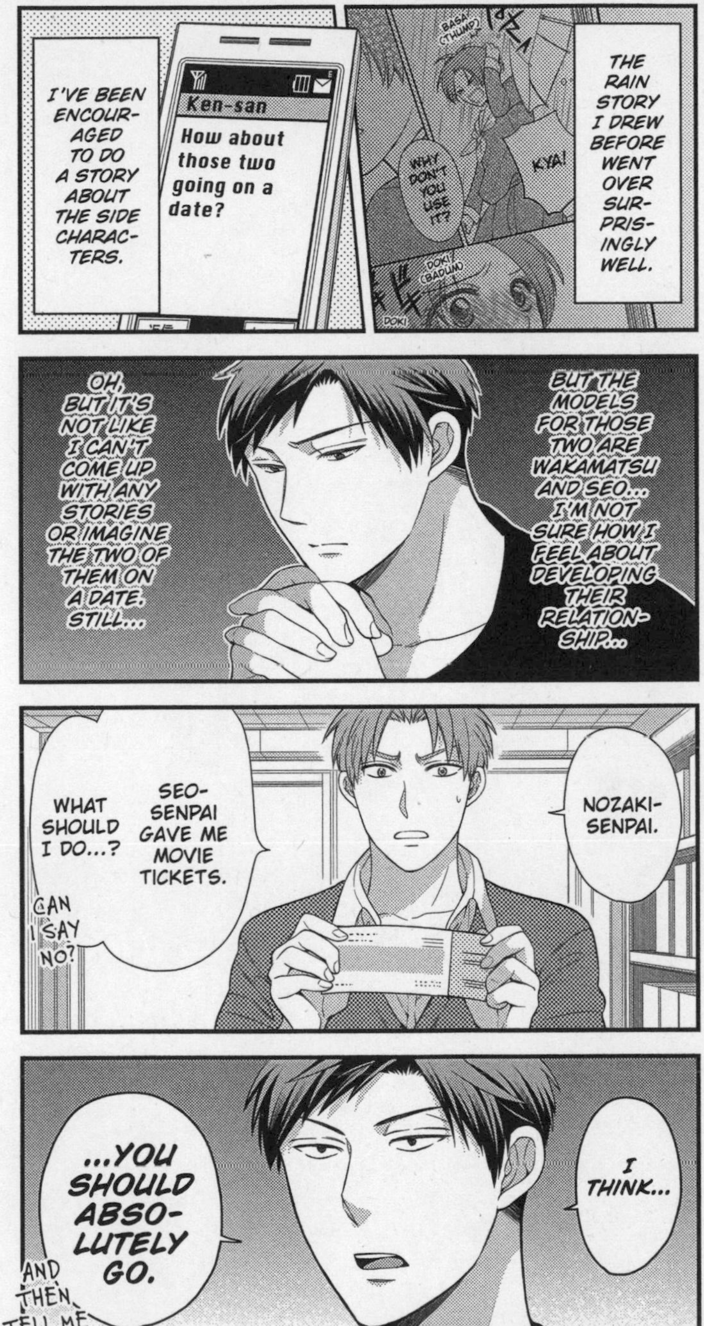
THE RAIN STORY I DREW BEFORE WENT OVER SURPRISINGLY WELL.
BASA (THUMP)
KYA!
WHY DON'T YOU USE IT?
DOKI (BADUM)
DOKI
Ken-san
How about those two going on a date?
I'VE BEEN ENCOURAGED TO DO A STORY ABOUT THE SIDE CHARACTERS.
BUT THE MODELS FOR THOSE TWO ARE WAKAMATSU AND SEO... I'M NOT SURE HOW I FEEL ABOUT DEVELOPING THEIR RELATIONSHIP...
OH, BUT IT'S NOT LIKE I CAN'T COME UP WITH ANY STORIES OR IMAGINE THE TWO OF THEM ON A DATE. STILL...
NOZAKI-SENPAI.
SEO-SENPAI GAVE ME MOVIE TICKETS.
WHAT SHOULD I DO...?
CAN I SAY NO?
I THINK...
...YOU SHOULD ABSOLUTELY GO.
AND THEN TELL ME HOW IT WENT.

VICTORY BIBLE

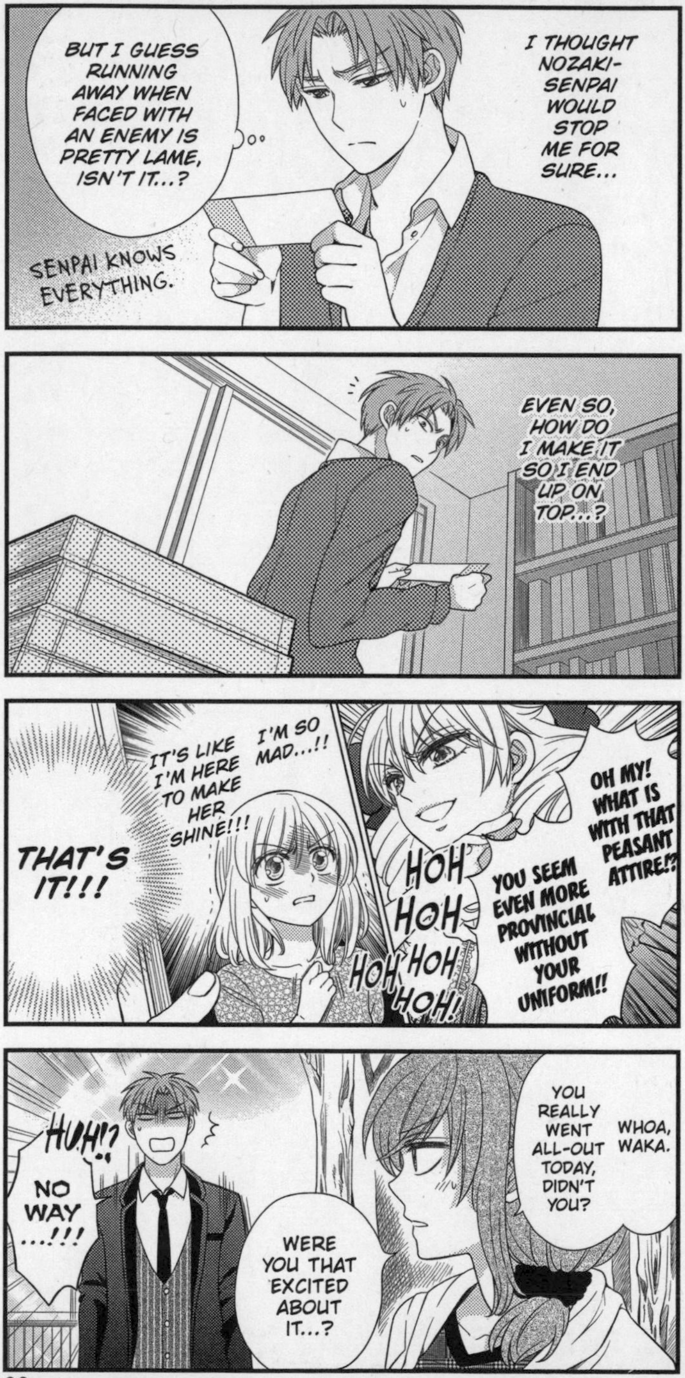
I THOUGHT NOZAKI-SENPAI WOULD STOP ME FOR SURE...
BUT I GUESS RUNNING AWAY WHEN FACED WITH AN ENEMY IS PRETTY LAME, ISN'T IT...?
SENPAI KNOWS EVERYTHING.
EVEN SO, HOW DO I MAKE IT SO I END UP ON TOP...?
OH MY! WHAT IS WITH THAT PEASANT ATTIRE!?
YOU SEEM EVEN MORE PROVINCIAL WITHOUT YOUR UNIFORM!!
HOH HOH HOH HOH HOH HOH!
I'M SO MAD...!!
IT'S LIKE I'M HERE TO MAKE HER SHINE!!!
THAT'S IT!!!
WHOA, WAKA.
YOU REALLY WENT ALL-OUT TODAY, DIDN'T YOU?
WERE YOU THAT EXCITED ABOUT IT...?
HUH!?
NO WAY ...!!!

FIGHT FOR THE ARMREST ①

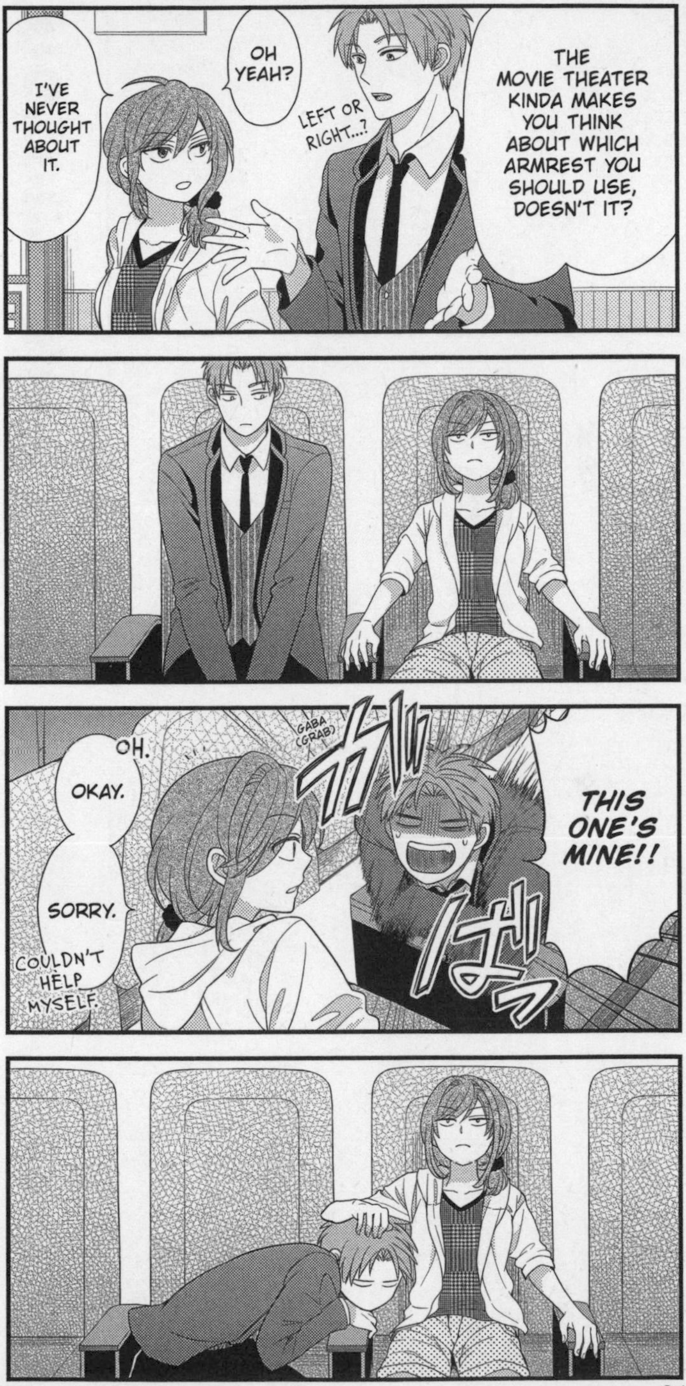
THE MOVIE THEATER KINDA MAKES YOU THINK ABOUT WHICH ARMREST YOU SHOULD USE, DOESN'T IT?
LEFT OR RIGHT...?
OH YEAH?
I'VE NEVER THOUGHT ABOUT IT.
GABA (GRAB)
ガッ
THIS ONE'S MINE!!
ばっ
OH.
OKAY.
SORRY.
COULDN'T HELP MYSELF.

FIGHT FOR THE ARMREST ②

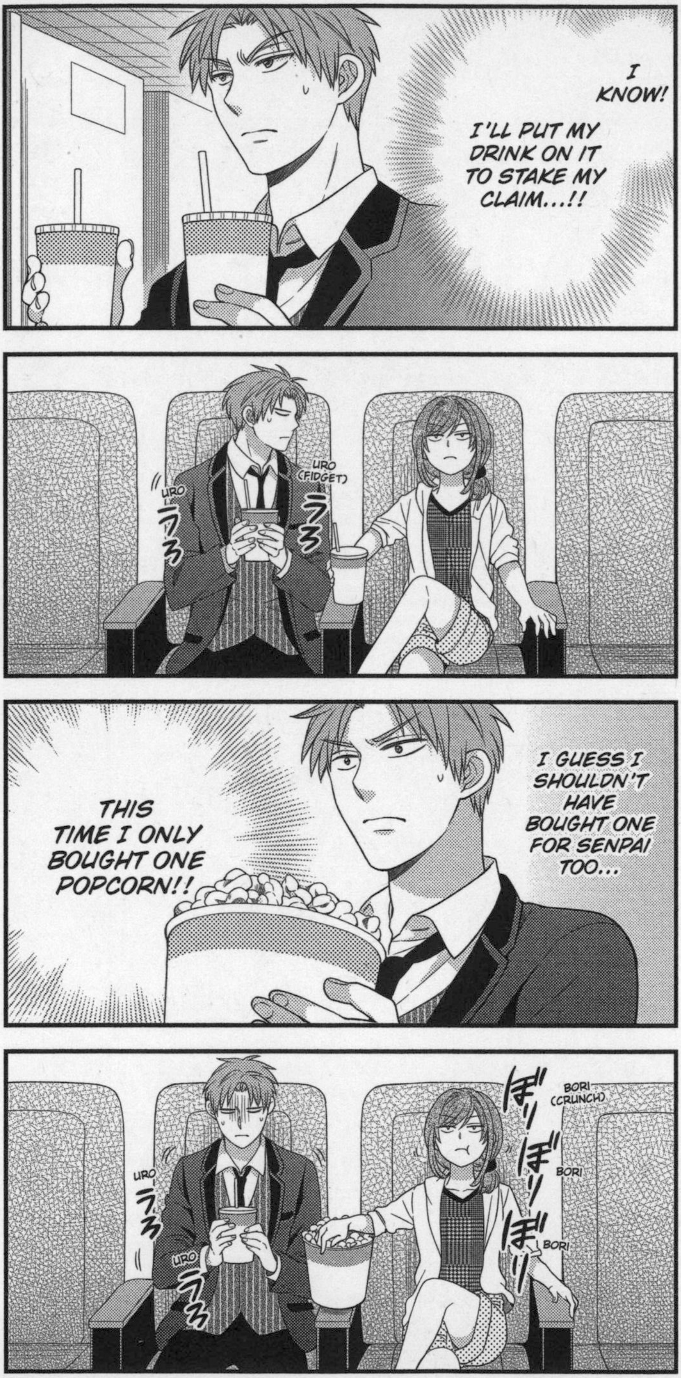

I KNOW!
I'LL PUT MY DRINK ON IT TO STAKE MY CLAIM...!!
URO (FIDGET)
ろろ
URO
ろろ
I GUESS I SHOULDN'T HAVE BOUGHT ONE FOR SENPAI TOO...
THIS TIME I ONLY BOUGHT ONE POPCORN!!
ぼリ
BORI (CRUNCH)
ぼリ
BORI
ぼリ
BORI
URO
ろろ
URO
ろろ

NEIGHBORLY CONCERN

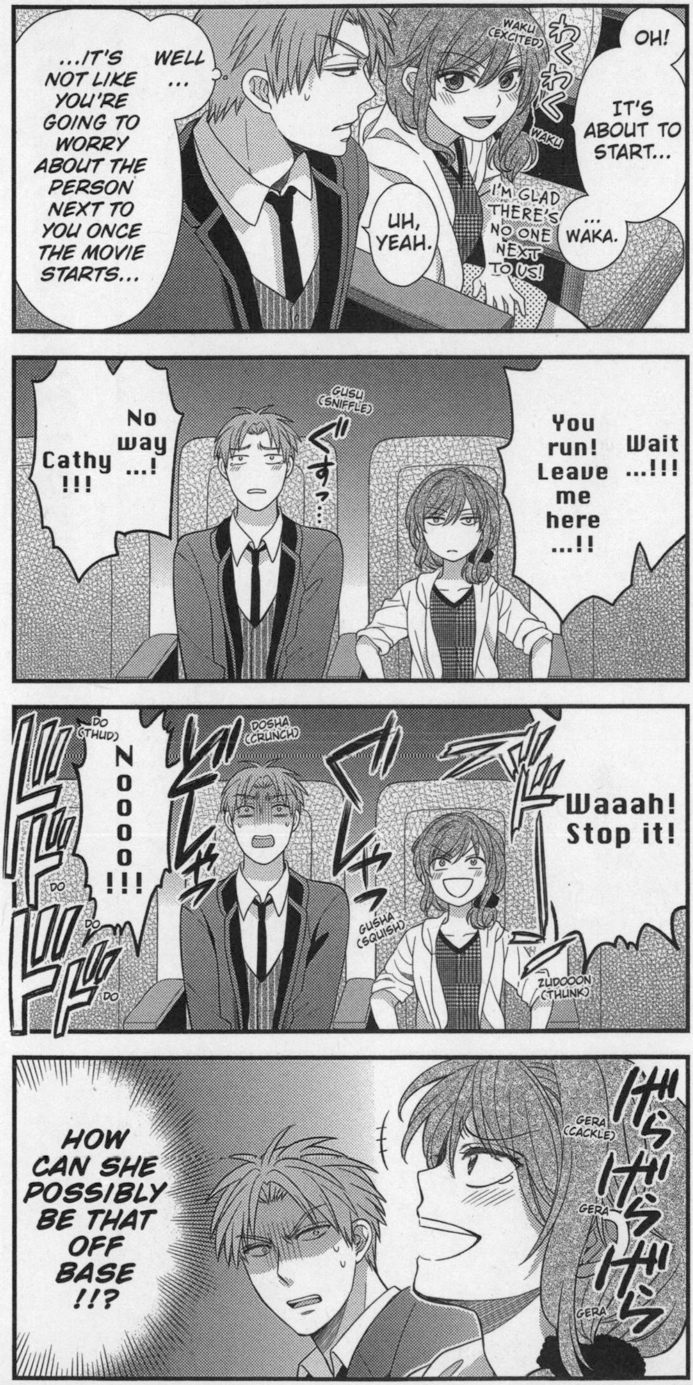
OH!
IT'S ABOUT TO START...
...WAKA.
わくわく
WAKU (EXCITED)
WAKU
I'M GLAD THERE'S NO ONE NEXT TO US!
UH, YEAH.
WELL ...
...IT'S NOT LIKE YOU'RE GOING TO WORRY ABOUT THE PERSON NEXT TO YOU ONCE THE MOVIE STARTS...
Wait ...!!!
You run! Leave me here ...!!
ぐすっ
GUSU (SNIFFLE)
No way ...!
Cathy !!!
Waaah! Stop it!
ZUDOOON (THUNK)
GUSHA (SQUISH)
DOSHA (CRUNCH)
NOOOO !!!
DO (THUD)
DO
DO
DO
げらげらげら
GERA (CACKLE)
GERA
GERA
HOW CAN SHE POSSIBLY BE THAT OFF BASE !!?

YUZUKI'S POINT OF VIEW

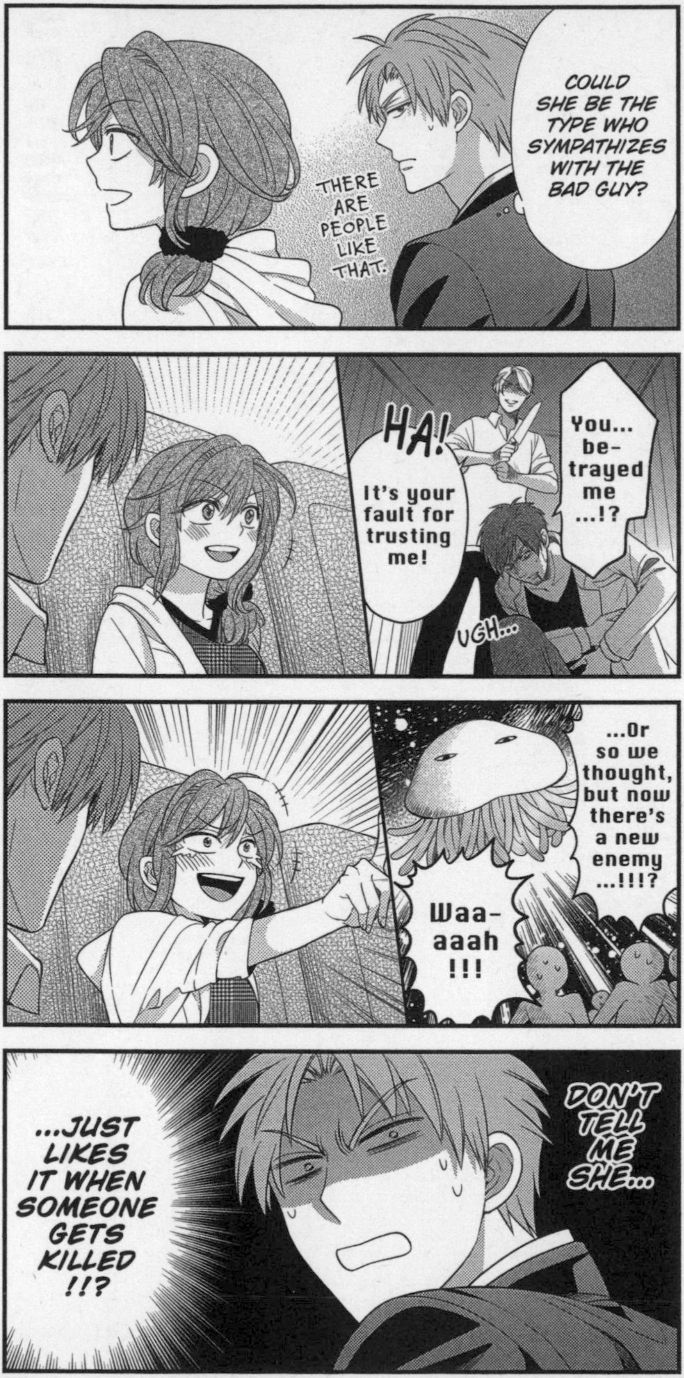
COULD SHE BE THE TYPE WHO SYMPATHIZES WITH THE BAD GUY?
THERE ARE PEOPLE LIKE THAT.
You... be-trayed me ...!?
HA!
It's your fault for trusting me!
UGH...
...Or so we thought, but now there's a new enemy ...!!!?
Waa-aaah !!!
DON'T TELL ME SHE...
...JUST LIKES IT WHEN SOMEONE GETS KILLED !!?

NAPPING ①

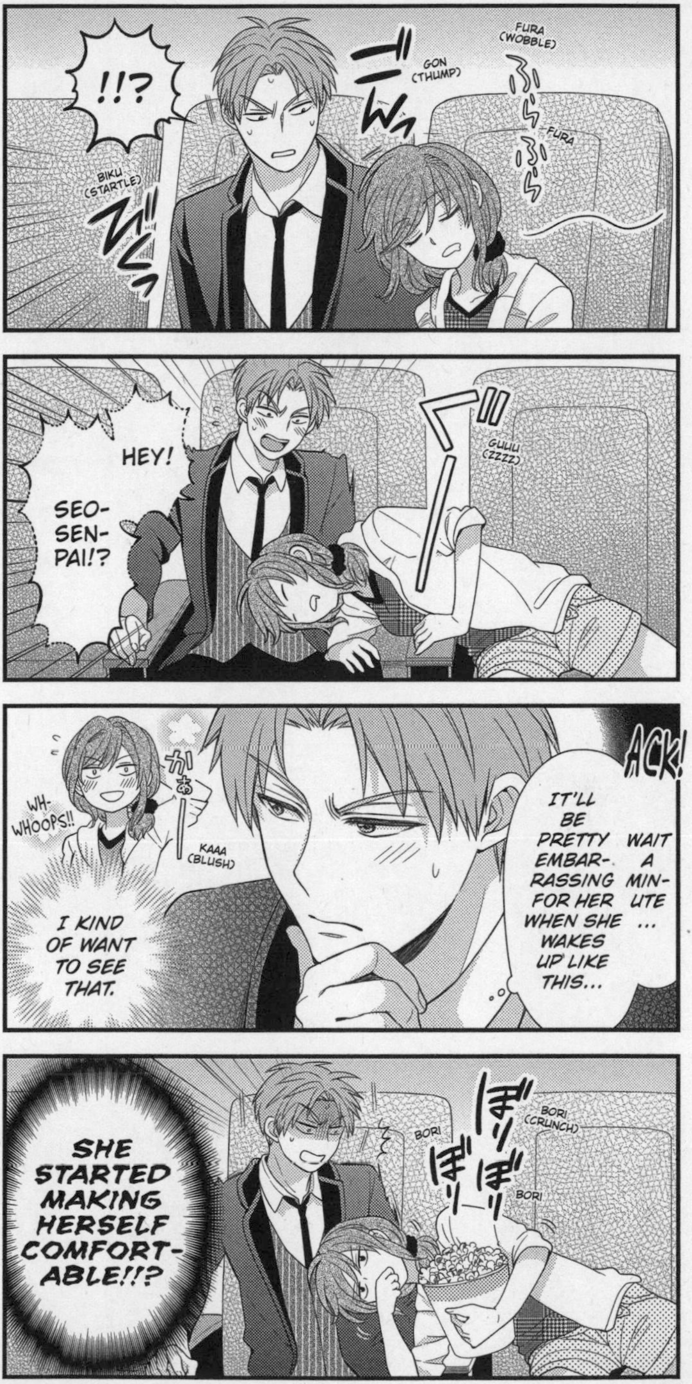
FURA (WOBBLE)
ふらふら
FURA
ゴンッ
GON (THUMP)
!!?
びくっ
BIKU (STARTLE)
グー
GUUU (ZZZZ)
HEY!
SEO-SENPAI!?
ACK!
WAIT A MINUTE...
IT'LL BE PRETTY EMBARRASSING FOR HER WHEN SHE WAKES UP LIKE THIS...
かぁー
KAAA (BLUSH)
WH-WHOOPS!!
I KIND OF WANT TO SEE THAT.
ぼりぼり
BORI (CRUNCH)
ぼりぼり
BORI
BORI
SHE STARTED MAKING HERSELF COMFORTABLE!!?

NAPPING ②

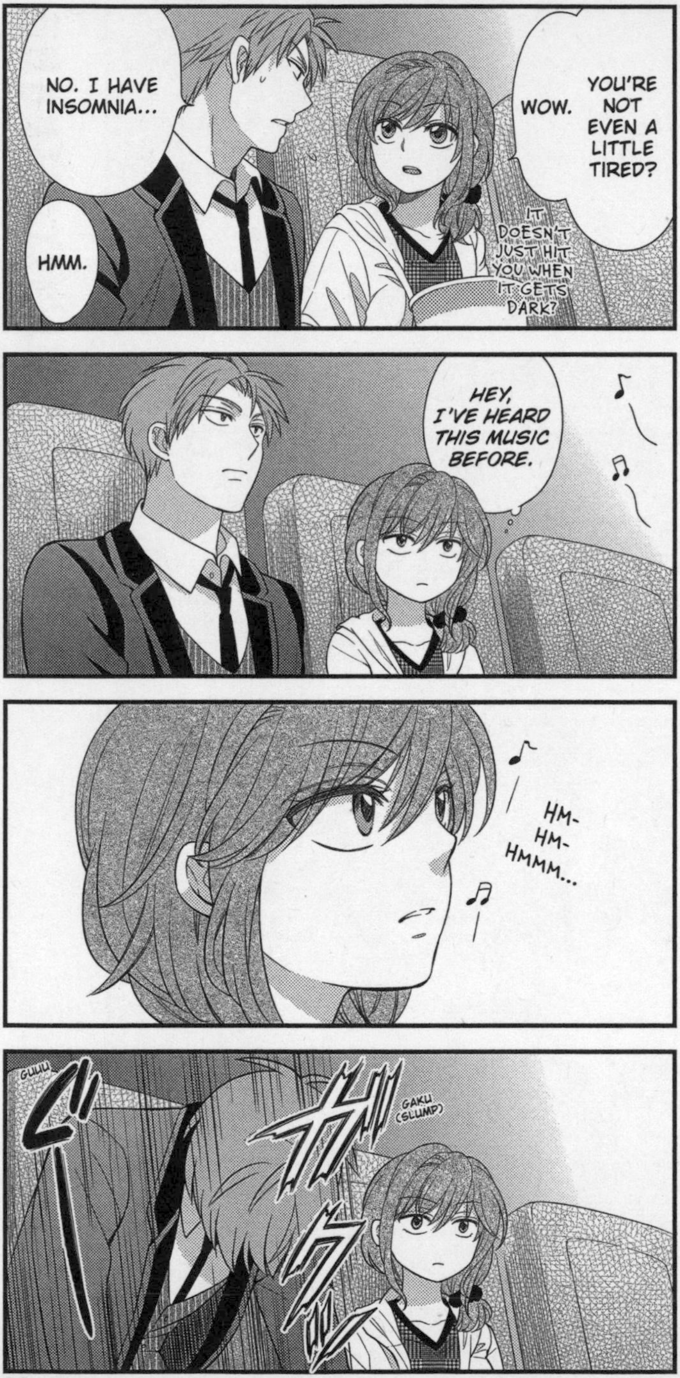
WOW. YOU'RE NOT EVEN A LITTLE TIRED?
IT DOESN'T JUST HIT YOU WHEN IT GETS DARK?
NO. I HAVE INSOMNIA...
HMM.
HEY, I'VE HEARD THIS MUSIC BEFORE.
HM-HM-HMMM...
GAKU (SLUMP)
GUUU

THE IMPORTANT SCENES

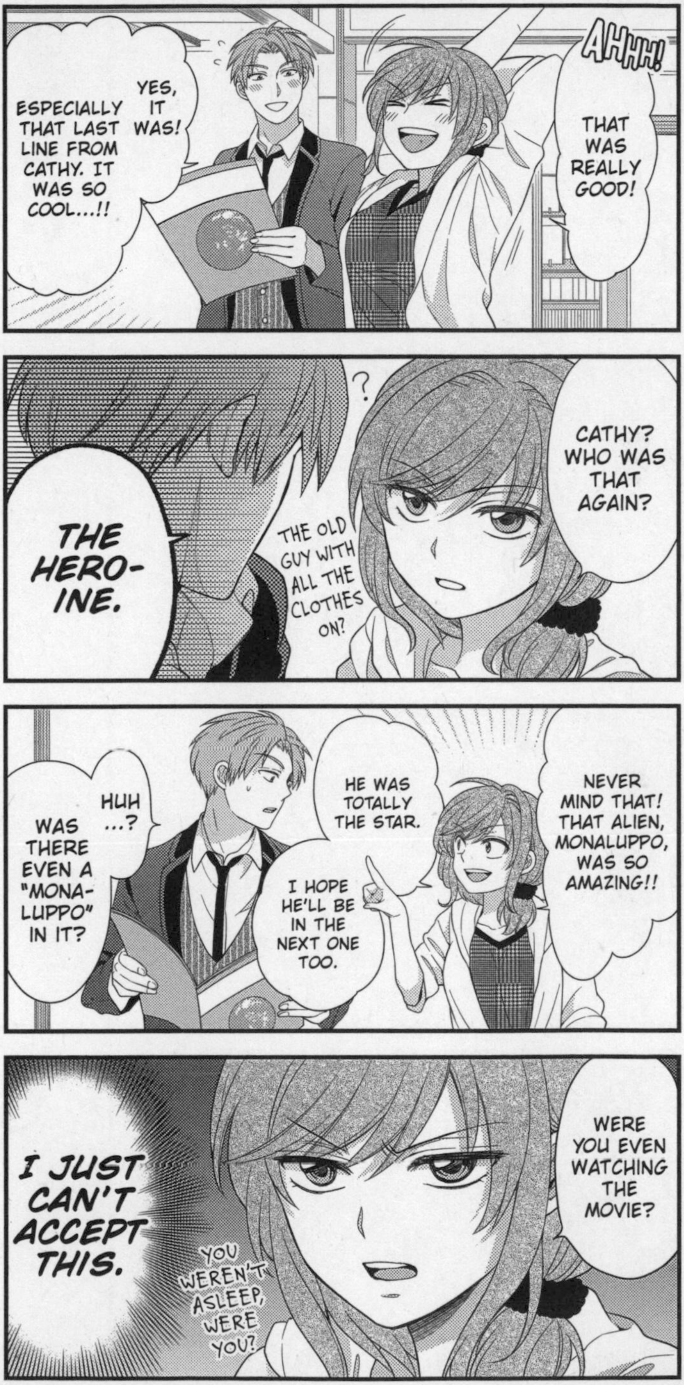
AHHH!
THAT WAS REALLY GOOD!
YES, IT WAS!
ESPECIALLY THAT LAST LINE FROM CATHY. IT WAS SO COOL...!!
CATHY? WHO WAS THAT AGAIN?
THE OLD GUY WITH ALL THE CLOTHES ON?
THE HERO-INE.
NEVER MIND THAT! THAT ALIEN, MONALUPPO, WAS SO AMAZING!!
HE WAS TOTALLY THE STAR.
I HOPE HE'LL BE IN THE NEXT ONE TOO.
HUH ...?
WAS THERE EVEN A "MONA-LUPPO" IN IT?
WERE YOU EVEN WATCHING THE MOVIE?
YOU WEREN'T ASLEEP, WERE YOU?
I JUST CAN'T ACCEPT THIS.

SHARING OPINIONS

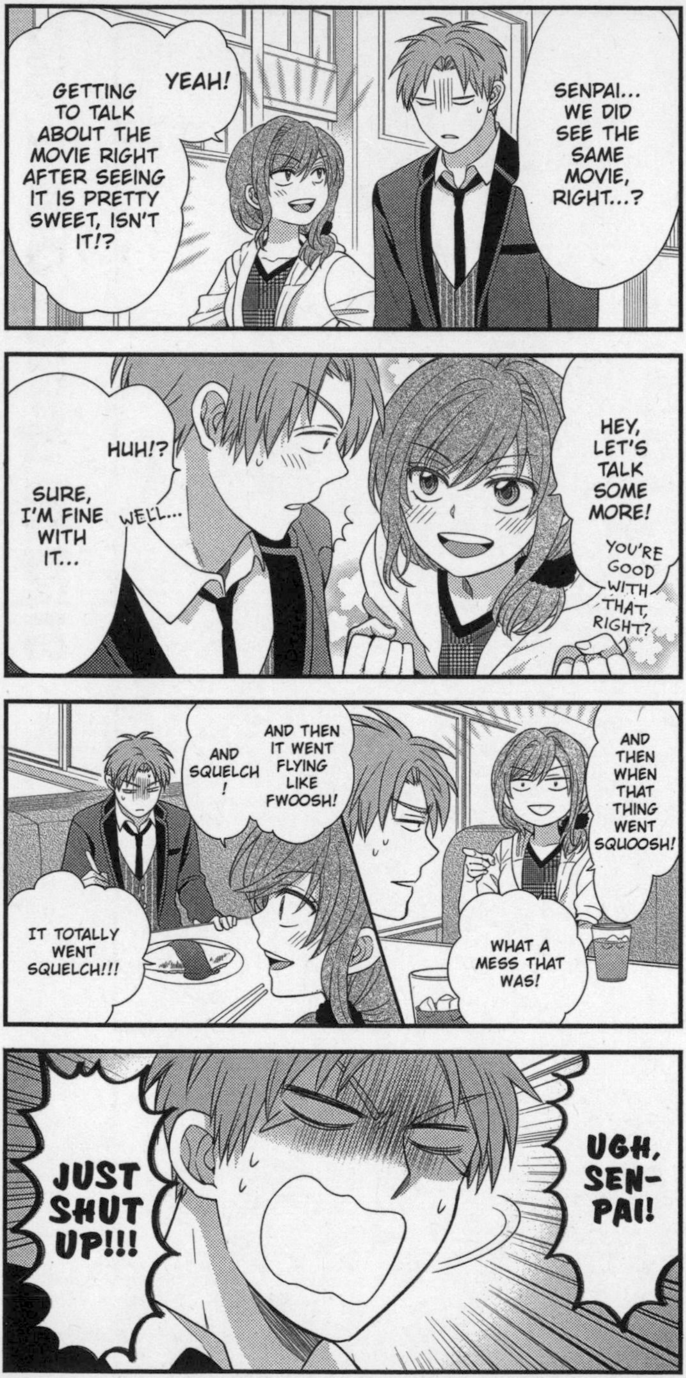
SENPAI... WE DID SEE THE SAME MOVIE, RIGHT...?
YEAH!
GETTING TO TALK ABOUT THE MOVIE RIGHT AFTER SEEING IT IS PRETTY SWEET, ISN'T IT!?
HEY, LET'S TALK SOME MORE!
YOU'RE GOOD WITH THAT, RIGHT?
HUH!?
WELL...
SURE, I'M FINE WITH IT...
AND THEN WHEN THAT THING WENT SQUOOSH!
WHAT A MESS THAT WAS!
AND THEN IT WENT FLYING LIKE FWOOSH!
AND SQUELCH!
IT TOTALLY WENT SQUELCH!!!
UGH, SEN-PAI!
JUST SHUT UP!!!

MY STAND-IN'S STAND IN

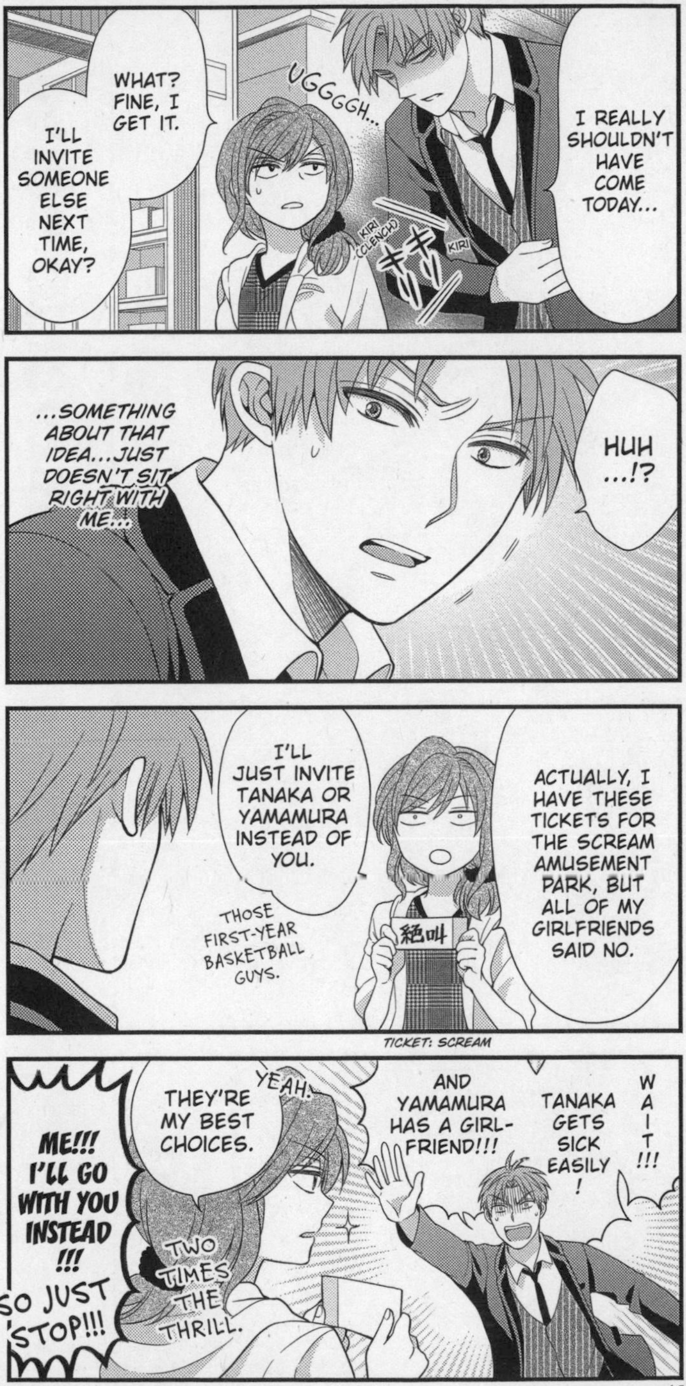
I REALLY SHOULDN'T HAVE COME TODAY...
UGGGGH...
KIRI (CLENCH)
KIRI
WHAT? FINE, I GET IT.
I'LL INVITE SOMEONE ELSE NEXT TIME, OKAY?
HUH ...!?
...SOMETHING ABOUT THAT IDEA...JUST DOESN'T SIT RIGHT WITH ME...
ACTUALLY, I HAVE THESE TICKETS FOR THE SCREAM AMUSEMENT PARK, BUT ALL OF MY GIRLFRIENDS SAID NO.
I'LL JUST INVITE TANAKA OR YAMAMURA INSTEAD OF YOU.
絶叫
THOSE FIRST-YEAR BASKETBALL GUYS.
TICKET: SCREAM
WAIT!!!
TANAKA GETS SICK EASILY!
AND YAMAMURA HAS A GIRLFRIEND!!!
YEAH!
THEY'RE MY BEST CHOICES.
TWO TIMES THE THRILL.
ME!!! I'LL GO WITH YOU INSTEAD!!!
SO JUST STOP!!!

THIS EPISODE'S RECAP

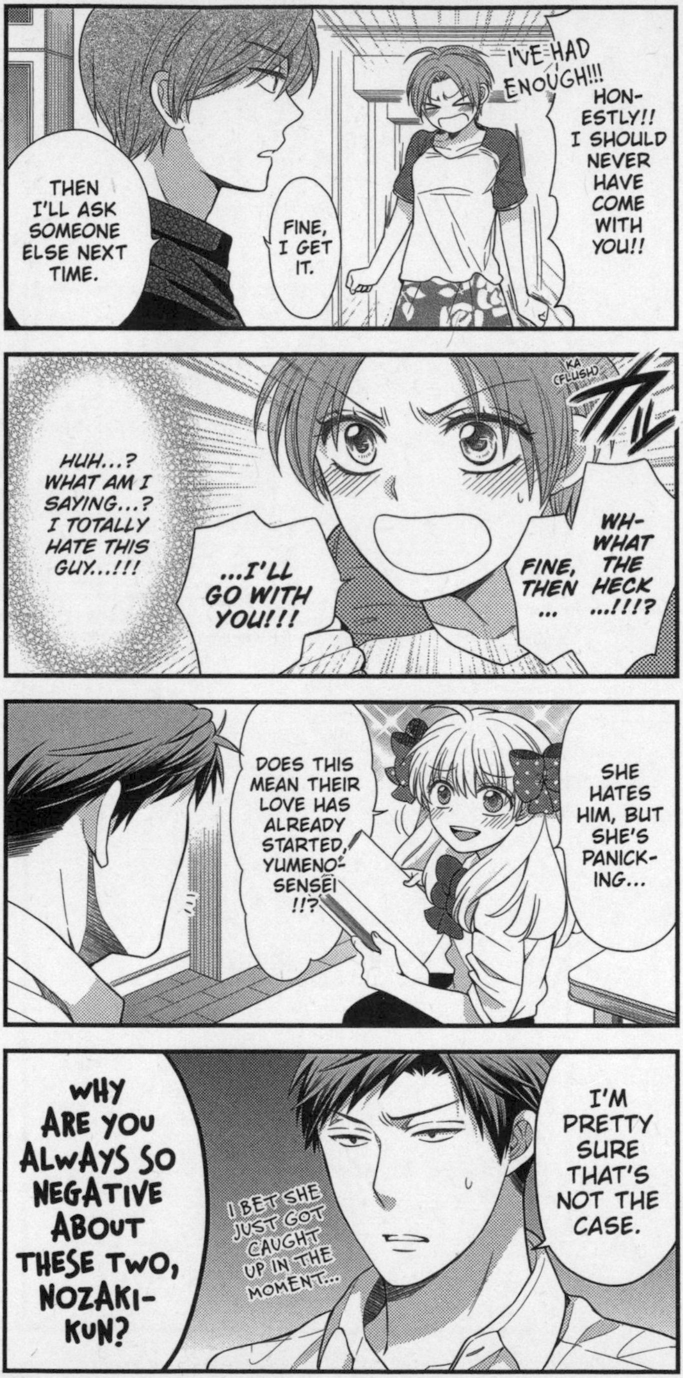
I'VE HAD ENOUGH!!!
HON-ESTLY!! I SHOULD NEVER HAVE COME WITH YOU!!
FINE, I GET IT.
THEN I'LL ASK SOMEONE ELSE NEXT TIME.
KA (FLUSH)
WH-WHAT THE HECK...!!!?
FINE, THEN...
...I'LL GO WITH YOU!!!
HUH...? WHAT AM I SAYING...? I TOTALLY HATE THIS GUY...!!!
SHE HATES HIM, BUT SHE'S PANICK-ING...
DOES THIS MEAN THEIR LOVE HAS ALREADY STARTED, YUMENO-SENSEI!!?
I'M PRETTY SURE THAT'S NOT THE CASE.
I BET SHE JUST GOT CAUGHT UP IN THE MOMENT...
WHY ARE YOU ALWAYS SO NEGATIVE ABOUT THESE TWO, NOZAKI-KUN?

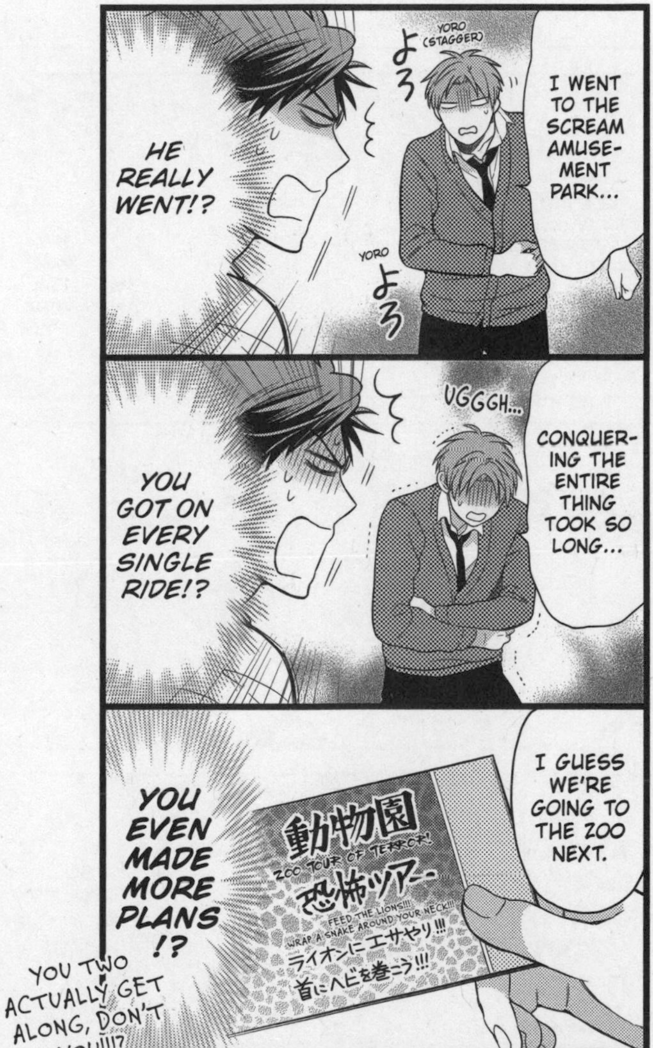
I WENT TO THE SCREAM AMUSE-MENT PARK...
よろ
YORO (STAGGER)
よろ
YORO
HE REALLY WENT!?
CONQUER-ING THE ENTIRE THING TOOK SO LONG...
UGGGH...
YOU GOT ON EVERY SINGLE RIDE!?
I GUESS WE'RE GOING TO THE ZOO NEXT.
動物園
恐怖ツアー
ZOO TOUR OF TERROR!
ライオンにエサやり!!!
FEED THE LIONS!!!
首にヘビを巻こう!!!
WRAP A SNAKE AROUND YOUR NECK!!!
YOU EVEN MADE MORE PLANS!?
YOU TWO ACTUALLY GET ALONG, DON'T YOU!!!?

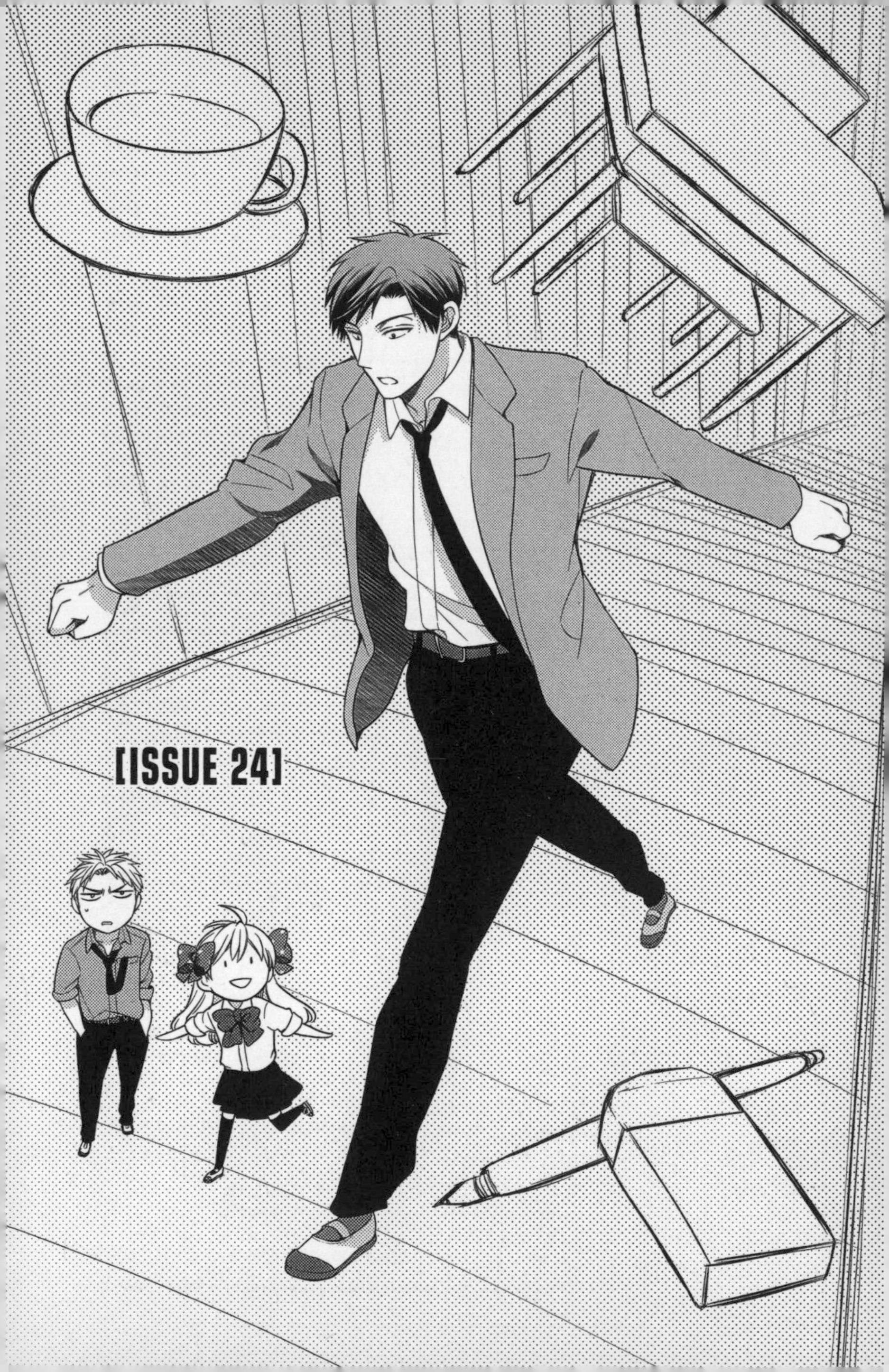
[ISSUE 24]

THE FIRST STEP TO BACKGROUNDS

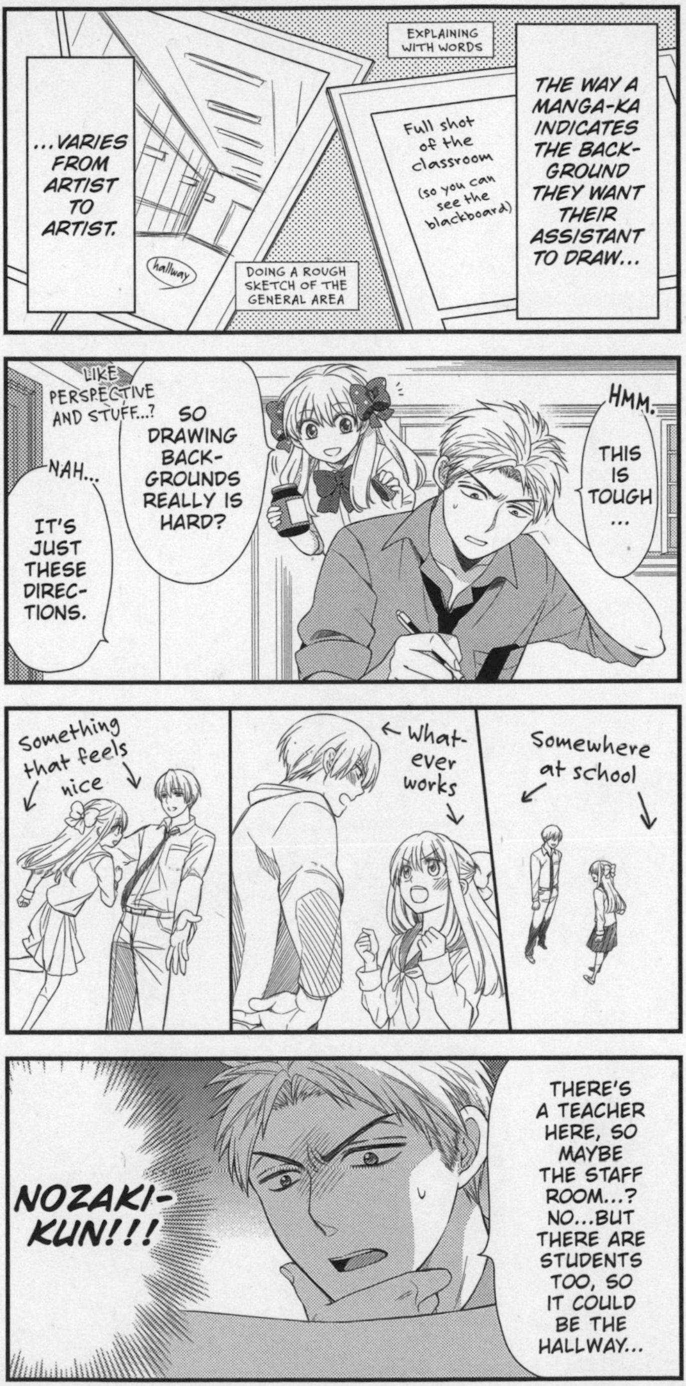
THE WAY A MANGA-KA INDICATES THE BACKGROUND THEY WANT THEIR ASSISTANT TO DRAW...
EXPLAINING WITH WORDS
Full shot of the classroom (so you can see the blackboard)
DOING A ROUGH SKETCH OF THE GENERAL AREA
hallway
...VARIES FROM ARTIST TO ARTIST.
HMM.
THIS IS TOUGH...
SO DRAWING BACKGROUNDS REALLY IS HARD?
LIKE PERSPECTIVE AND STUFF...?
NAH...
IT'S JUST THESE DIRECTIONS.
Somewhere at school
Whatever works
Something that feels nice
THERE'S A TEACHER HERE, SO MAYBE THE STAFF ROOM...? NO...BUT THERE ARE STUDENTS TOO, SO IT COULD BE THE HALLWAY...
NOZAKI-KUN!!!

THE ARTIST'S OPINION

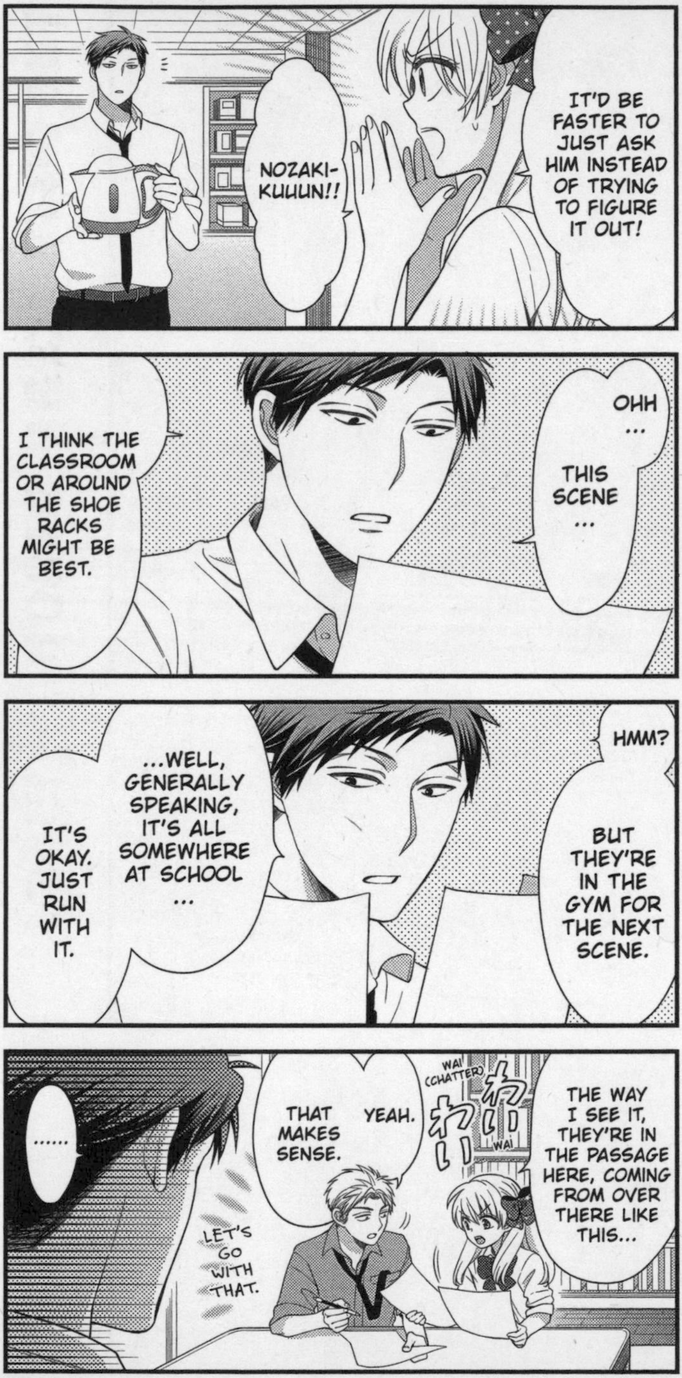
IT'D BE FASTER TO JUST ASK HIM INSTEAD OF TRYING TO FIGURE IT OUT!
NOZAKI-KUUUN!!
OHH ... THIS SCENE ...
I THINK THE CLASSROOM OR AROUND THE SHOE RACKS MIGHT BE BEST.
HMM? BUT THEY'RE IN THE GYM FOR THE NEXT SCENE.
...WELL, GENERALLY SPEAKING, IT'S ALL SOMEWHERE AT SCHOOL ...
IT'S OKAY. JUST RUN WITH IT.
THE WAY I SEE IT, THEY'RE IN THE PASSAGE HERE, COMING FROM OVER THERE LIKE THIS...
WAI (CHATTER) WAI
YEAH.
THAT MAKES SENSE.
LET'S GO WITH THAT.
......

THE PATH TO HIS DEBUT

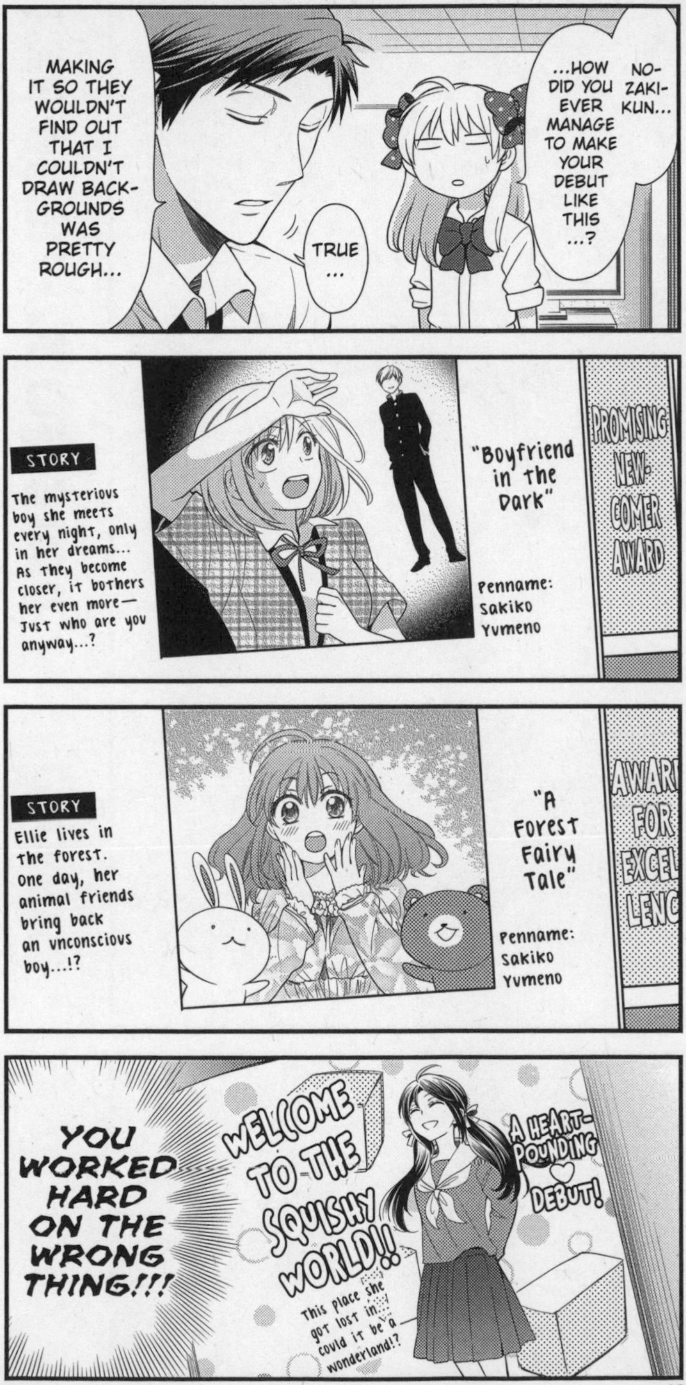
NO-ZAKI-KUN...
...HOW DID YOU EVER MANAGE TO MAKE YOUR DEBUT LIKE THIS ...?
TRUE ...
MAKING IT SO THEY WOULDN'T FIND OUT THAT I COULDN'T DRAW BACK-GROUNDS WAS PRETTY ROUGH...
PROMISING NEW-COMER AWARD
"Boyfriend in the Dark"
Penname: Sakiko Yumeno
STORY
The mysterious boy she meets every night, only in her dreams... As they become closer, it bothers her even more—Just who are you anyway...?
AWAR
FOR
EXCEL
LENC
"A Forest Fairy Tale"
Penname: Sakiko Yumeno
STORY
Ellie lives in the forest. One day, her animal friends bring back an unconscious boy...!?
A HEART-POUNDING ♡ DEBUT!
WELCOME TO THE SQUISHY WORLD!!
This place she got lost in...! could it be a wonderland!?
YOU WORKED HARD ON THE WRONG THING!!!

I'VE MADE PROGRESS

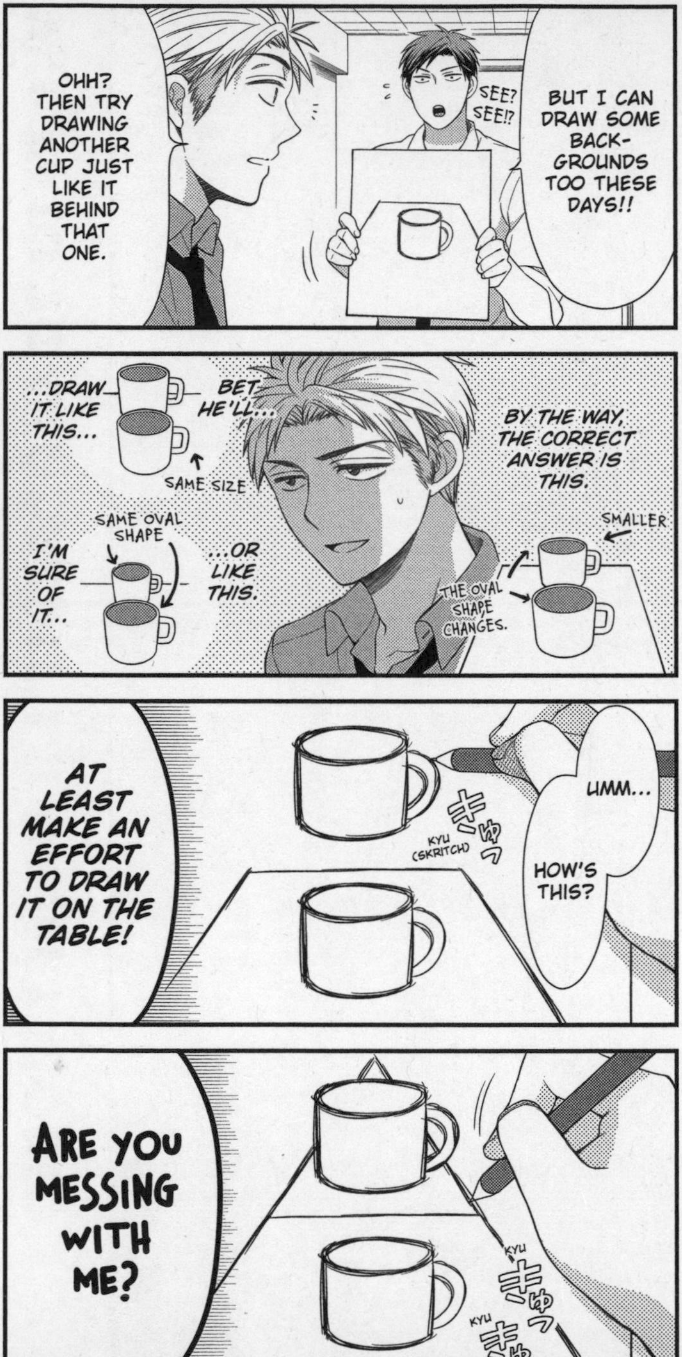
BUT I CAN DRAW SOME BACK-GROUNDS TOO THESE DAYS!!
SEE? SEE!?
OHH? THEN TRY DRAWING ANOTHER CUP JUST LIKE IT BEHIND THAT ONE.
BY THE WAY, THE CORRECT ANSWER IS THIS.
SMALLER
THE OVAL SHAPE CHANGES.
BET HE'LL...
...DRAW IT LIKE THIS...
SAME SIZE
...OR LIKE THIS.
SAME OVAL SHAPE
I'M SURE OF IT...
UMM...
HOW'S THIS?
KYU (SKRITCH)
AT LEAST MAKE AN EFFORT TO DRAW IT ON THE TABLE!
KYU
KYU
ARE YOU MESSING WITH ME?

IF YOU LOOK CLOSELY, IT'S A CREEPY WORLD

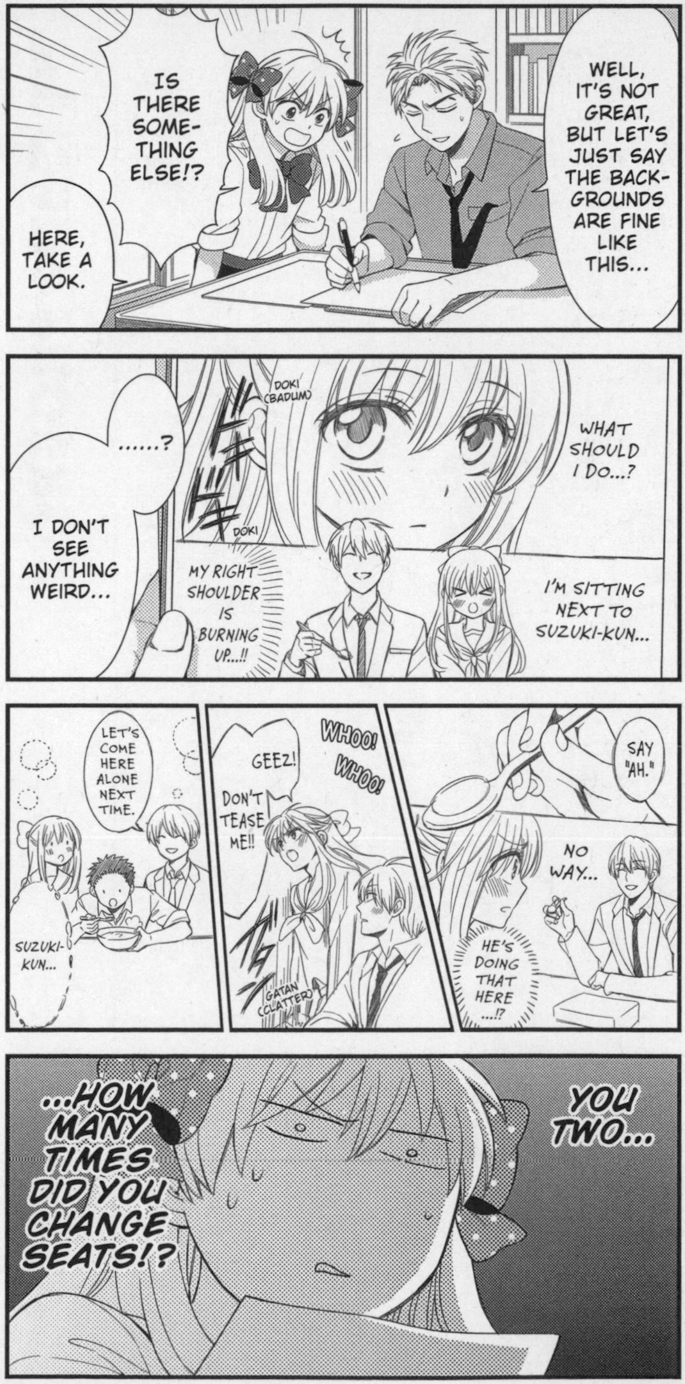
WELL, IT'S NOT GREAT, BUT LET'S JUST SAY THE BACKGROUNDS ARE FINE LIKE THIS...
IS THERE SOMETHING ELSE!?
HERE, TAKE A LOOK.
WHAT SHOULD I DO...?
DOKI (BADUM)
I'M SITTING NEXT TO SUZUKI-KUN...
MY RIGHT SHOULDER IS BURNING UP...!!
DOKI
......?
I DON'T SEE ANYTHING WEIRD...
SAY "AH."
NO WAY...
HE'S DOING THAT HERE ...!?
WHOO!
WHOO!
GEEZ!
DON'T TEASE ME!!
GATAN (CLATTER)
LET'S COME HERE ALONE NEXT TIME.
SUZUKI-KUN...
YOU TWO...
...HOW MANY TIMES DID YOU CHANGE SEATS!?

UNRELIABLE EDITOR

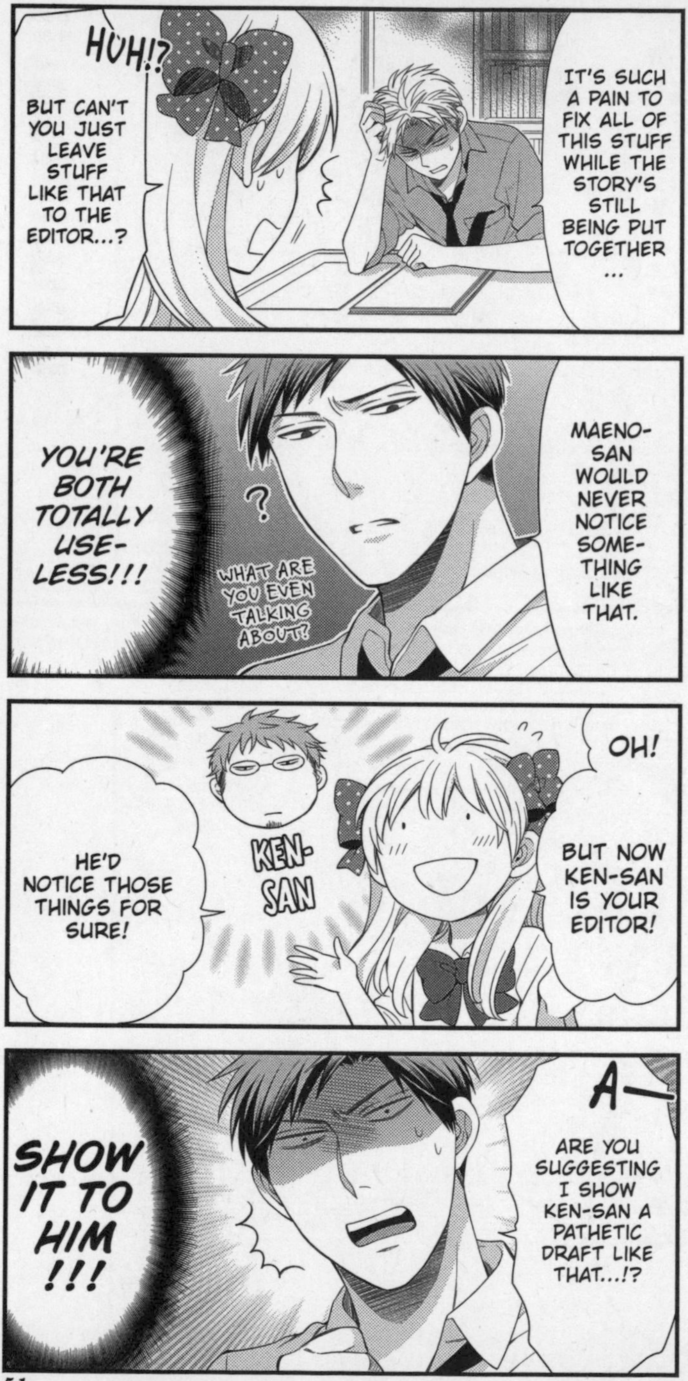

IT'S SUCH A PAIN TO FIX ALL OF THIS STUFF WHILE THE STORY'S STILL BEING PUT TOGETHER ...
HUH!?
BUT CAN'T YOU JUST LEAVE STUFF LIKE THAT TO THE EDITOR...?
MAENO-SAN WOULD NEVER NOTICE SOMETHING LIKE THAT.
?
WHAT ARE YOU EVEN TALKING ABOUT?
YOU'RE BOTH TOTALLY USELESS!!!
OH!
BUT NOW KEN-SAN IS YOUR EDITOR!
KEN-SAN
HE'D NOTICE THOSE THINGS FOR SURE!
A—
ARE YOU SUGGESTING I SHOW KEN-SAN A PATHETIC DRAFT LIKE THAT...!?
SHOW IT TO HIM!!!

IMAGINATION

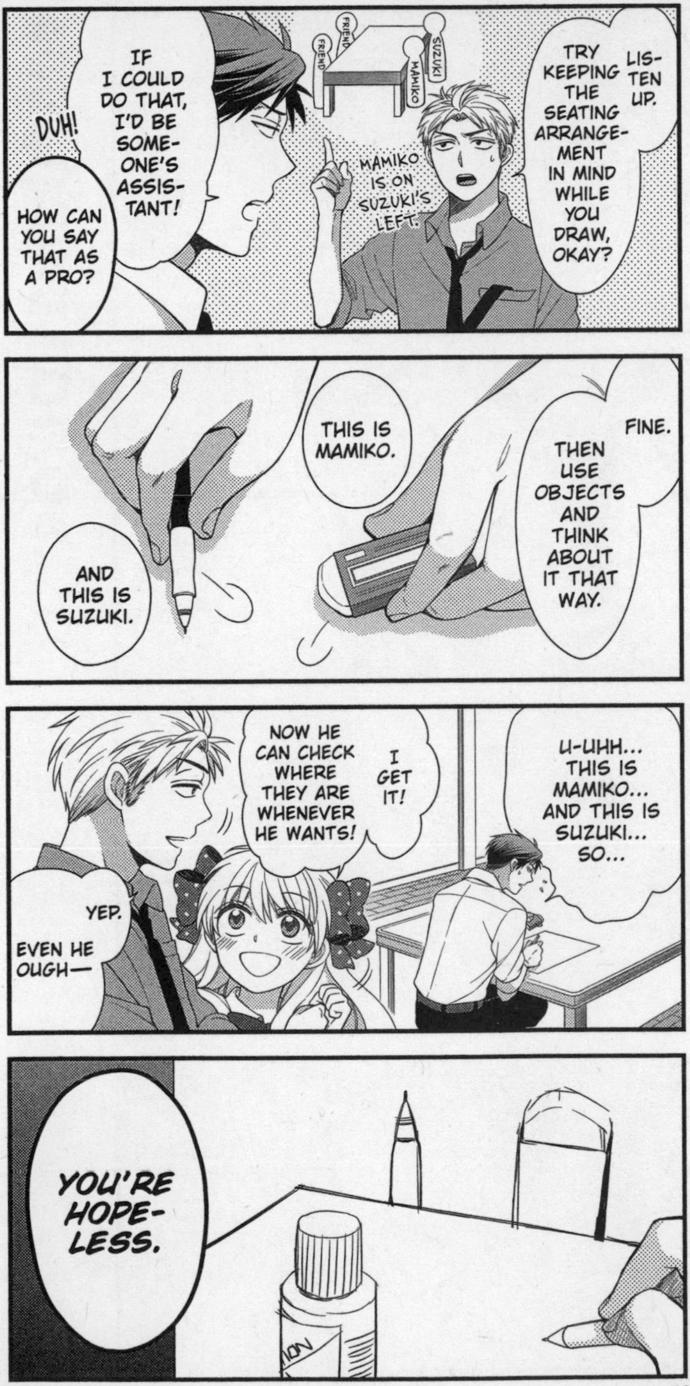
LISTEN UP.
TRY KEEPING THE SEATING ARRANGEMENT IN MIND WHILE YOU DRAW, OKAY?
SUZUKI
MAMIKO
FRIEND
FRIEND
MAMIKO IS ON SUZUKI'S LEFT.
IF I COULD DO THAT, I'D BE SOMEONE'S ASSISTANT!
DUH!
HOW CAN YOU SAY THAT AS A PRO?
FINE.
THEN USE OBJECTS AND THINK ABOUT IT THAT WAY.
THIS IS MAMIKO.
AND THIS IS SUZUKI.
U-UHH... THIS IS MAMIKO... AND THIS IS SUZUKI... SO...
I GET IT!
NOW HE CAN CHECK WHERE THEY ARE WHENEVER HE WANTS!
YEP.
EVEN HE OUGH—
YOU'RE HOPELESS.

THE MODELS ON HAND

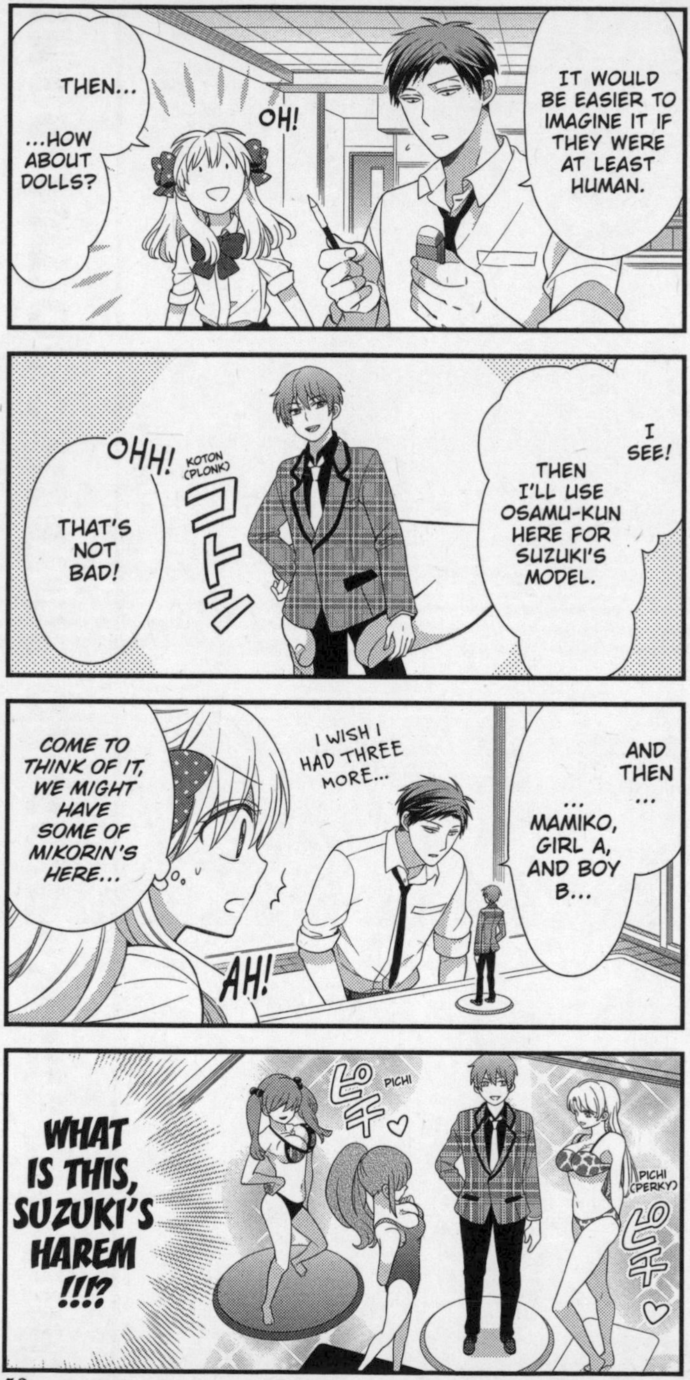
IT WOULD BE EASIER TO IMAGINE IT IF THEY WERE AT LEAST HUMAN.
OH!
THEN...
...HOW ABOUT DOLLS?
I SEE!
THEN I'LL USE OSAMU-KUN HERE FOR SUZUKI'S MODEL.
KOTON (PLONK)
コトン
OHH!
THAT'S NOT BAD!
AND THEN ...
... MAMIKO, GIRL A, AND BOY B...
I WISH I HAD THREE MORE...
COME TO THINK OF IT, WE MIGHT HAVE SOME OF MIKORIN'S HERE...
AH!
PICHI (PERKY)
ピチ
PICHI
ピチ
WHAT IS THIS, SUZUKI'S HAREM!!!?

THE RESULT OF OBSERVING CAREFULLY WHILE DRAWING

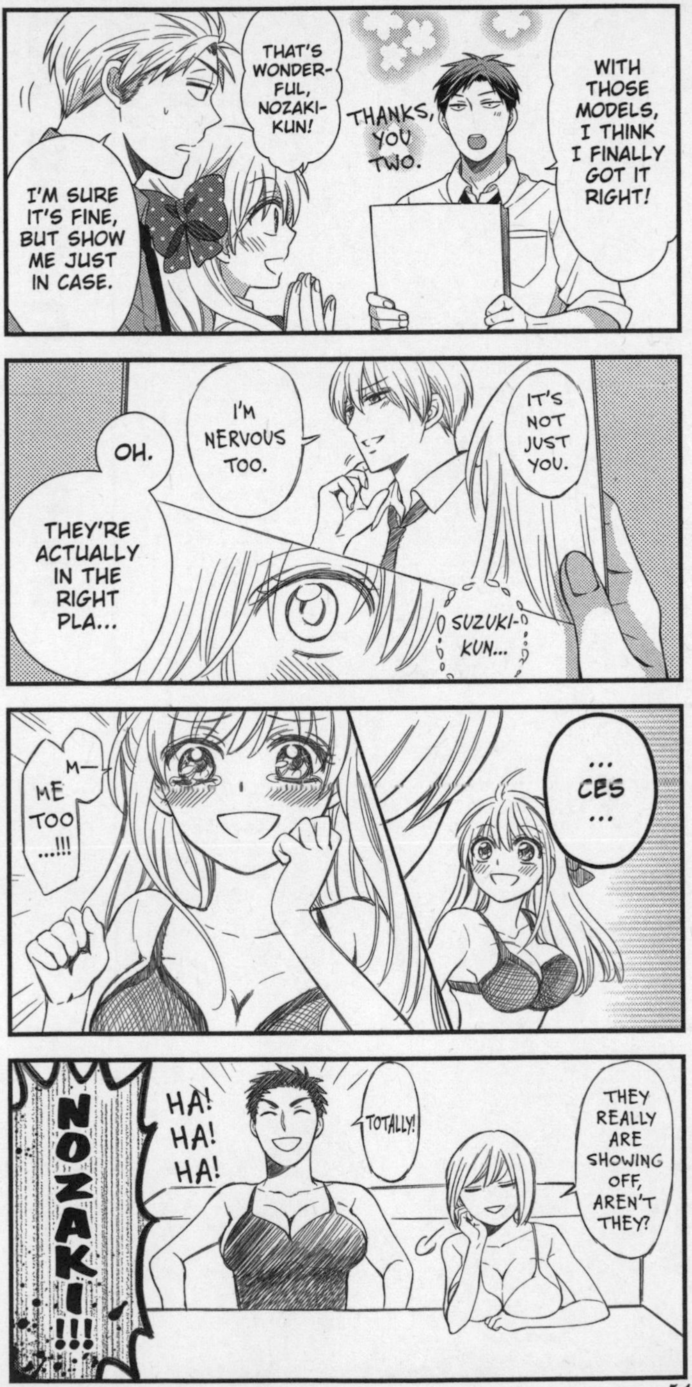
WITH THOSE MODELS, I THINK I FINALLY GOT IT RIGHT!
THANKS, YOU TWO.
THAT'S WONDERFUL, NOZAKI-KUN!
I'M SURE IT'S FINE, BUT SHOW ME JUST IN CASE.
IT'S NOT JUST YOU.
I'M NERVOUS TOO.
SUZUKI-KUN...
OH.
THEY'RE ACTUALLY IN THE RIGHT PLA...
...CES...
M— ME TOO...!!!
THEY REALLY ARE SHOWING OFF, AREN'T THEY?
TOTALLY!
HA! HA! HA!
NOZAKI!!!

INSTINCTIVELY

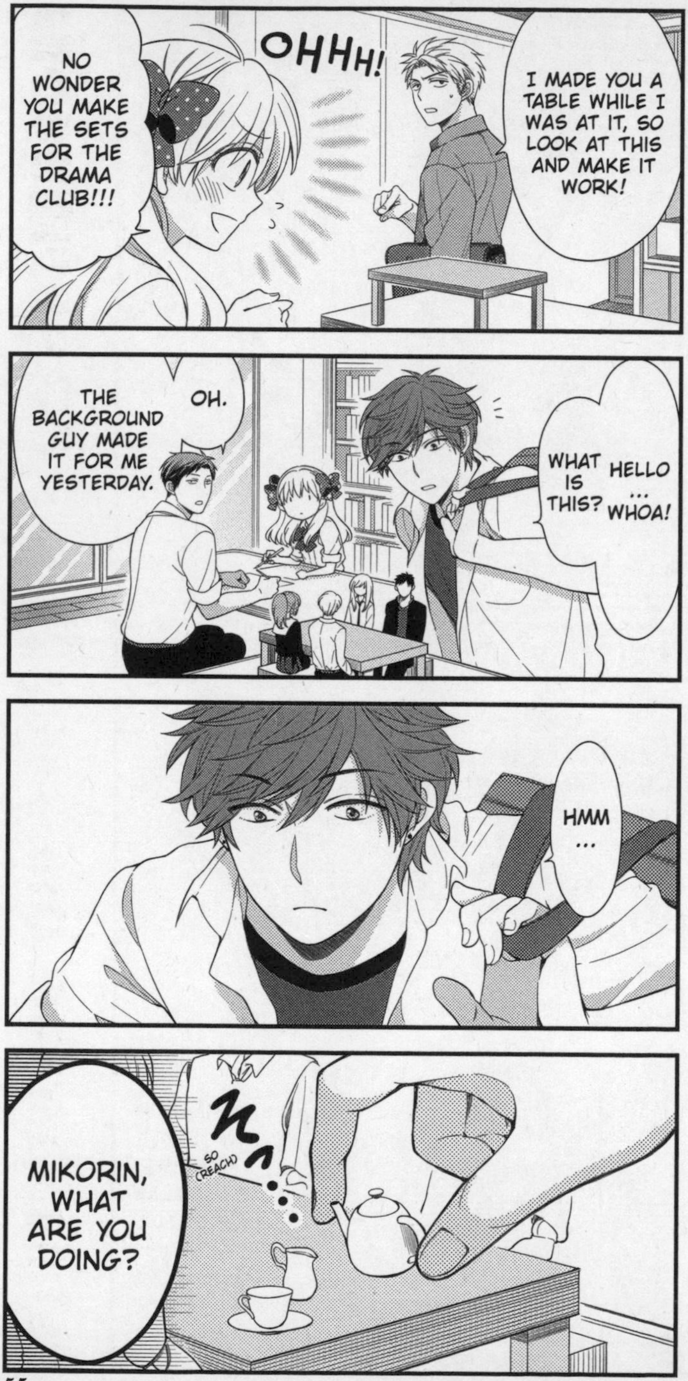

I MADE YOU A TABLE WHILE I WAS AT IT, SO LOOK AT THIS AND MAKE IT WORK!
OHHHH!
NO WONDER YOU MAKE THE SETS FOR THE DRAMA CLUB!!!
HELLO... WHOA!
WHAT IS THIS?
OH.
THE BACKGROUND GUY MADE IT FOR ME YESTERDAY.
HMM...
SO (REACH)
MIKORIN, WHAT ARE YOU DOING?

EXCHANGING○○

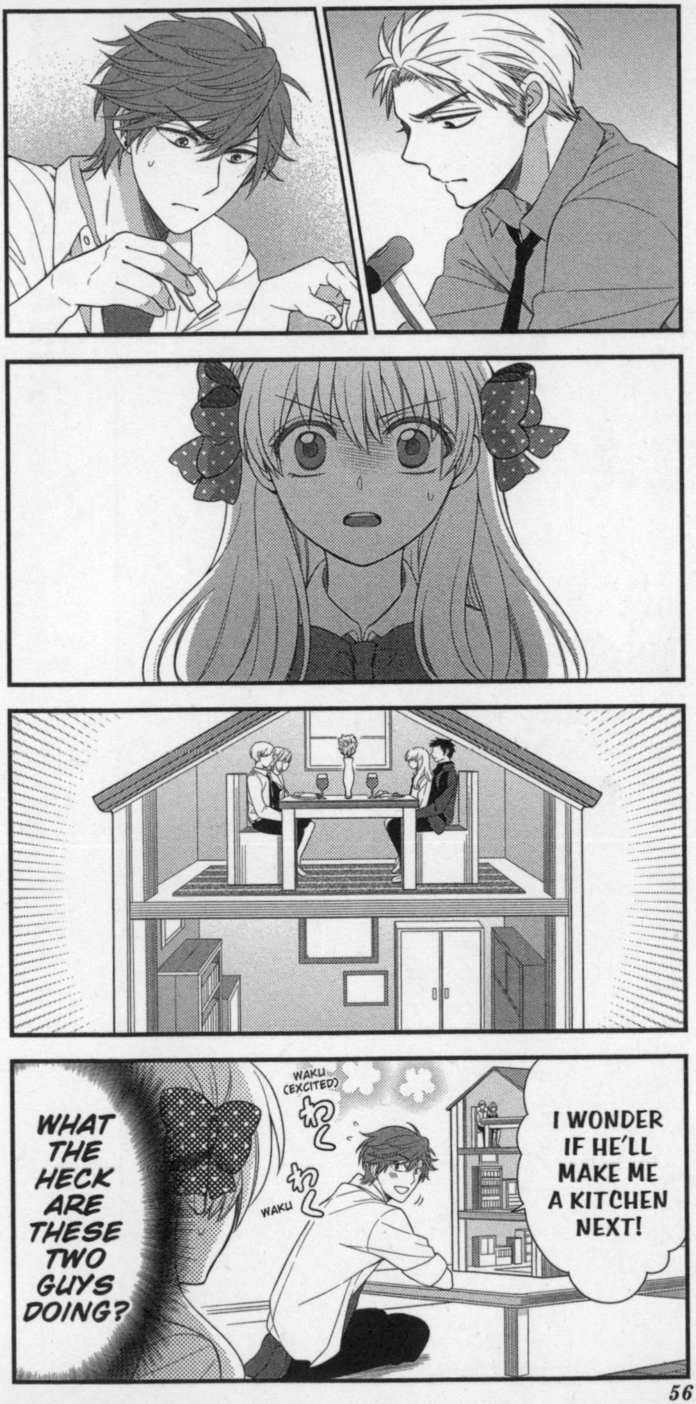
I WONDER IF HE'LL MAKE ME A KITCHEN NEXT!
WAKU (EXCITED)
わく
わく
WAKU
WHAT THE HECK ARE THESE TWO GUYS DOING?

THE HOBBIES OF HIGH SCHOOL BOYS

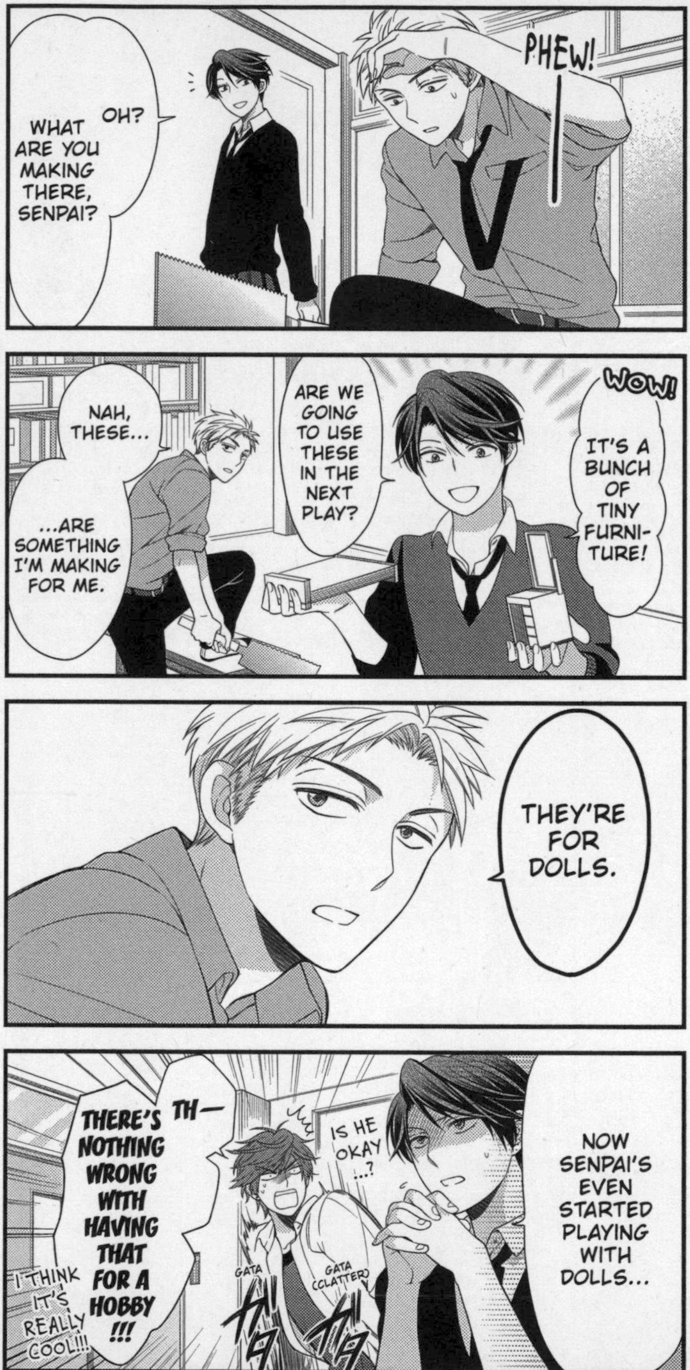
PHEW!
OH?
WHAT ARE YOU MAKING THERE, SENPAI?
WOW!
IT'S A BUNCH OF TINY FURNITURE!
ARE WE GOING TO USE THESE IN THE NEXT PLAY?
NAH, THESE...
...ARE SOMETHING I'M MAKING FOR ME.
THEY'RE FOR DOLLS.
NOW SENPAI'S EVEN STARTED PLAYING WITH DOLLS...
IS HE OKAY ...?
GATA (CLATTER)
TH—
THERE'S NOTHING WRONG WITH HAVING THAT FOR A HOBBY !!!
GATA
I THINK IT'S REALLY COOL!!!

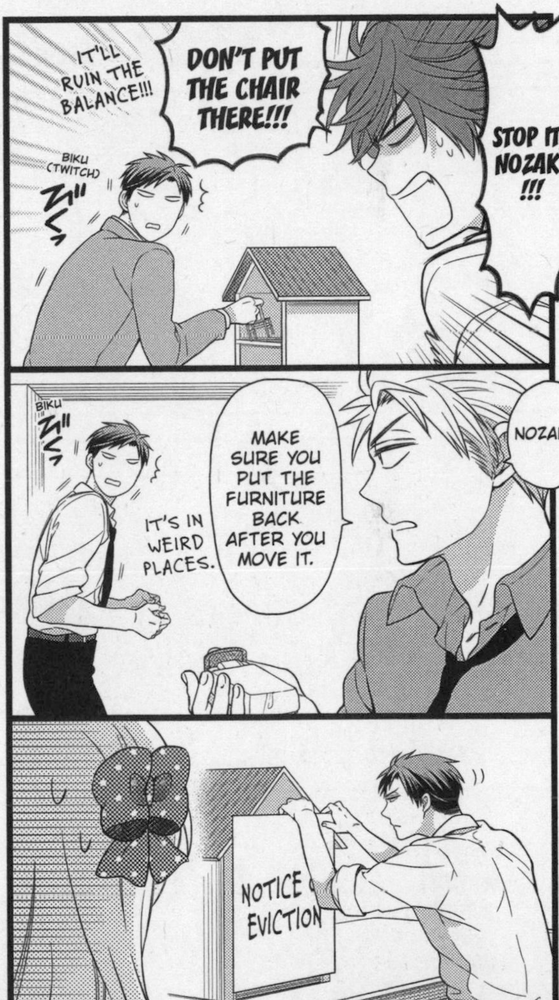
STOP IT, NOZAKI!!!
DON'T PUT THE CHAIR THERE!!!
IT'LL RUIN THE BALANCE!!!
BIKU (TWITCH)
NOZAKI.
MAKE SURE YOU PUT THE FURNITURE BACK AFTER YOU MOVE IT.
IT'S IN WEIRD PLACES.
BIKU
NOTICE
EVICTION

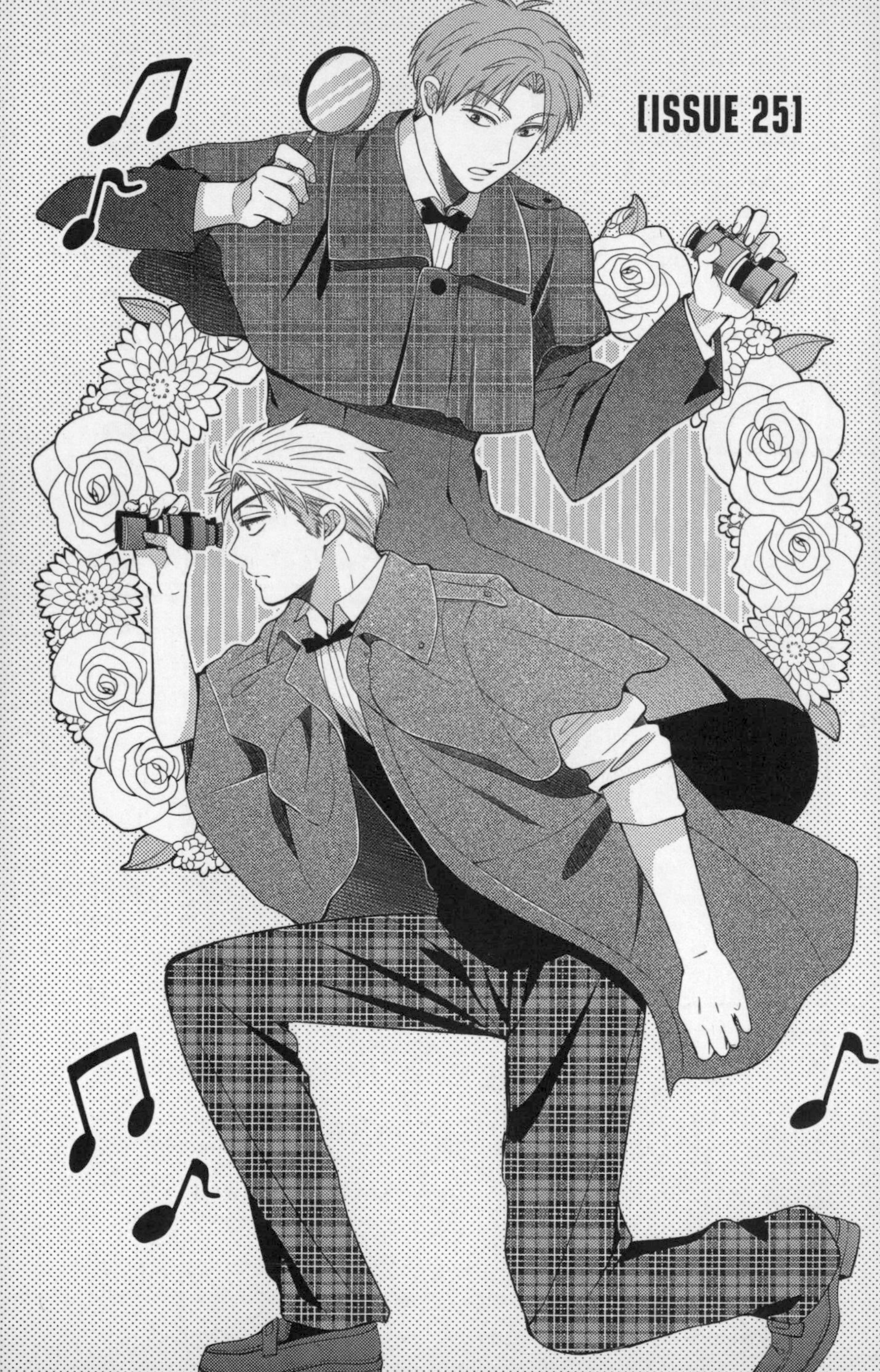
[ISSUE 25]

AN EXCITING WEAKNESS

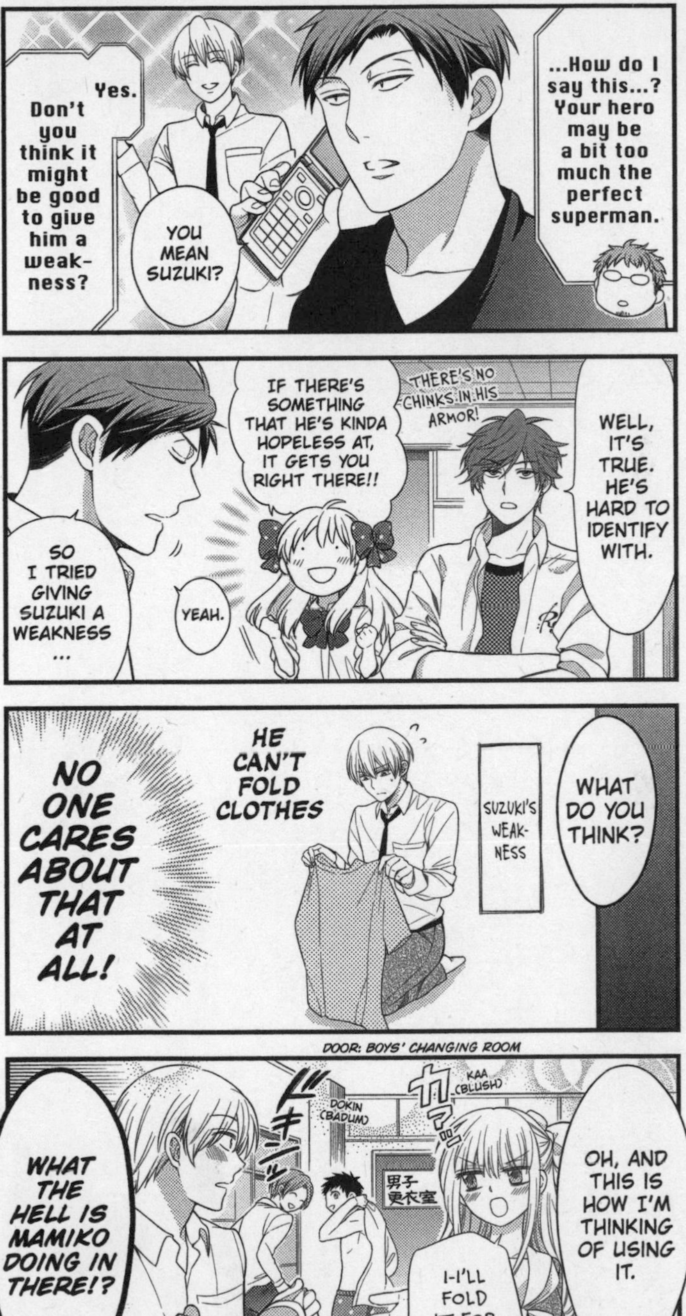
...How do I say this...? Your hero may be a bit too much the perfect superman.
YOU MEAN SUZUKI?
Yes. Don't you think it might be good to give him a weak-ness?
WELL, IT'S TRUE. HE'S HARD TO IDENTIFY WITH.
THERE'S NO CHINKS IN HIS ARMOR!
IF THERE'S SOMETHING THAT HE'S KINDA HOPELESS AT, IT GETS YOU RIGHT THERE!!
YEAH.
SO I TRIED GIVING SUZUKI A WEAKNESS ...
WHAT DO YOU THINK?
SUZUKI'S WEAK-NESS
HE CAN'T FOLD CLOTHES
NO ONE CARES ABOUT THAT AT ALL!
DOOR: BOYS' CHANGING ROOM
OH, AND THIS IS HOW I'M THINKING OF USING IT.
KAA (BLUSH)
男子更衣室
DOKIN (BADUM)
I-I'LL FOLD IT FOR YOU!!!
WHAT THE HELL IS MAMIKO DOING IN THERE!?

THE GAP

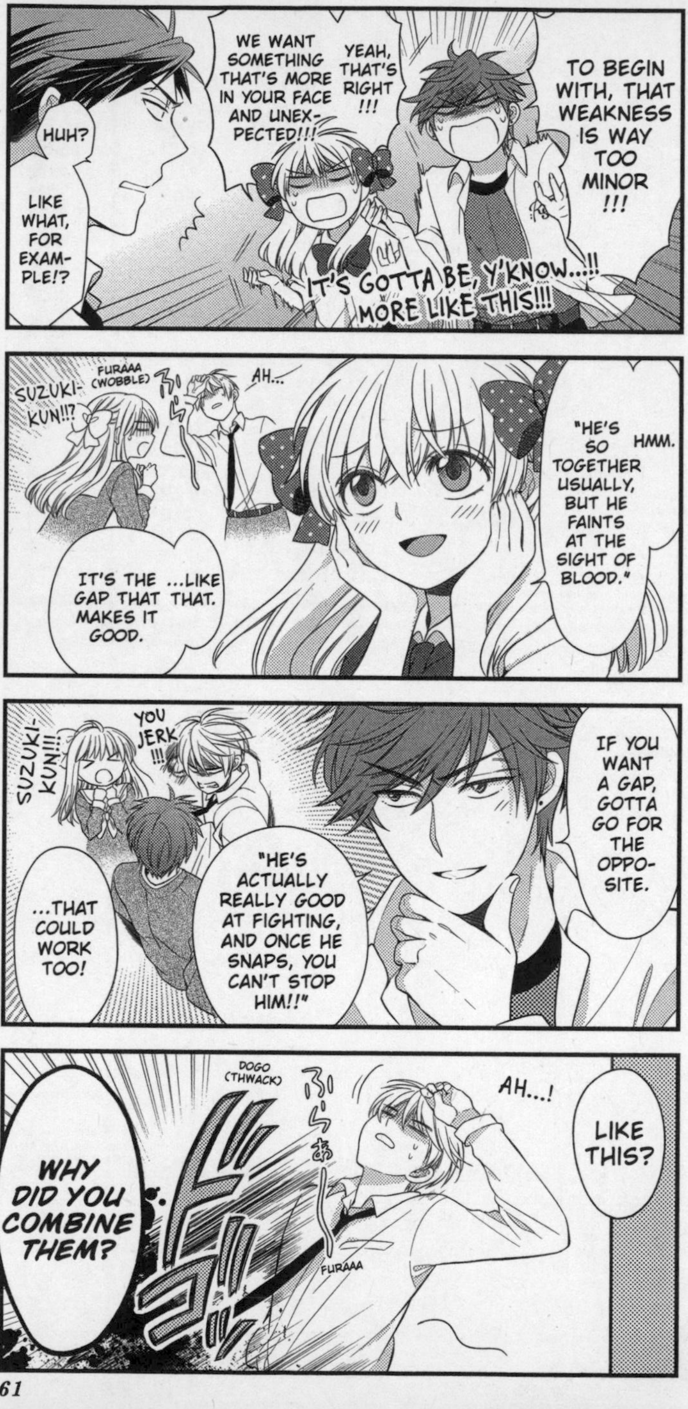
TO BEGIN WITH, THAT WEAKNESS IS WAY TOO MINOR!!!
YEAH, THAT'S RIGHT!!!
WE WANT SOMETHING THAT'S MORE IN YOUR FACE AND UNEXPECTED!!!
HUH?
LIKE WHAT, FOR EXAMPLE!?
IT'S GOTTA BE, Y'KNOW...!! MORE LIKE THIS!!!
HMM.
"HE'S SO TOGETHER USUALLY, BUT HE FAINTS AT THE SIGHT OF BLOOD."
AH...
FURAAA (WOBBLE)
SUZUKI-KUN!!?
...LIKE THAT.
IT'S THE GAP THAT MAKES IT GOOD.
IF YOU WANT A GAP, GOTTA GO FOR THE OPPOSITE.
YOU JERK!!!
SUZUKI-KUN!!!
"HE'S ACTUALLY REALLY GOOD AT FIGHTING, AND ONCE HE SNAPS, YOU CAN'T STOP HIM!!"
...THAT COULD WORK TOO!
LIKE THIS?
AH...!
DOGO (THWACK)
FURAAA
WHY DID YOU COMBINE THEM?

HER NICKNAME

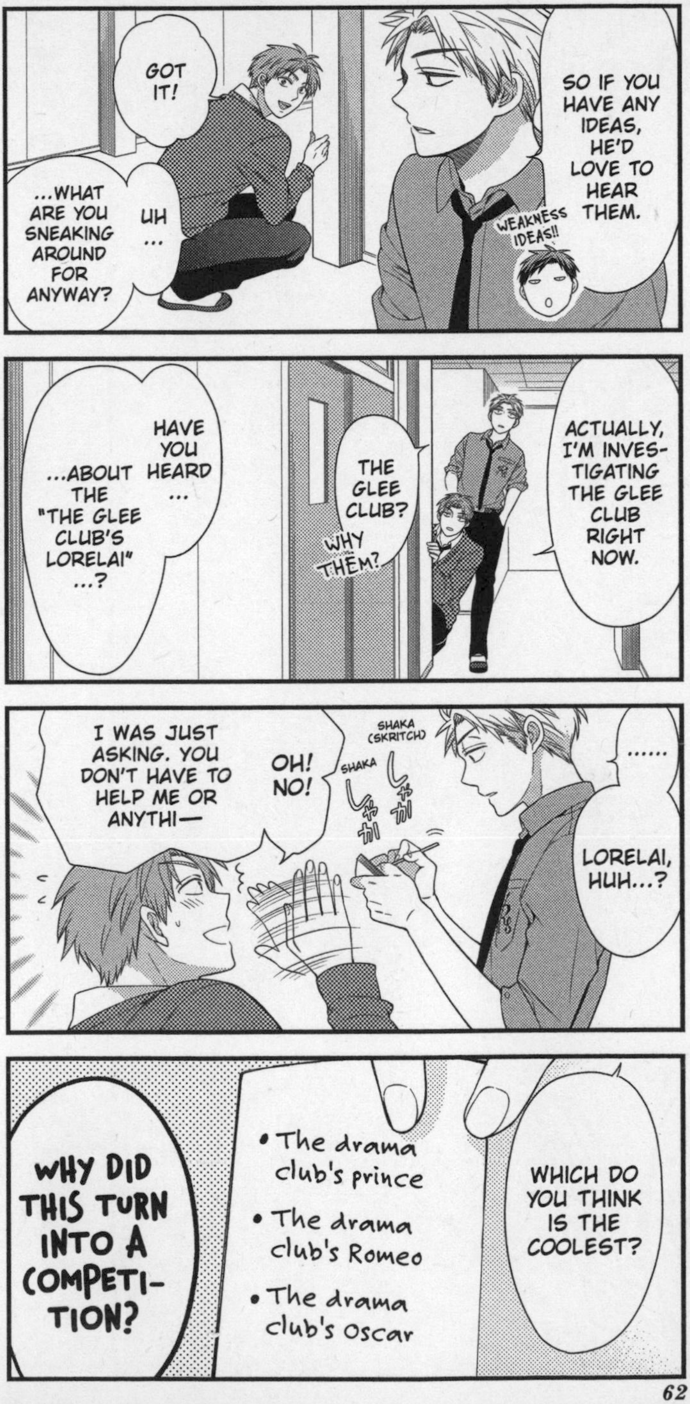

SO IF YOU HAVE ANY IDEAS, HE'D LOVE TO HEAR THEM.
WEAKNESS IDEAS!!
GOT IT!
UH ...
...WHAT ARE YOU SNEAKING AROUND FOR ANYWAY?
ACTUALLY, I'M INVESTIGATING THE GLEE CLUB RIGHT NOW.
THE GLEE CLUB?
WHY THEM?
HAVE YOU HEARD ...
...ABOUT THE "THE GLEE CLUB'S LORELAI" ...?
......
LORELAI, HUH...?
SHAKA (SKRITCH)
しゃか
SHAKA
しゃか
OH! NO!
I WAS JUST ASKING. YOU DON'T HAVE TO HELP ME OR ANYTHI—
WHICH DO YOU THINK IS THE COOLEST?
• The drama club's prince
• The drama club's Romeo
• The drama club's Oscar
WHY DID THIS TURN INTO A COMPETITION?

*OSCAR IS A REFERENCE TO THE PROTAGONIST OF THE SHOUJO MANGA CLASSIC THE ROSE OF VERSAILLES BY RIYOKO IKEDA, WHICH IS SET IN FRANCE DURING THE FRENCH REVOLUTION. OSCAR IS A WOMAN WHO WAS BROUGHT UP AS A MAN BY HER FATHER TO SUCCEED HIM IN HIS POST AT THE ROYAL COURT. SHE WORKS AS COMMANDER OF THE ROYAL GUARD IN THE COURT OF MARIE ANTOINETTE AND IS PORTRAYED IN MEN'S GARB.

HORI-SENPAI'S INVESTIGATION REPORT

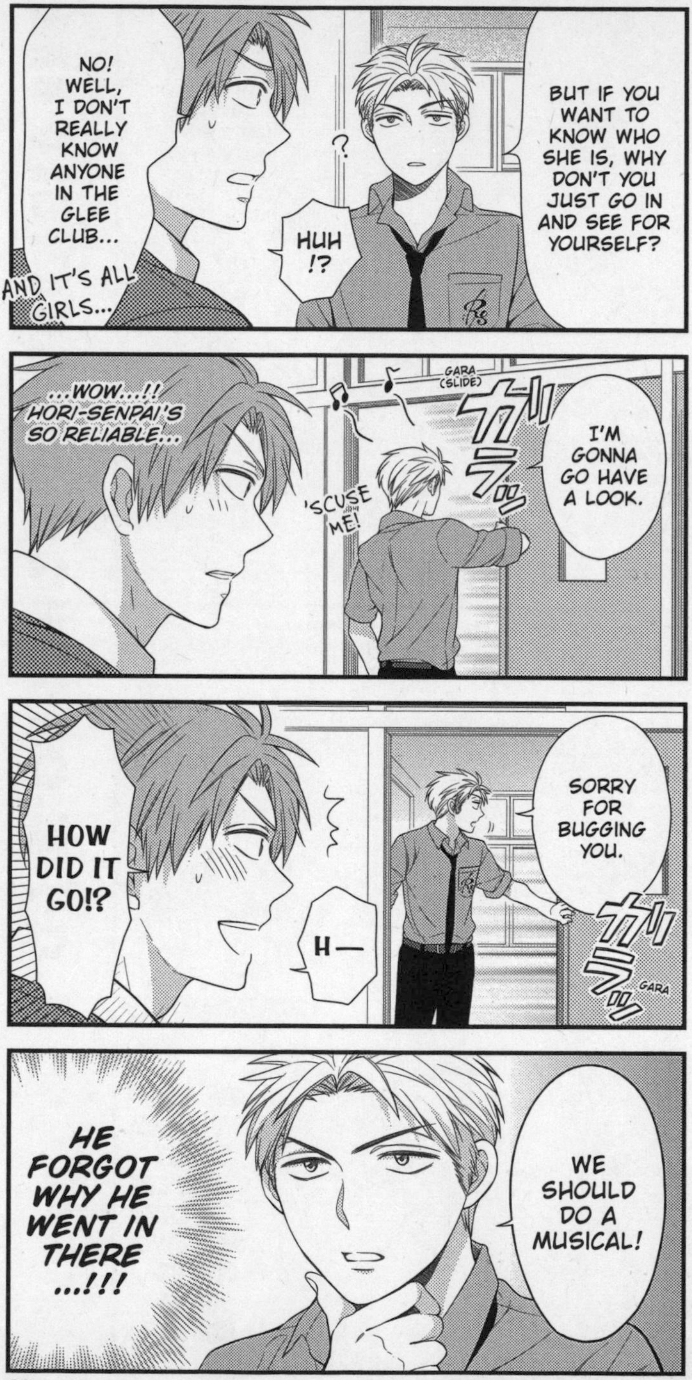
BUT IF YOU WANT TO KNOW WHO SHE IS, WHY DON'T YOU JUST GO IN AND SEE FOR YOURSELF?
?
HUH !?
NO! WELL, I DON'T REALLY KNOW ANYONE IN THE GLEE CLUB...
AND IT'S ALL GIRLS...
I'M GONNA GO HAVE A LOOK.
GARA (SLIDE)
'SCUSE ME!
...WOW...!! HORI-SENPAI'S SO RELIABLE...
GARA
SORRY FOR BUGGING YOU.
H—
HOW DID IT GO!?
WE SHOULD DO A MUSICAL!
HE FORGOT WHY HE WENT IN THERE ...!!!

THE REASON THAT COMES TO MIND

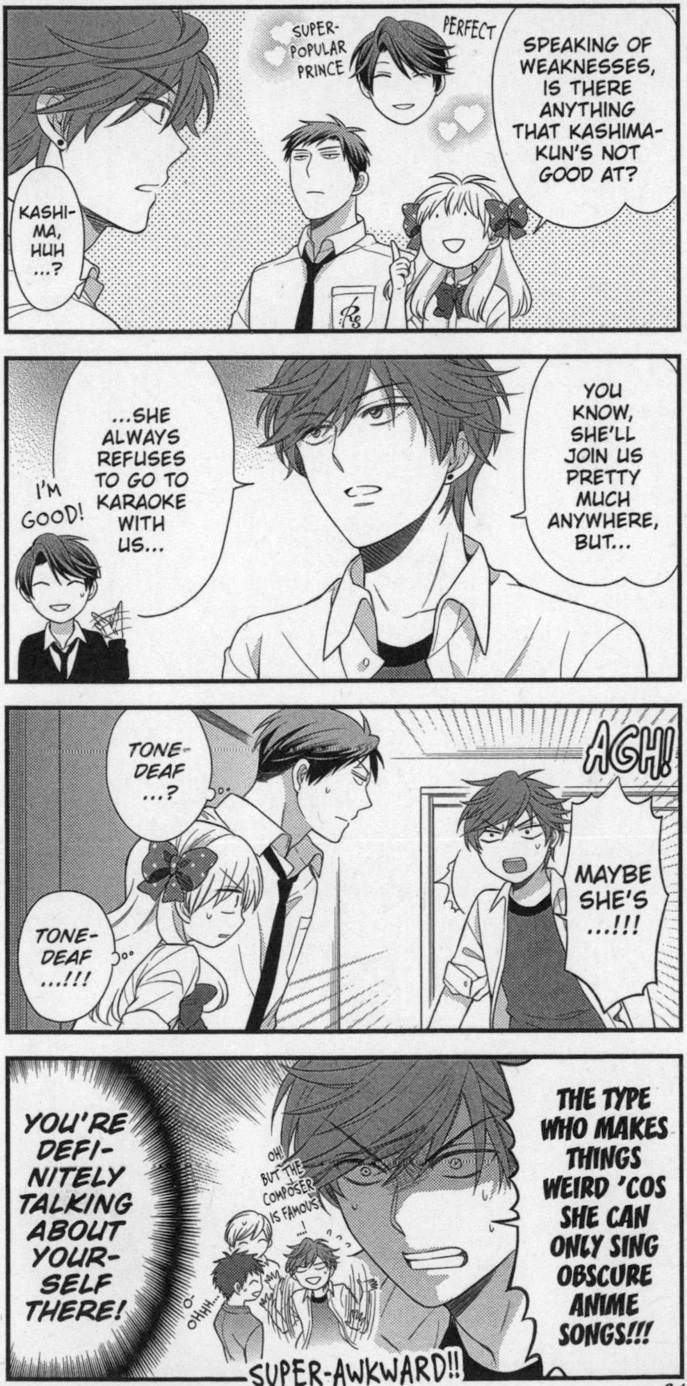
SPEAKING OF WEAKNESSES, IS THERE ANYTHING THAT KASHIMA-KUN'S NOT GOOD AT?
PERFECT
SUPER-POPULAR PRINCE
KASHIMA, HUH ...?
YOU KNOW, SHE'LL JOIN US PRETTY MUCH ANYWHERE, BUT...
...SHE ALWAYS REFUSES TO GO TO KARAOKE WITH US...
I'M GOOD!
AGH!
MAYBE SHE'S ...!!!
TONE-DEAF ...?
TONE-DEAF ...!!!
THE TYPE WHO MAKES THINGS WEIRD 'COS SHE CAN ONLY SING OBSCURE ANIME SONGS!!!
OH! BUT THE COMPOSER IS FAMOUS ...!
O-OHHH...
YOU'RE DEFI-NITELY TALKING ABOUT YOUR-SELF THERE!
SUPER-AWKWARD!!

LET DOWN

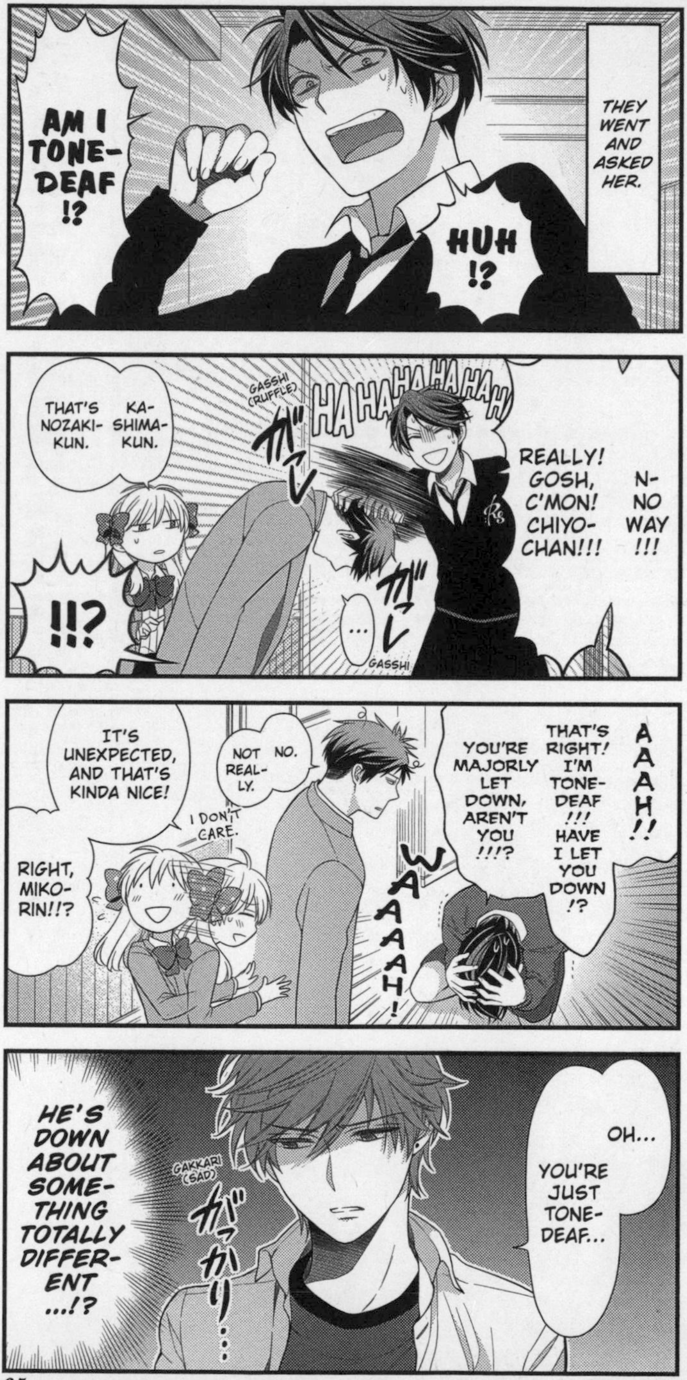
THEY WENT AND ASKED HER.
HUH !?
AM I TONE-DEAF !?
N-NO WAY !!!
REALLY! GOSH, C'MON! CHIYO-CHAN!!!
HAHAHAHAHAH
GASSHI (RUFFLE)
KA-SHIMA-KUN.
THAT'S NOZAKI-KUN.
...
GASSHI
!!?
AAAAH!!
THAT'S RIGHT! I'M TONE-DEAF!!! HAVE I LET YOU DOWN !?
YOU'RE MAJORLY LET DOWN, AREN'T YOU !!!?
WAAAAAH!
NO.
NOT REAL-LY.
IT'S UNEXPECTED, AND THAT'S KINDA NICE!
I DON'T CARE.
RIGHT, MIKO-RIN!!?
OH...
YOU'RE JUST TONE-DEAF...
GAKKARI (SAD)
HE'S DOWN ABOUT SOME-THING TOTALLY DIFFER-ENT ...!?

TOO HIGH A HURDLE

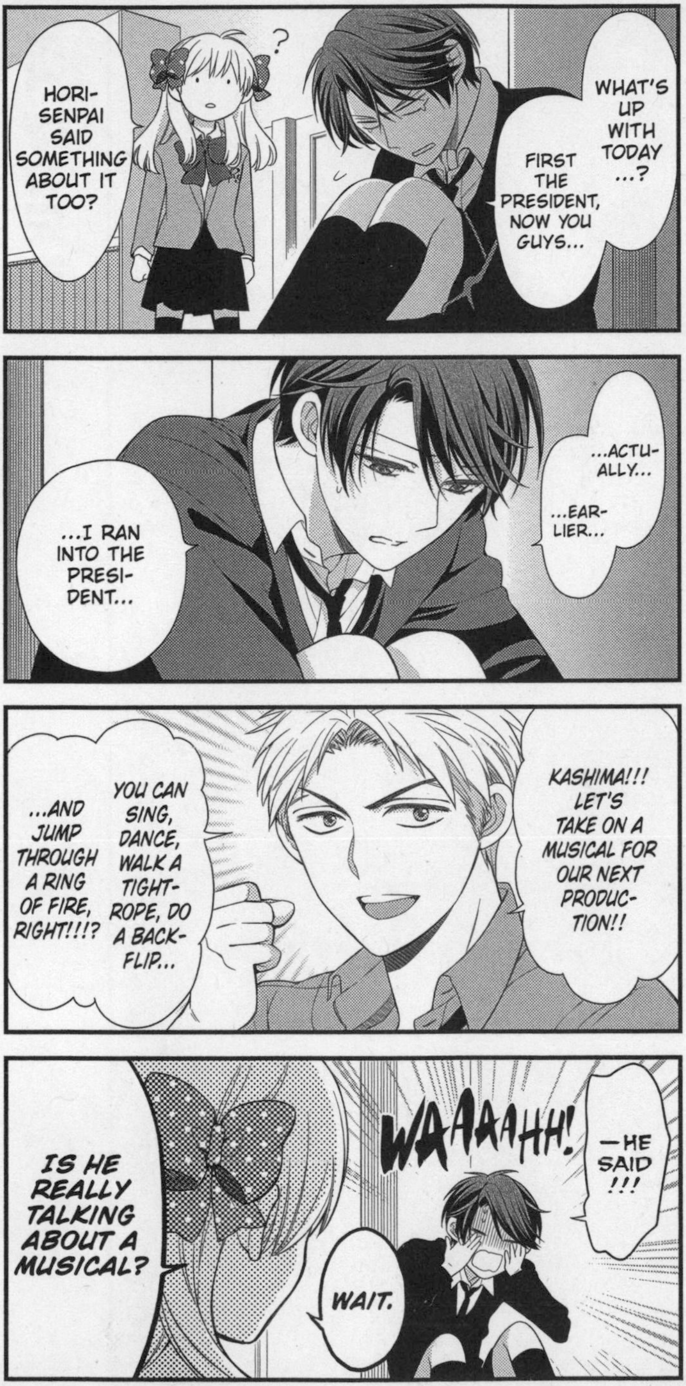
WHAT'S UP WITH TODAY...?
FIRST THE PRESIDENT, NOW YOU GUYS...
HORI-SENPAI SAID SOMETHING ABOUT IT TOO?
...ACTUALLY...
...EARLIER...
...I RAN INTO THE PRESIDENT...
KASHIMA!!! LET'S TAKE ON A MUSICAL FOR OUR NEXT PRODUCTION!!
YOU CAN SING, DANCE, WALK A TIGHTROPE, DO A BACKFLIP...
...AND JUMP THROUGH A RING OF FIRE, RIGHT!!!?
—HE SAID!!!
WAAAAHH!
WAIT.
IS HE REALLY TALKING ABOUT A MUSICAL?

USED TO IT

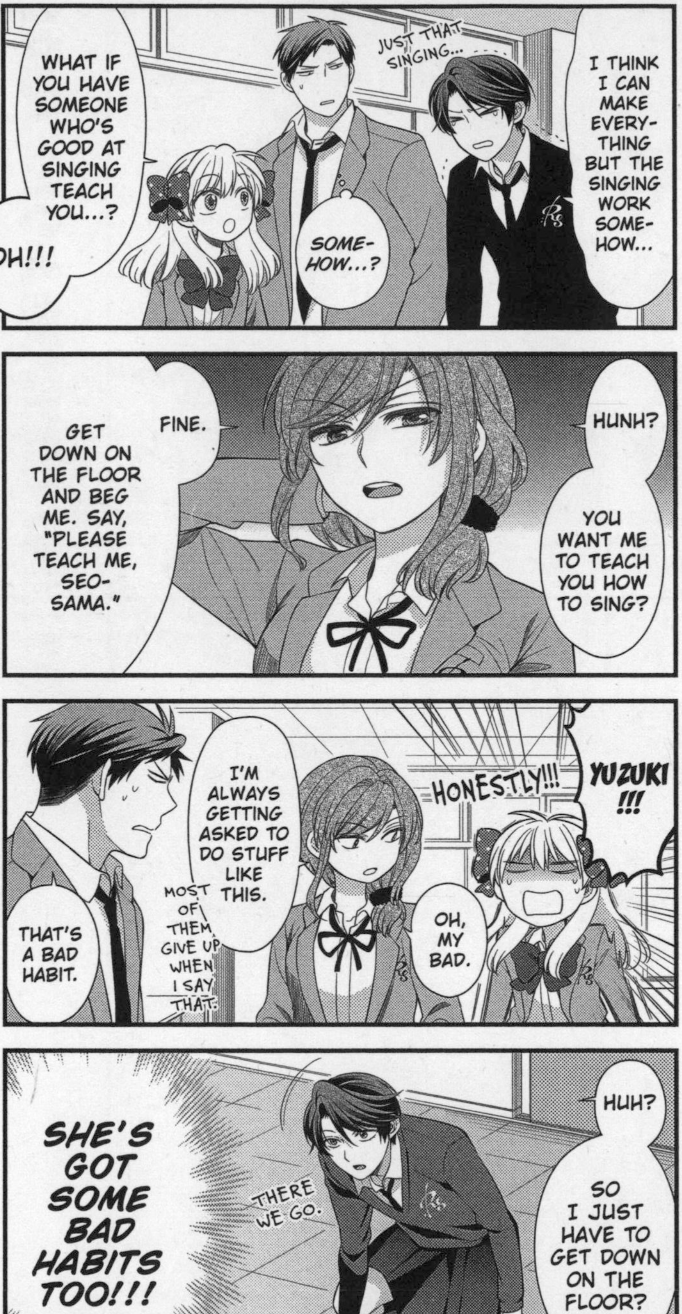
I THINK I CAN MAKE EVERY-THING BUT THE SINGING WORK SOME-HOW...
JUST THAT SINGING...
SOME-HOW...?
WHAT IF YOU HAVE SOMEONE WHO'S GOOD AT SINGING TEACH YOU...?
OH!!!
HUNH?
YOU WANT ME TO TEACH YOU HOW TO SING?
FINE.
GET DOWN ON THE FLOOR AND BEG ME. SAY, "PLEASE TEACH ME, SEO-SAMA."
YUZUKI!!!
HONESTLY!!!
OH, MY BAD.
I'M ALWAYS GETTING ASKED TO DO STUFF LIKE THIS.
MOST OF THEM GIVE UP WHEN I SAY THAT.
THAT'S A BAD HABIT.
HUH?
SO I JUST HAVE TO GET DOWN ON THE FLOOR?
THERE WE GO.
SHE'S GOT SOME BAD HABITS TOO!!!

JUDGING THE RAW MATERIAL

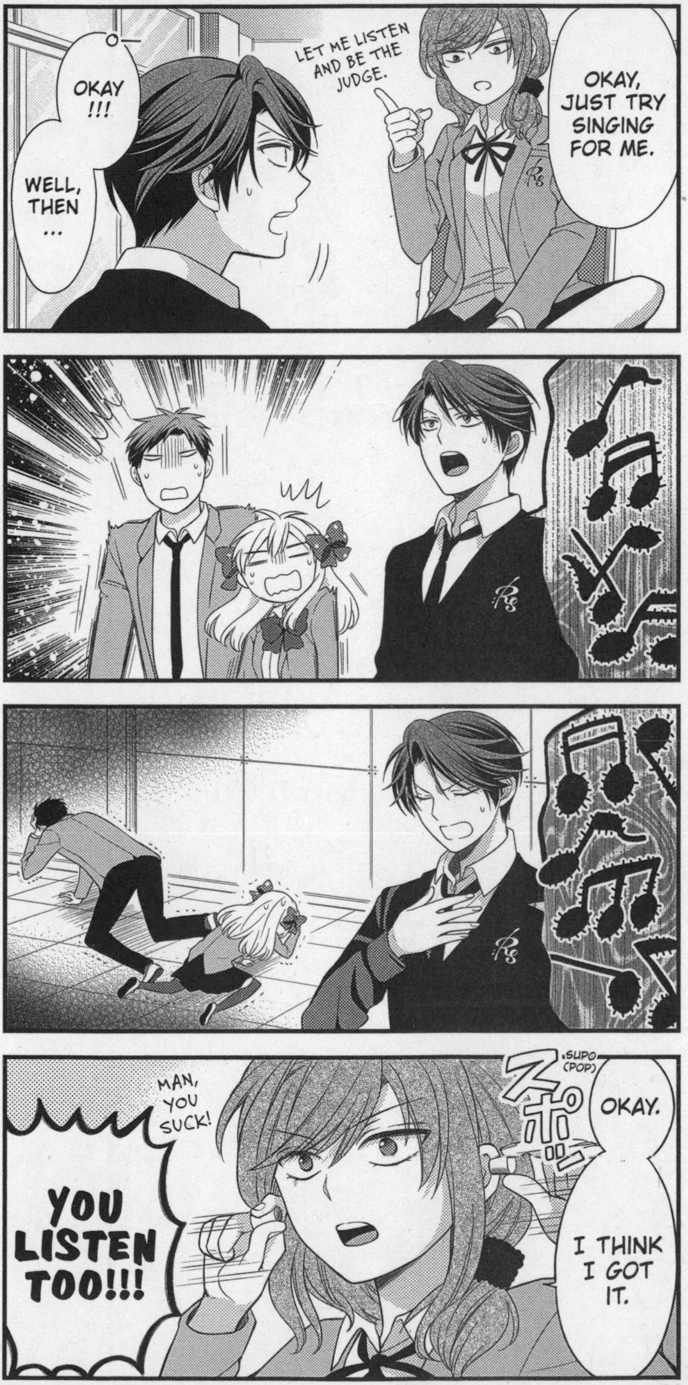
OKAY, JUST TRY SINGING FOR ME.
LET ME LISTEN AND BE THE JUDGE.
OKAY !!!
WELL, THEN ...
OKAY.
I THINK I GOT IT.
SUPO (POP)
MAN, YOU SUCK!
YOU LISTEN TOO!!!

CHOICES

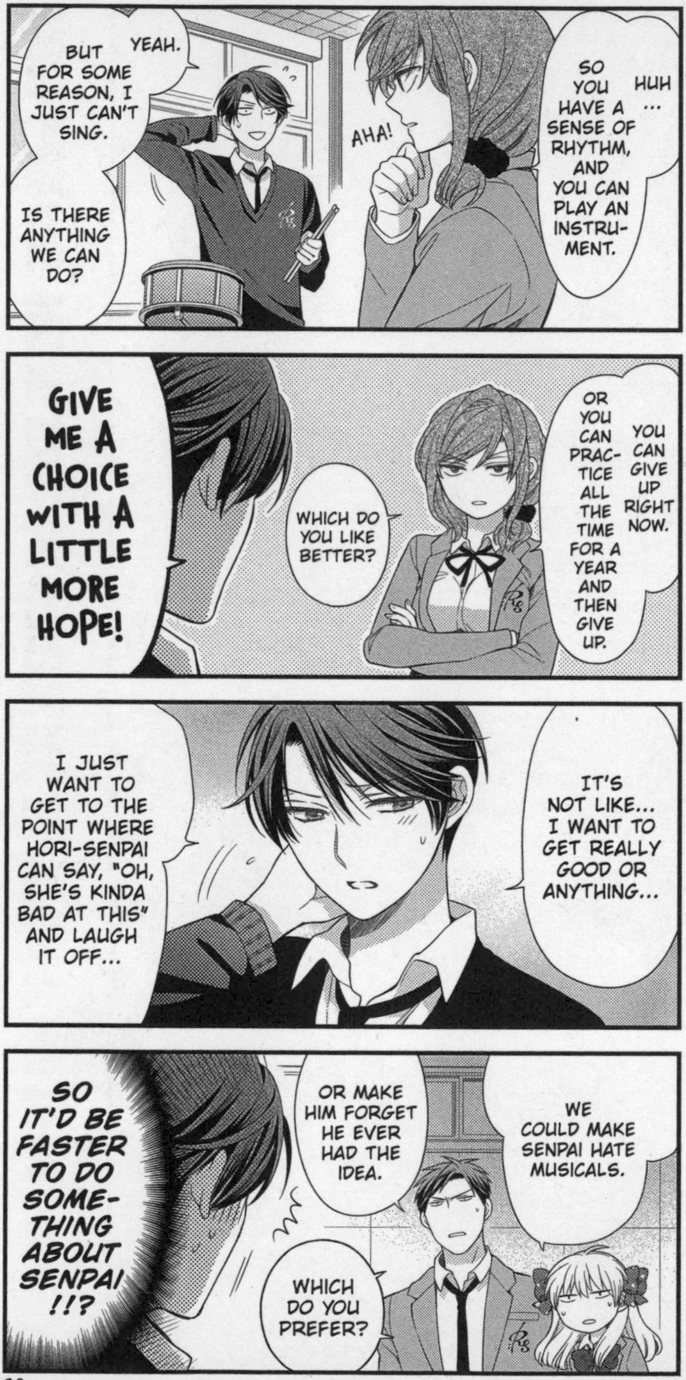

HUH ...
SO YOU HAVE A SENSE OF RHYTHM, AND YOU CAN PLAY AN INSTRUMENT.
AHA!
YEAH.
BUT FOR SOME REASON, I JUST CAN'T SING.
IS THERE ANYTHING WE CAN DO?
YOU CAN GIVE UP RIGHT NOW.
OR YOU CAN PRACTICE ALL THE TIME FOR A YEAR AND THEN GIVE UP.
WHICH DO YOU LIKE BETTER?
GIVE ME A CHOICE WITH A LITTLE MORE HOPE!
IT'S NOT LIKE... I WANT TO GET REALLY GOOD OR ANYTHING...
I JUST WANT TO GET TO THE POINT WHERE HORI-SENPAI CAN SAY, "OH, SHE'S KINDA BAD AT THIS" AND LAUGH IT OFF...
WE COULD MAKE SENPAI HATE MUSICALS.
OR MAKE HIM FORGET HE EVER HAD THE IDEA.
WHICH DO YOU PREFER?
SO IT'D BE FASTER TO DO SOMETHING ABOUT SENPAI!!?

WEIGHING HER STRENGTHS AND WEAKNESSES

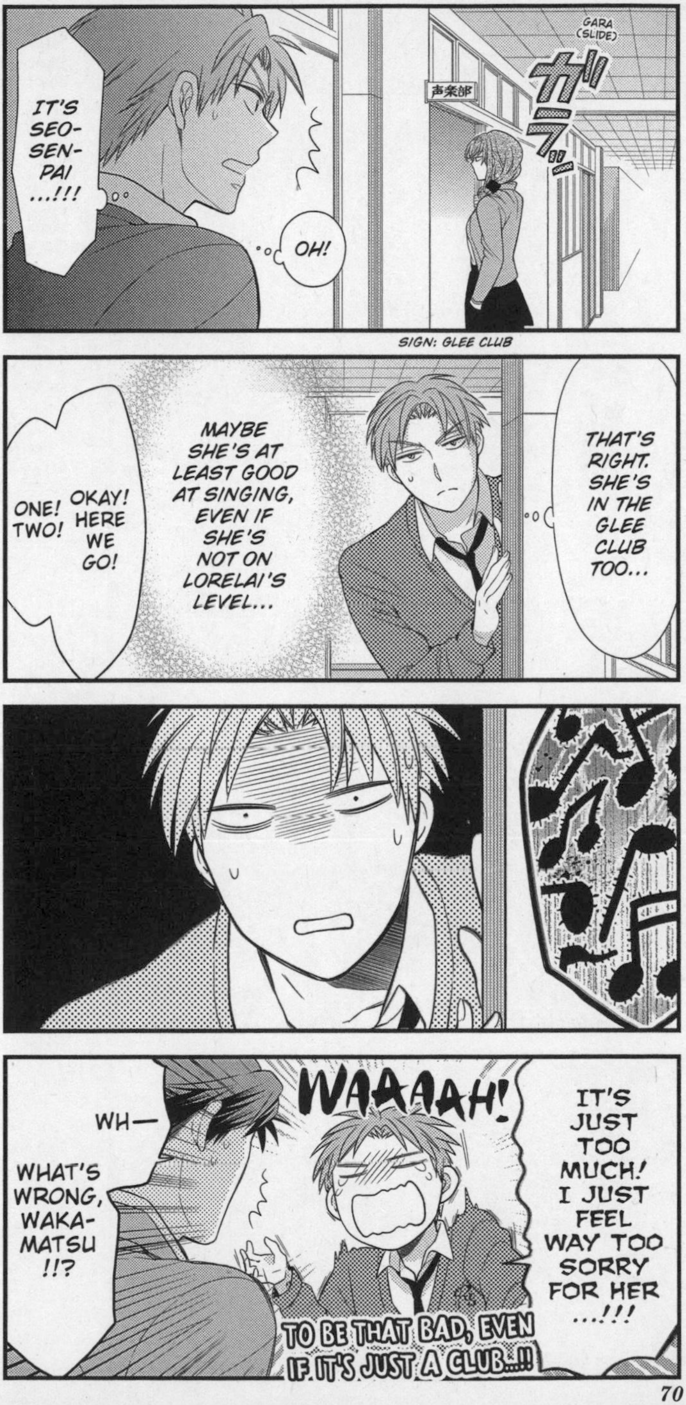
GARA (SLIDE)
ガラ
声楽部
OH!
IT'S SEO-SENPAI...!!!
SIGN: GLEE CLUB
THAT'S RIGHT. SHE'S IN THE GLEE CLUB TOO...
MAYBE SHE'S AT LEAST GOOD AT SINGING, EVEN IF SHE'S NOT ON LORELAI'S LEVEL...
OKAY! HERE WE GO!
ONE! TWO!
WAAAAH!
IT'S JUST TOO MUCH! I JUST FEEL WAY TOO SORRY FOR HER...!!!
WH—
WHAT'S WRONG, WAKAMATSU!!?
TO BE THAT BAD, EVEN IF IT'S JUST A CLUB...!!

WAKAMATSU'S KINDNESS

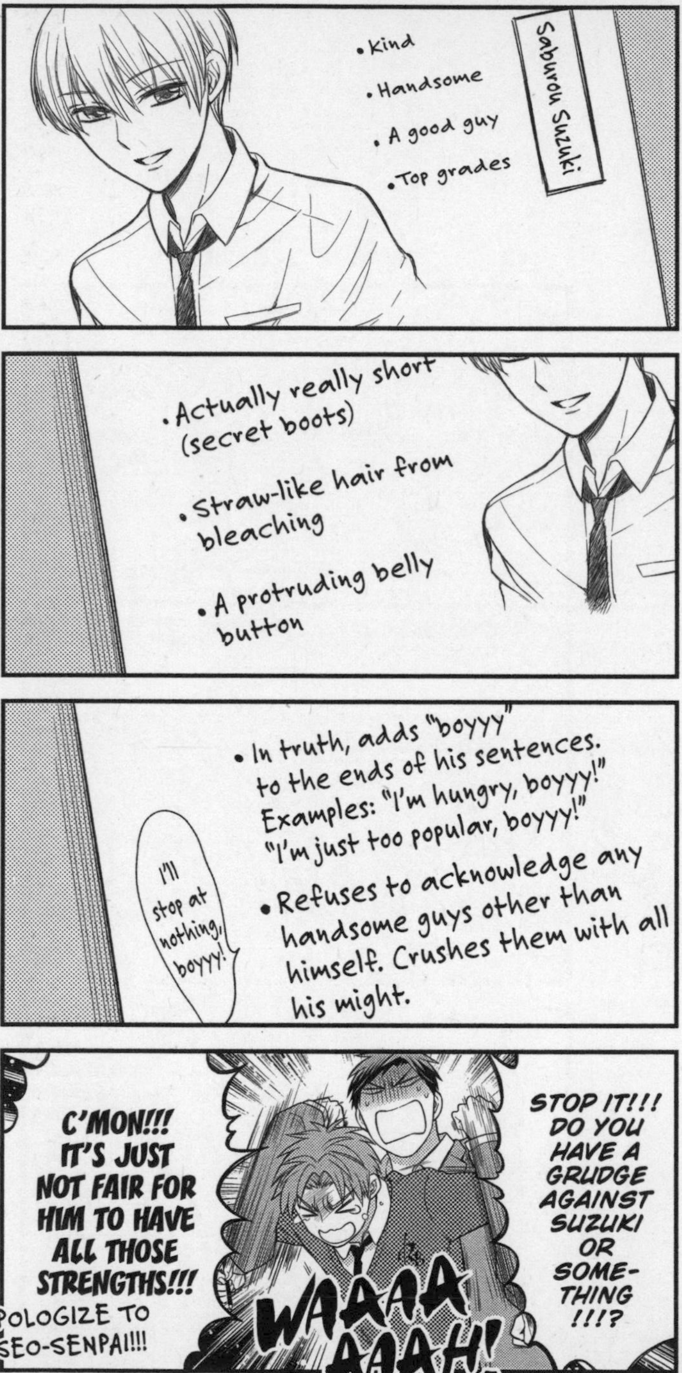

Saburou Suzuki
•Kind
•Handsome
•A good guy
•Top grades
•Actually really short (secret boots)
•Straw-like hair from bleaching
•A protruding belly button
•In truth, adds "boyyy" to the ends of his sentences. Examples: "I'm hungry, boyyy!" "I'm just too popular, boyyy!"
•Refuses to acknowledge any handsome guys other than himself. Crushes them with all his might.
I'll stop at nothing, boyyy!
STOP IT!!! DO YOU HAVE A GRUDGE AGAINST SUZUKI OR SOME-THING!!!?
C'MON!!! IT'S JUST NOT FAIR FOR HIM TO HAVE ALL THOSE STRENGTHS!!!
WAAAA AAAH!
APOLOGIZE TO SEO-SENPAI!!!

ANSWER UNKNOWN

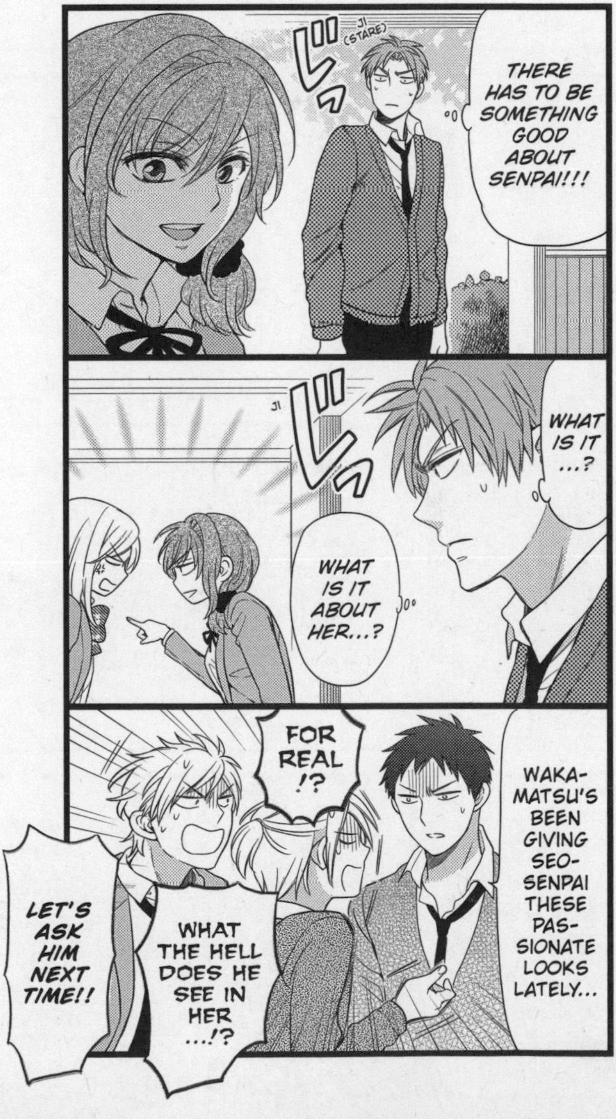
THERE HAS TO BE SOMETHING GOOD ABOUT SENPAI!!!
JI (STARE)
WHAT IS IT ...?
JI
WHAT IS IT ABOUT HER...?
WAKA-MATSU'S BEEN GIVING SEO-SENPAI THESE PAS-SIONATE LOOKS LATELY...
FOR REAL !?
WHAT THE HELL DOES HE SEE IN HER ...!?
LET'S ASK HIM NEXT TIME!!

[ISSUE 26]

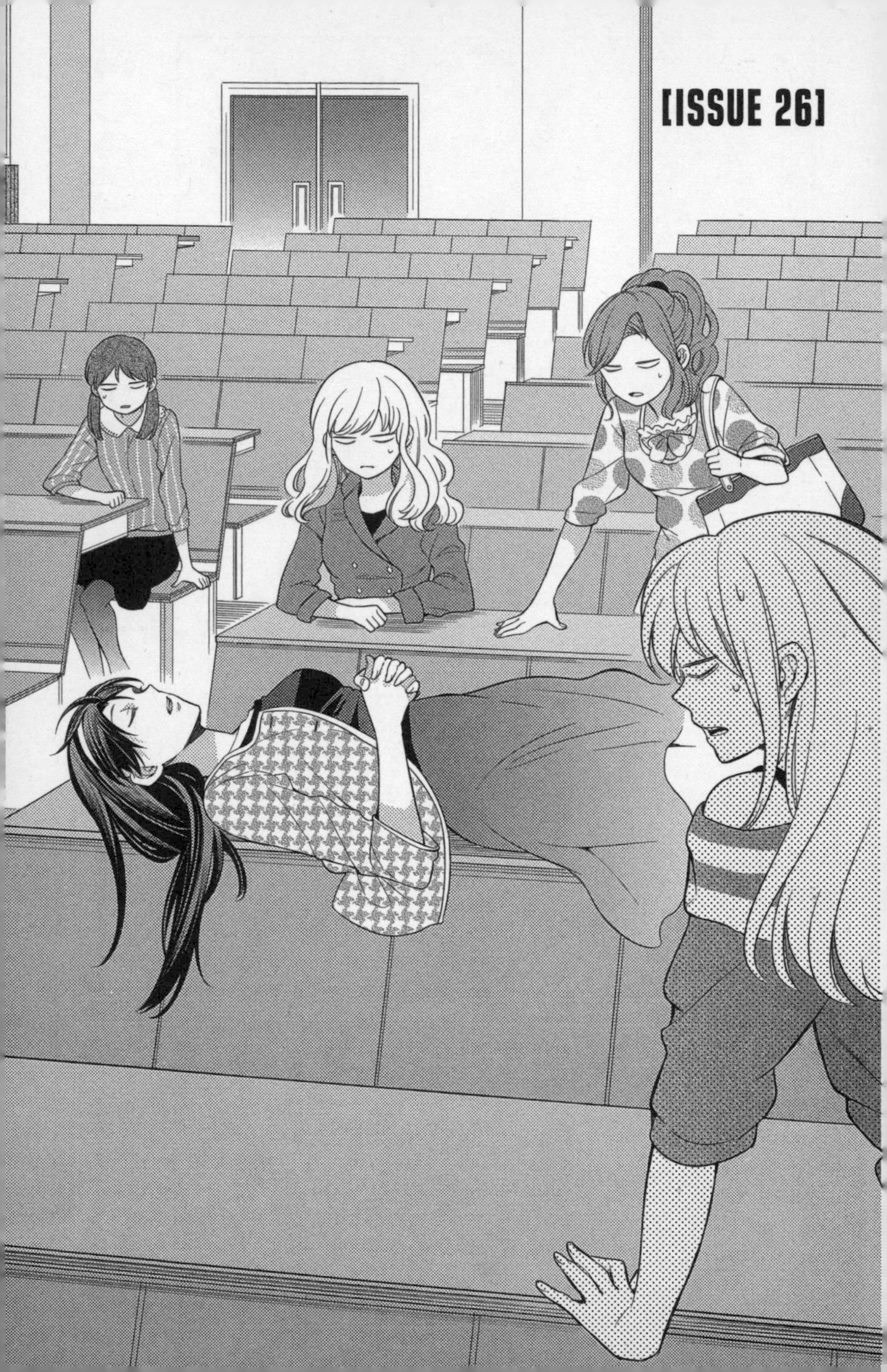

SECRETIVE YUKARI

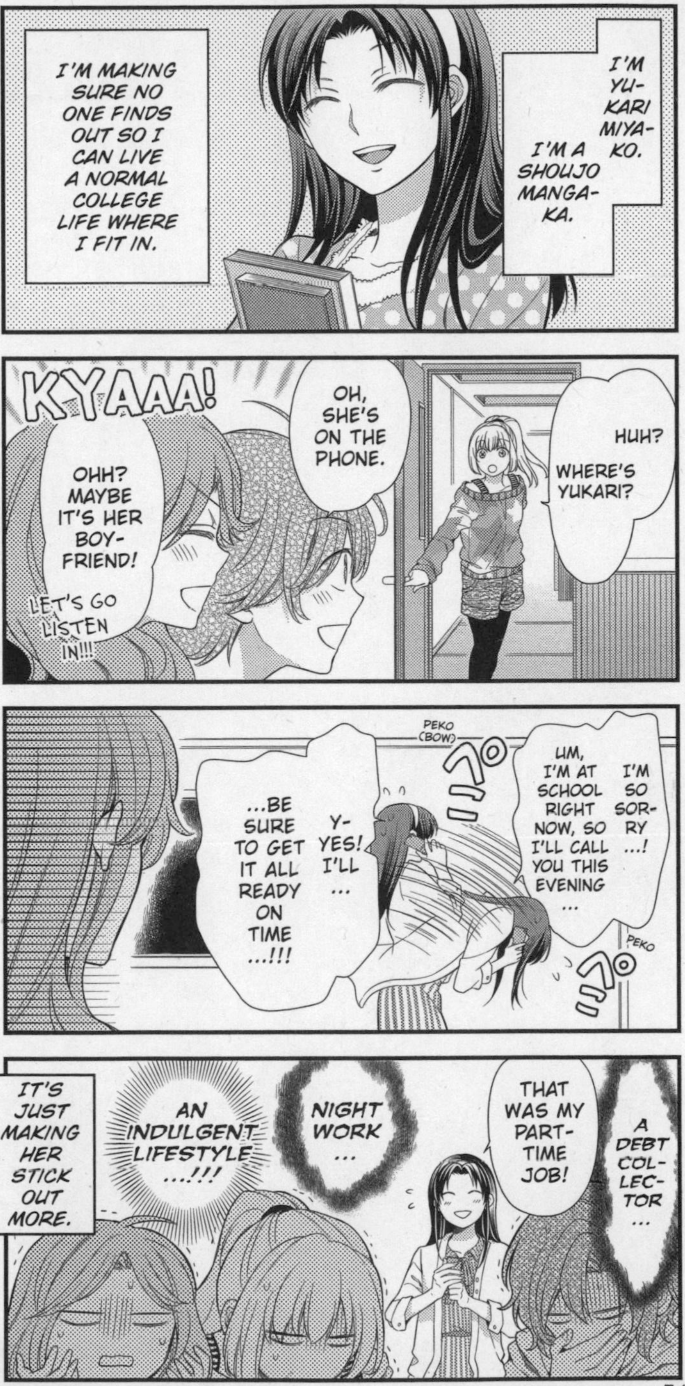
I'M YUKARI MIYAKO.
I'M A SHOUJO MANGAKA.
I'M MAKING SURE NO ONE FINDS OUT SO I CAN LIVE A NORMAL COLLEGE LIFE WHERE I FIT IN.
HUH? WHERE'S YUKARI?
OH, SHE'S ON THE PHONE.
KYAAA!
OHH? MAYBE IT'S HER BOYFRIEND!
LET'S GO LISTEN IN!!!
I'M SO SORRY ...!
UM, I'M AT SCHOOL RIGHT NOW, SO I'LL CALL YOU THIS EVENING ...
PEKO
PEKO (BOW)
Y-YES! I'LL ...
...BE SURE TO GET IT ALL READY ON TIME ...!!!
A DEBT COLLECTOR ...
THAT WAS MY PART-TIME JOB!
NIGHT WORK ...
AN INDULGENT LIFESTYLE ...!!!
IT'S JUST MAKING HER STICK OUT MORE.

PLOT IDEAS

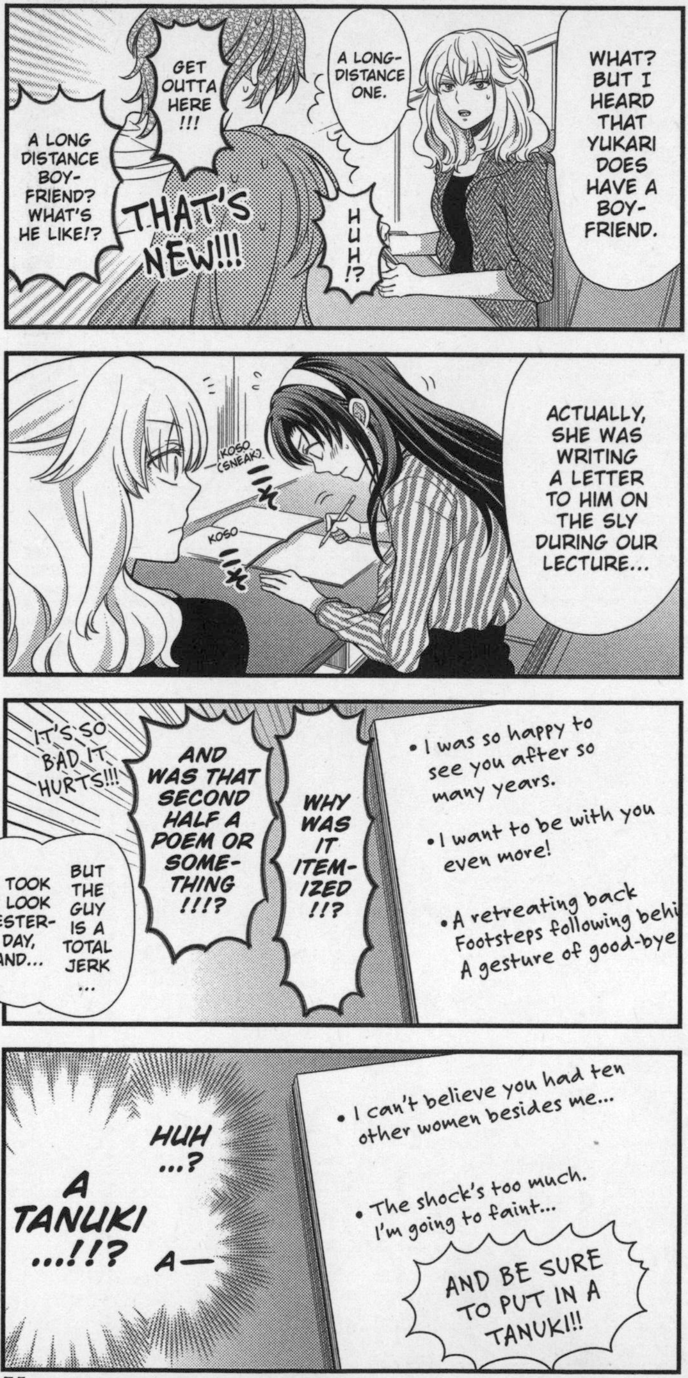

WHAT? BUT I HEARD THAT YUKARI DOES HAVE A BOY-FRIEND.
A LONG-DISTANCE ONE.
HUH!?
THAT'S NEW!!!
GET OUTTA HERE!!!
A LONG DISTANCE BOY-FRIEND? WHAT'S HE LIKE!?
ACTUALLY, SHE WAS WRITING A LETTER TO HIM ON THE SLY DURING OUR LECTURE...
KOSO (SNEAK)
KOSO
• I was so happy to see you after so many years.
• I want to be with you even more!
• A retreating back
Footsteps following behi
A gesture of good-bye
WHY WAS IT ITEMIZED!!?
AND WAS THAT SECOND HALF A POEM OR SOME-THING!!!?
IT'S SO BAD IT HURTS!!!
BUT THE GUY IS A TOTAL JERK...
I TOOK A LOOK YESTER-DAY, AND...
• I can't believe you had ten other women besides me...
• The shock's too much. I'm going to faint...
AND BE SURE TO PUT IN A TANUKI!!!
HUH...?
A—
A TANUKI...!!?

A REAL LIVE HIGH SCHOOL GIRL

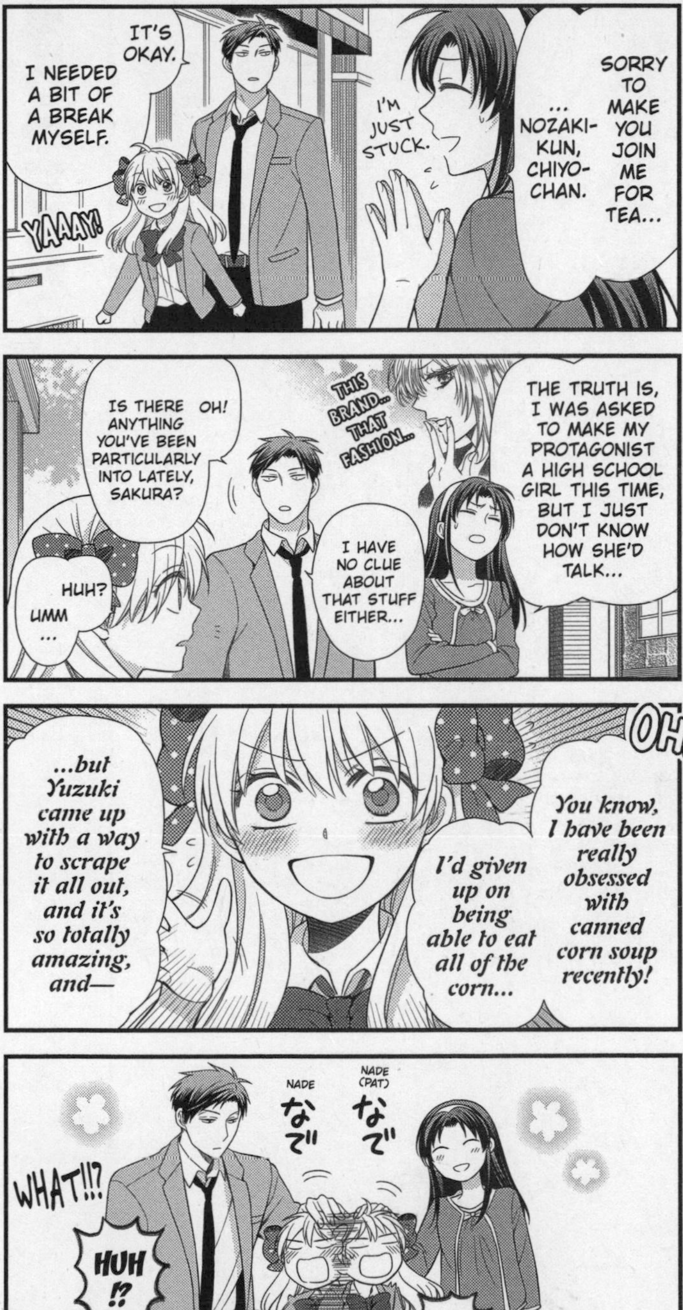
SORRY TO MAKE YOU JOIN ME FOR TEA...
... NOZAKI-KUN, CHIYO-CHAN.
I'M JUST STUCK.
IT'S OKAY.
I NEEDED A BIT OF A BREAK MYSELF.
YAAAY!
THE TRUTH IS, I WAS ASKED TO MAKE MY PROTAGONIST A HIGH SCHOOL GIRL THIS TIME, BUT I JUST DON'T KNOW HOW SHE'D TALK...
THIS BRAND... THAT FASHION...
I HAVE NO CLUE ABOUT THAT STUFF EITHER...
OH!
IS THERE ANYTHING YOU'VE BEEN PARTICULARLY INTO LATELY, SAKURA?
HUH?
UMM ...
OH!
You know, I have been really obsessed with canned corn soup recently!
I'd given up on being able to eat all of the corn...
...but Yuzuki came up with a way to scrape it all out, and it's so totally amazing, and—
NADE (PAT)
なで
NADE
なで
WHAT!!?
HUH !!?
HUH !?

DISTRIBUTORS OF THE INFORMATION THE CREATOR WANTS TO CONVEY

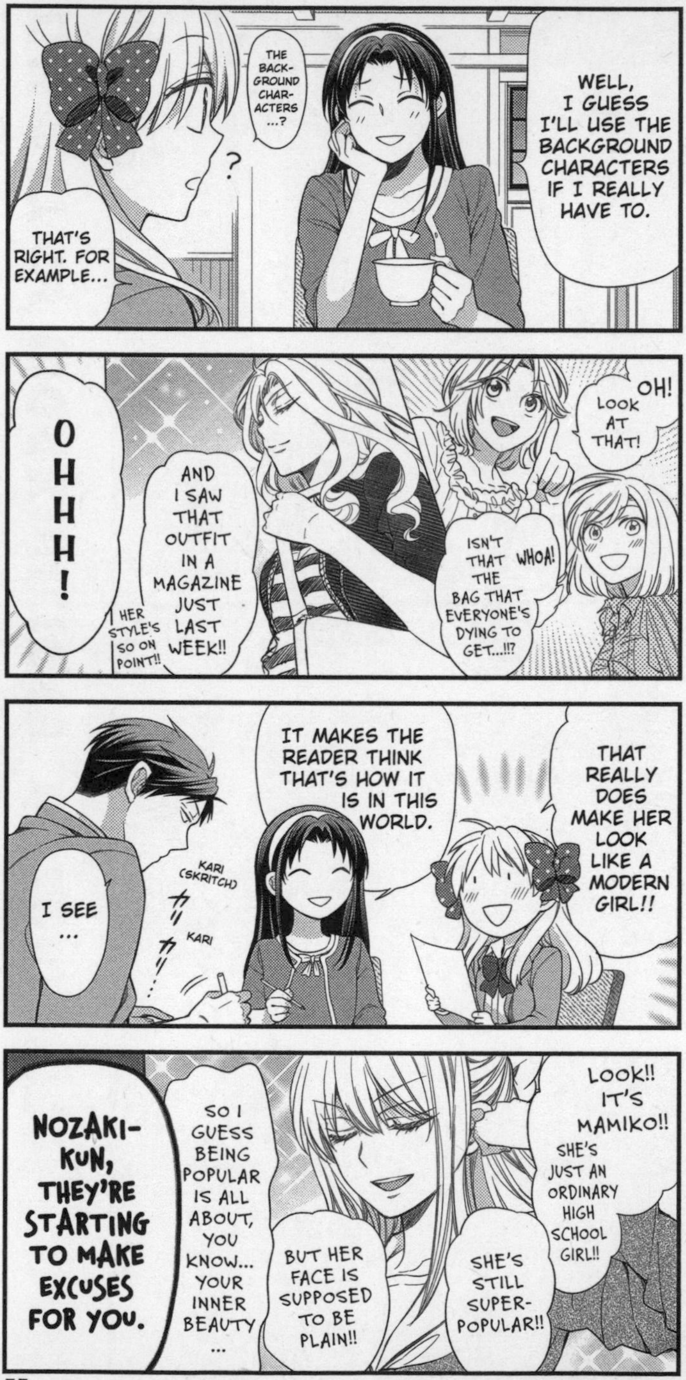
WELL, I GUESS I'LL USE THE BACKGROUND CHARACTERS IF I REALLY HAVE TO.
THE BACK-GROUND CHAR-ACTERS ...?
?
THAT'S RIGHT. FOR EXAMPLE...
OH! LOOK AT THAT!
ISN'T THAT THE BAG THAT EVERYONE'S DYING TO GET...!!?
WHOA!
AND I SAW THAT OUTFIT IN A MAGAZINE JUST LAST WEEK!!
HER STYLE'S SO ON POINT!!
OHHH!
THAT REALLY DOES MAKE HER LOOK LIKE A MODERN GIRL!!
IT MAKES THE READER THINK THAT'S HOW IT IS IN THIS WORLD.
KARI (SKRITCH)
KARI
I SEE...
LOOK!! IT'S MAMIKO!!
SHE'S JUST AN ORDINARY HIGH SCHOOL GIRL!!
SHE'S STILL SUPER-POPULAR!!
BUT HER FACE IS SUPPOSED TO BE PLAIN!!
SO I GUESS BEING POPULAR IS ALL ABOUT, YOU KNOW... YOUR INNER BEAUTY...
NOZAKI-KUN, THEY'RE STARTING TO MAKE EXCUSES FOR YOU.

THE ART OF WORKING IT IN, NOZAKI-STYLE

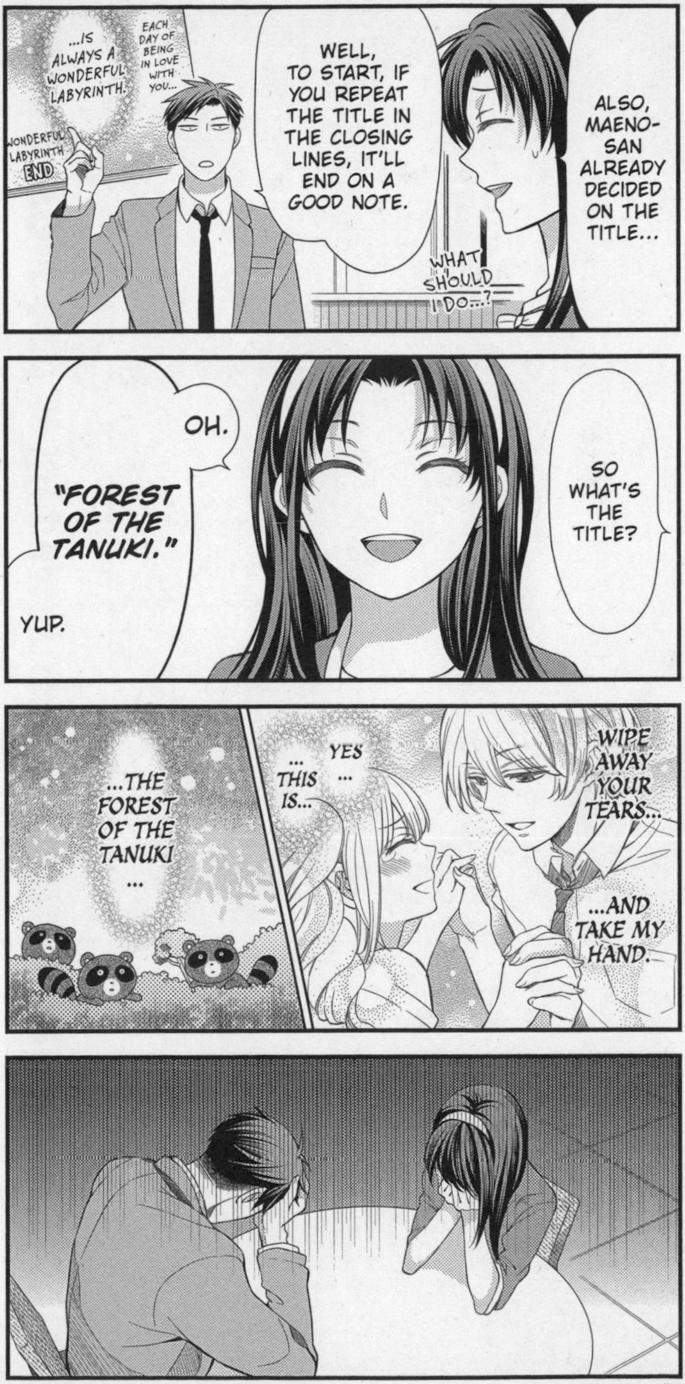
ALSO, MAENO-SAN ALREADY DECIDED ON THE TITLE...
WHAT SHOULD I DO...?
WELL, TO START, IF YOU REPEAT THE TITLE IN THE CLOSING LINES, IT'LL END ON A GOOD NOTE.
EACH DAY OF BEING IN LOVE WITH YOU...
...IS ALWAYS A WONDERFUL LABYRINTH.
WONDERFUL LABYRINTH
END
SO WHAT'S THE TITLE?
OH.
"FOREST OF THE TANUKI."
YUP.
WIPE AWAY YOUR TEARS...
...AND TAKE MY HAND.
YES...
...THIS IS...
...THE FOREST OF THE TANUKI...

AN INTRUDER

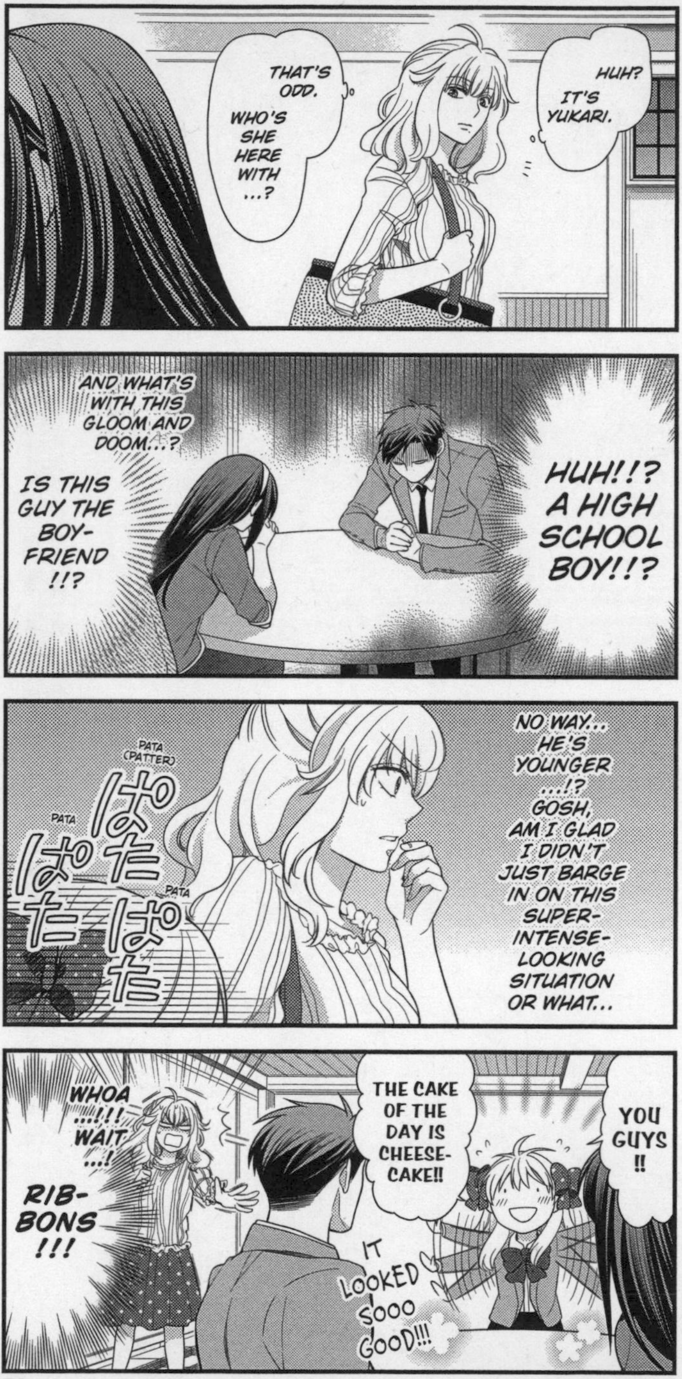
HUH? IT'S YUKARI.
THAT'S ODD.
WHO'S SHE HERE WITH ...?
HUH!!? A HIGH SCHOOL BOY!!?
AND WHAT'S WITH THIS GLOOM AND DOOM...?
IS THIS GUY THE BOY-FRIEND !!?
NO WAY... HE'S YOUNGER ...!? GOSH, AM I GLAD I DIDN'T JUST BARGE IN ON THIS SUPER-INTENSE-LOOKING SITUATION OR WHAT...
ぱた PATA (PATTER)
ぱた PATA
ぱた PATA
ぱた
YOU GUYS !!
THE CAKE OF THE DAY IS CHEESE-CAKE!!
IT LOOKED SOOO GOOD!!!
WHOA ...!!! WAIT ...!
RIB-BONS !!!

IT'S ABOUT SUZUKI AND MAMIKO

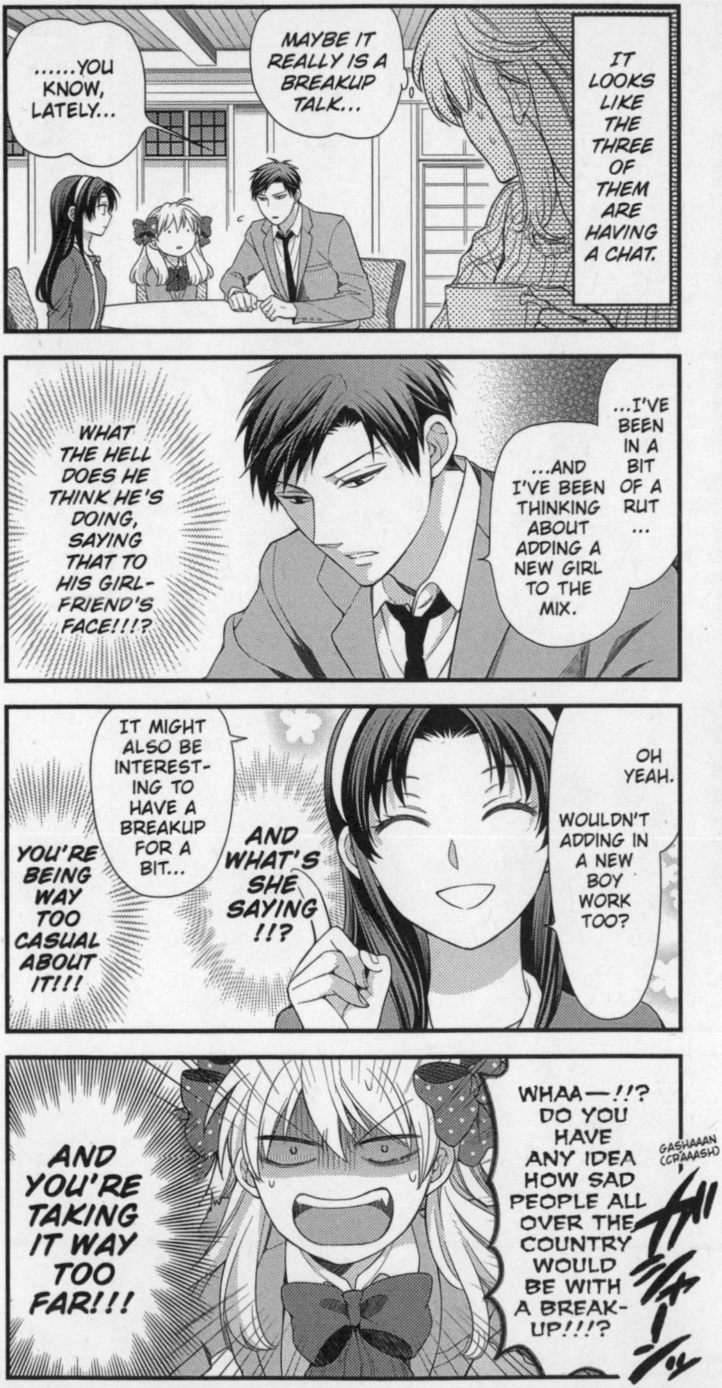
IT LOOKS LIKE THE THREE OF THEM ARE HAVING A CHAT.
MAYBE IT REALLY IS A BREAKUP TALK...
......YOU KNOW, LATELY...
...I'VE BEEN IN A BIT OF A RUT ...
...AND I'VE BEEN THINKING ABOUT ADDING A NEW GIRL TO THE MIX.
WHAT THE HELL DOES HE THINK HE'S DOING, SAYING THAT TO HIS GIRL-FRIEND'S FACE!!!?
OH YEAH.
WOULDN'T ADDING IN A NEW BOY WORK TOO?
IT MIGHT ALSO BE INTERESTING TO HAVE A BREAKUP FOR A BIT...
AND WHAT'S SHE SAYING!!?
YOU'RE BEING WAY TOO CASUAL ABOUT IT!!!
GASHAAAN (CRAAASH)
WHAA—!!? DO YOU HAVE ANY IDEA HOW SAD PEOPLE ALL OVER THE COUNTRY WOULD BE WITH A BREAK-UP!!!?
AND YOU'RE TAKING IT WAY TOO FAR!!!

A SERIOUS OPINION

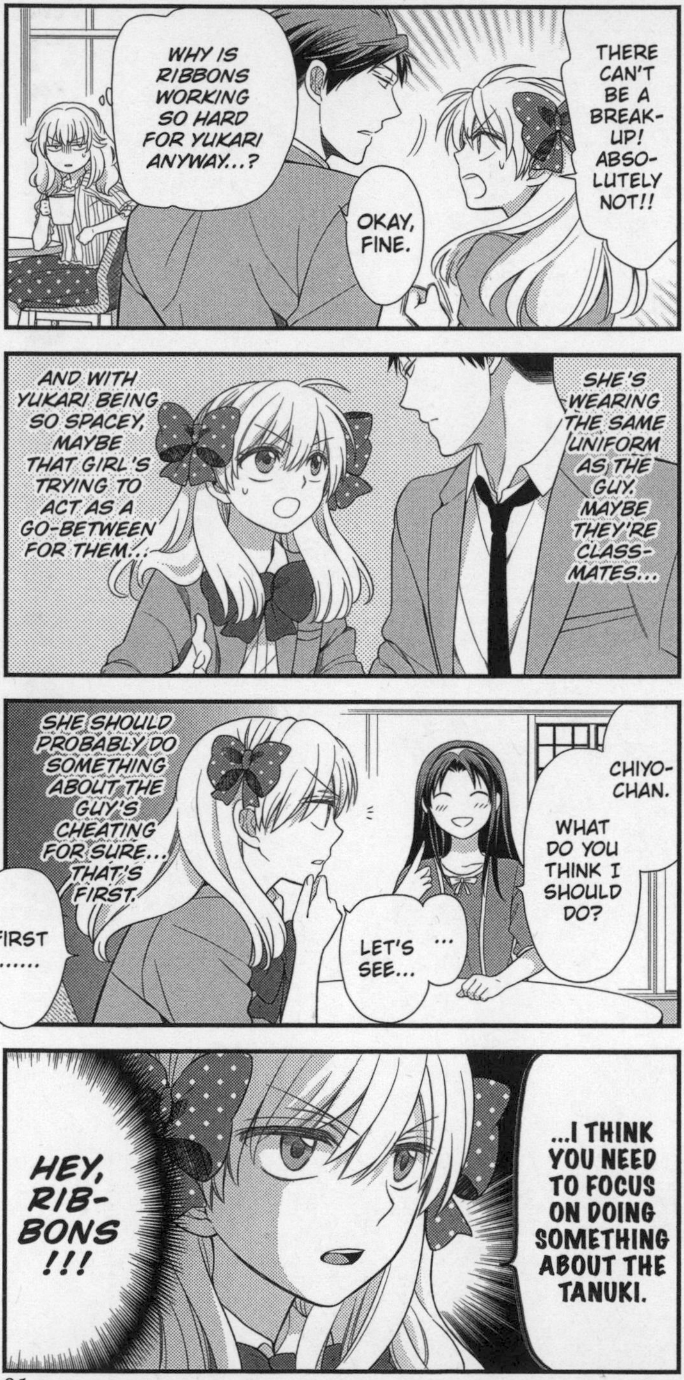
THERE CAN'T BE A BREAK-UP! ABSOLUTELY NOT!!
OKAY, FINE.
WHY IS RIBBONS WORKING SO HARD FOR YUKARI ANYWAY...?
SHE'S WEARING THE SAME UNIFORM AS THE GUY. MAYBE THEY'RE CLASSMATES...
AND WITH YUKARI BEING SO SPACEY, MAYBE THAT GIRL'S TRYING TO ACT AS A GO-BETWEEN FOR THEM...
CHIYO-CHAN.
WHAT DO YOU THINK I SHOULD DO?
...
LET'S SEE...
SHE SHOULD PROBABLY DO SOMETHING ABOUT THE GUY'S CHEATING FOR SURE... THAT'S FIRST.
FIRST ......
...I THINK YOU NEED TO FOCUS ON DOING SOMETHING ABOUT THE TANUKI.
HEY, RIB-BONS!!!

IT'S ABOUT THE CHARACTERS' OUTFITS

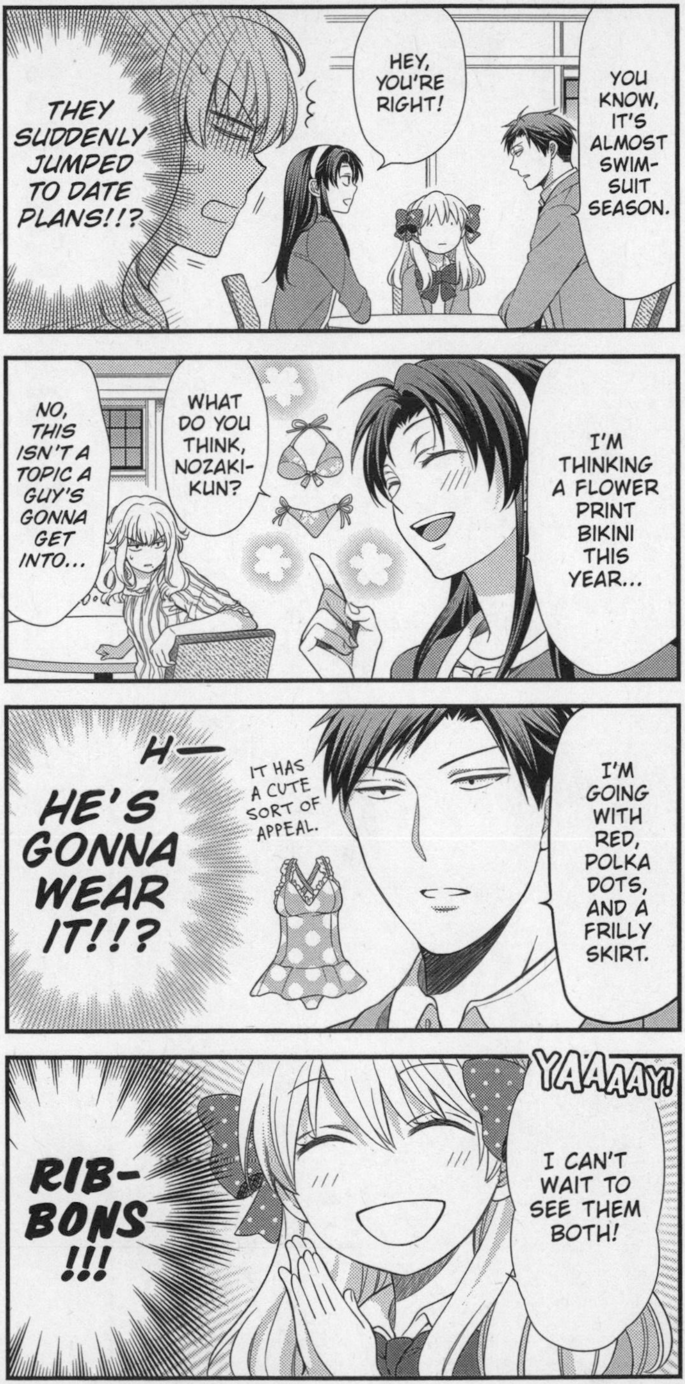
YOU KNOW, IT'S ALMOST SWIM-SUIT SEASON.
HEY, YOU'RE RIGHT!
THEY SUDDENLY JUMPED TO DATE PLANS!!?
I'M THINKING A FLOWER PRINT BIKINI THIS YEAR...
WHAT DO YOU THINK, NOZAKI-KUN?
NO, THIS ISN'T A TOPIC A GUY'S GONNA GET INTO...
I'M GOING WITH RED, POLKA DOTS, AND A FRILLY SKIRT.
IT HAS A CUTE SORT OF APPEAL.
H— HE'S GONNA WEAR IT!!?
YAAAAY!
I CAN'T WAIT TO SEE THEM BOTH!
RIB-BONS!!!

WANDERING OFF SOMEWHERE!

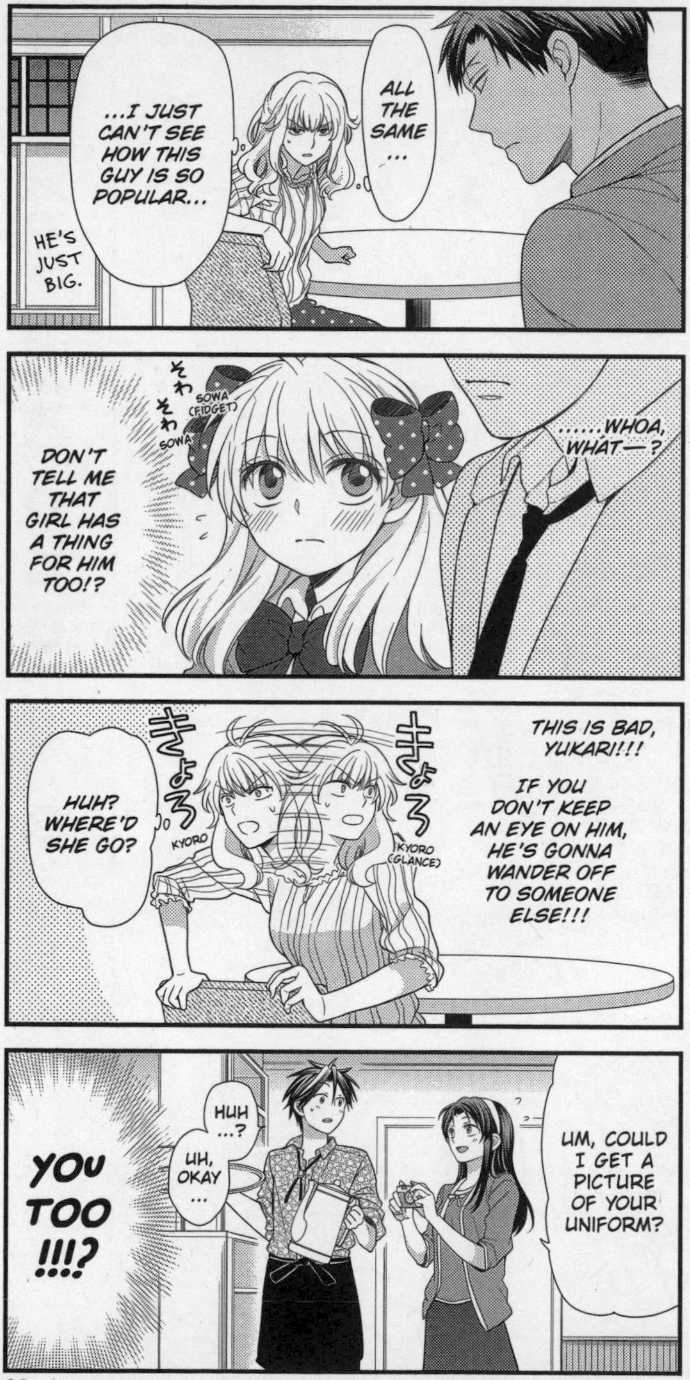
ALL THE SAME...
...I JUST CAN'T SEE HOW THIS GUY IS SO POPULAR...
HE'S JUST BIG.
......WHOA, WHAT—?
そわ SOWA (FIDGET)
そわ SOWA
DON'T TELL ME THAT GIRL HAS A THING FOR HIM TOO!?
THIS IS BAD, YUKARI!!!
IF YOU DON'T KEEP AN EYE ON HIM, HE'S GONNA WANDER OFF TO SOMEONE ELSE!!!
きょろ KYORO (GLANCE)
きょろ KYORO
HUH? WHERE'D SHE GO?
UM, COULD I GET A PICTURE OF YOUR UNIFORM?
HUH...?
UH, OKAY...
YOU TOO!!!?

EACH AND EVERY ONE OF THEM

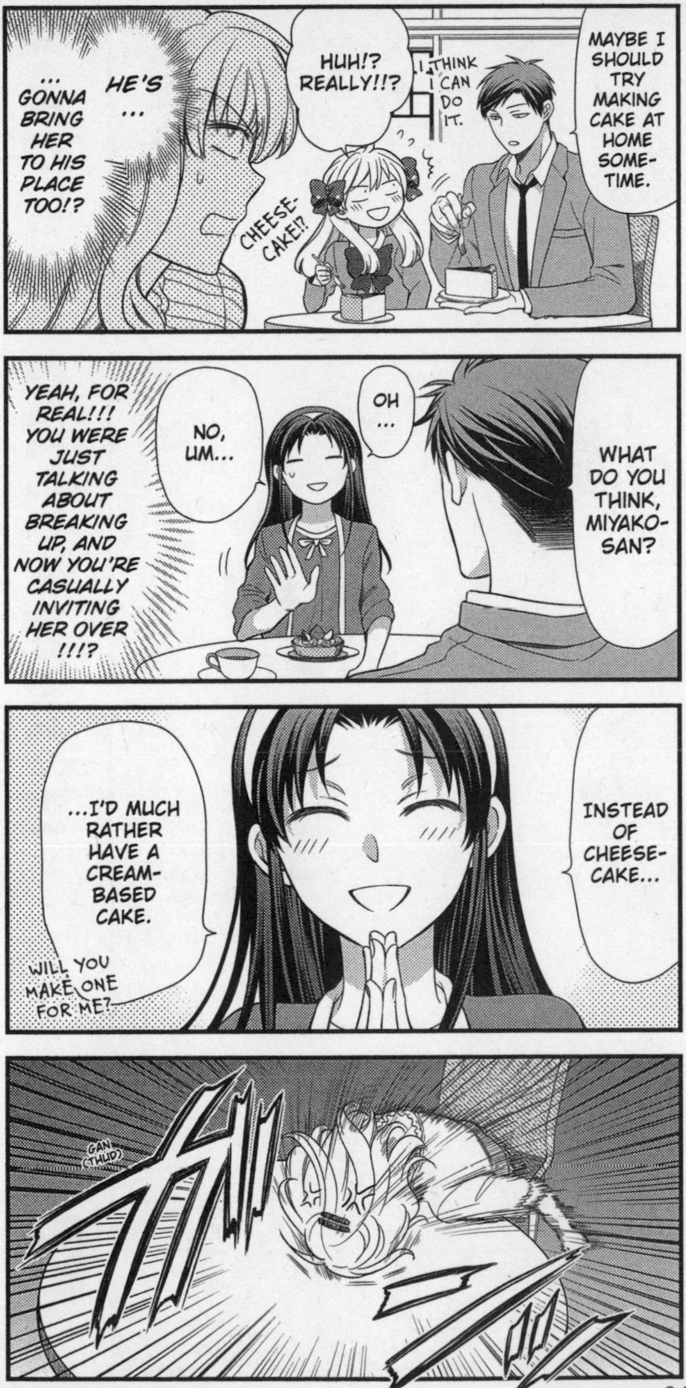
MAYBE I SHOULD TRY MAKING CAKE AT HOME SOMETIME.
I THINK I CAN DO IT.
HUH!? REALLY!!?
CHEESE-CAKE!?
HE'S ...
... GONNA BRING HER TO HIS PLACE TOO!?
WHAT DO YOU THINK, MIYAKO-SAN?
OH ...
NO, UM...
YEAH, FOR REAL!!! YOU WERE JUST TALKING ABOUT BREAKING UP, AND NOW YOU'RE CASUALLY INVITING HER OVER !!!?
INSTEAD OF CHEESE-CAKE...
...I'D MUCH RATHER HAVE A CREAM-BASED CAKE.
WILL YOU MAKE ONE FOR ME?
GAN (THUD)

THE DISASTER NEXT DOOR

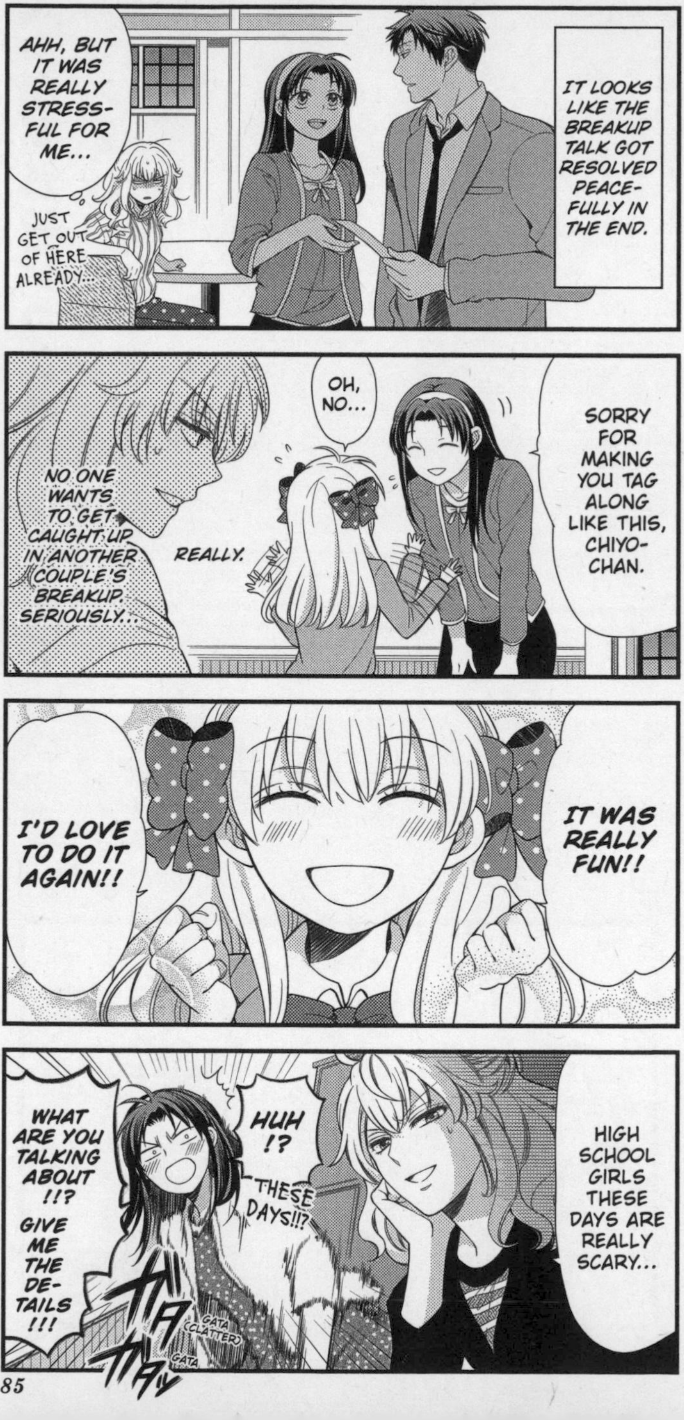
IT LOOKS LIKE THE BREAKUP TALK GOT RESOLVED PEACEFULLY IN THE END.
AHH, BUT IT WAS REALLY STRESSFUL FOR ME...
JUST GET OUT OF HERE ALREADY...
SORRY FOR MAKING YOU TAG ALONG LIKE THIS, CHIYO-CHAN.
OH, NO...
REALLY.
NO ONE WANTS TO GET CAUGHT UP IN ANOTHER COUPLE'S BREAKUP. SERIOUSLY...
IT WAS REALLY FUN!!
I'D LOVE TO DO IT AGAIN!!
HIGH SCHOOL GIRLS THESE DAYS ARE REALLY SCARY...
HUH!?
THESE DAYS!!?
WHAT ARE YOU TALKING ABOUT!!? GIVE ME THE DETAILS!!!
GATA (CLATTER)
GATA

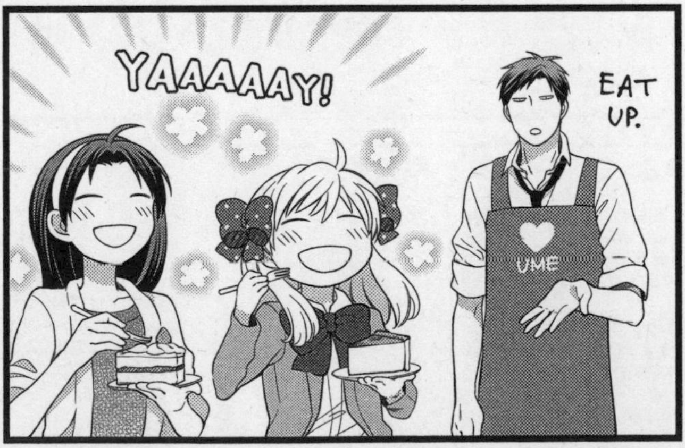
EAT UP.
YAAAAAY!
UME

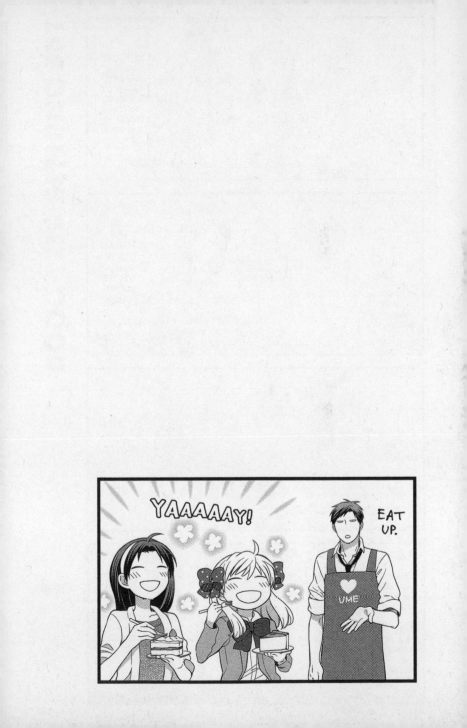

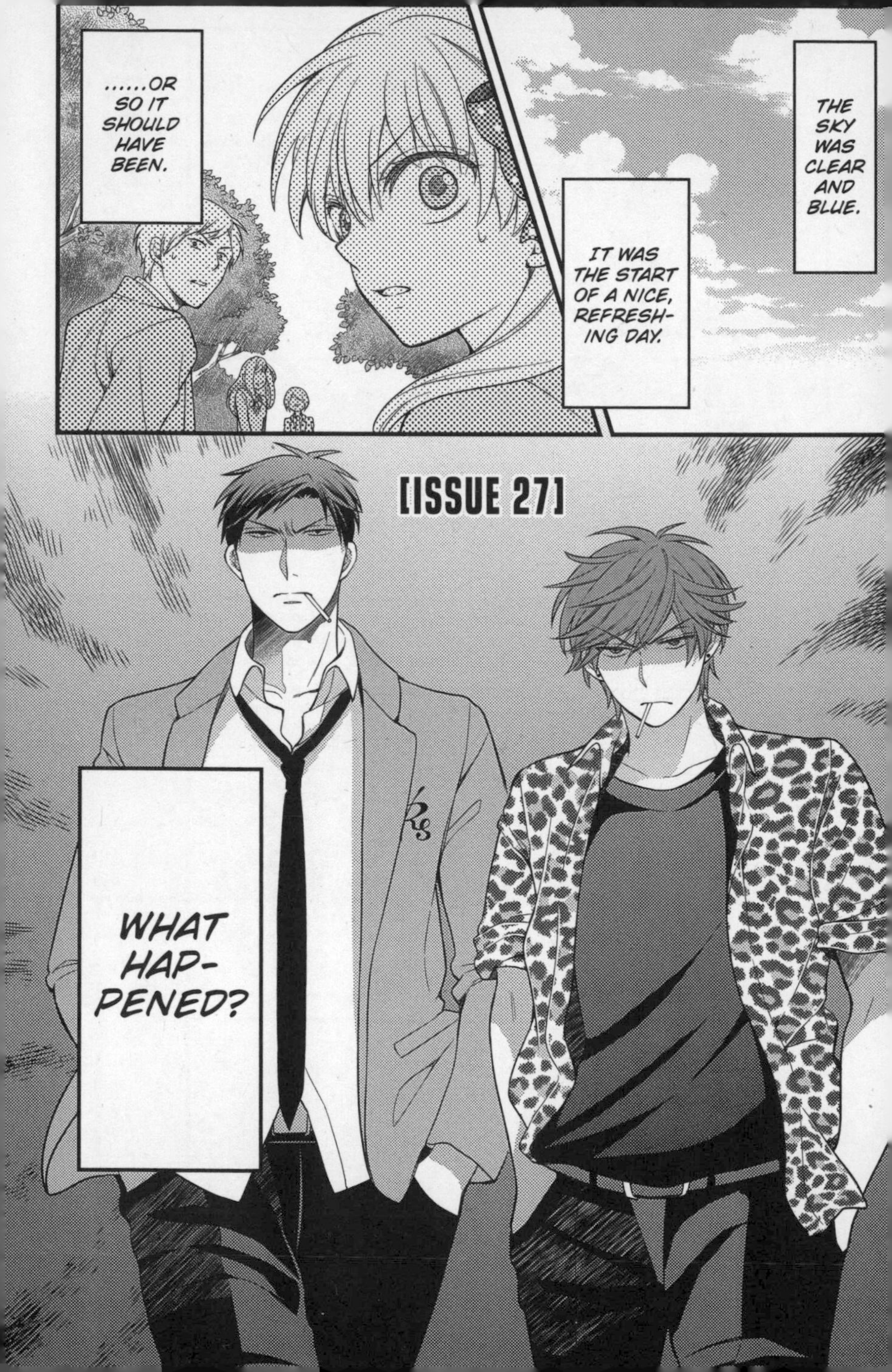
THE SKY WAS CLEAR AND BLUE.
IT WAS THE START OF A NICE, REFRESHING DAY.
......OR SO IT SHOULD HAVE BEEN.
[ISSUE 27]
WHAT HAPPENED?

CHIYO'S POSITION

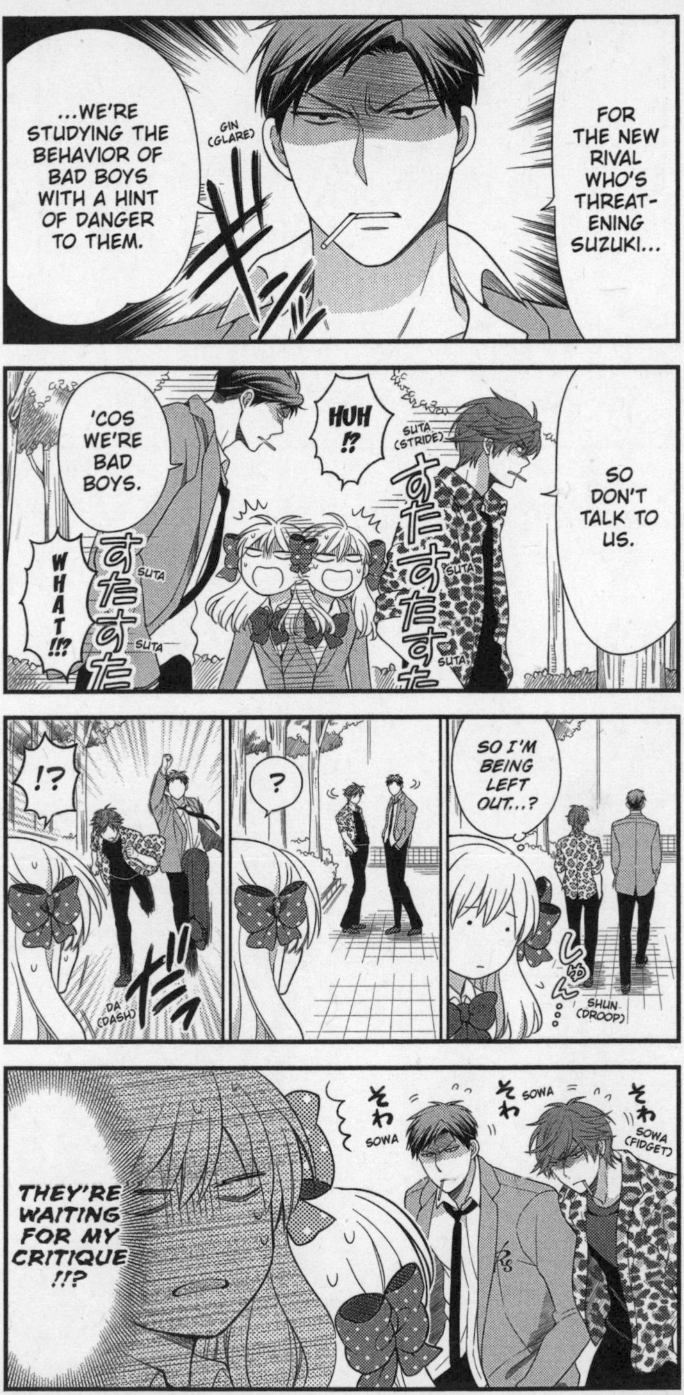

FOR THE NEW RIVAL WHO'S THREAT-ENING SUZUKI...
GIN (GLARE)
...WE'RE STUDYING THE BEHAVIOR OF BAD BOYS WITH A HINT OF DANGER TO THEM.
SO DON'T TALK TO US.
すたすたすた
SUTA (STRIDE)
SUTA
SUTA
HUH!?
'COS WE'RE BAD BOYS.
すたすた
SUTA
SUTA
WHAT!!?
SO I'M BEING LEFT OUT...?
しゅん...
SHUN (DROOP)
?
!?
ダッ
DA (DASH)
そわ
SOWA (FIDGET)
そわ
SOWA
そわ
SOWA
THEY'RE WAITING FOR MY CRITIQUE!!?

WE'LL KEEP ON FIGHTING

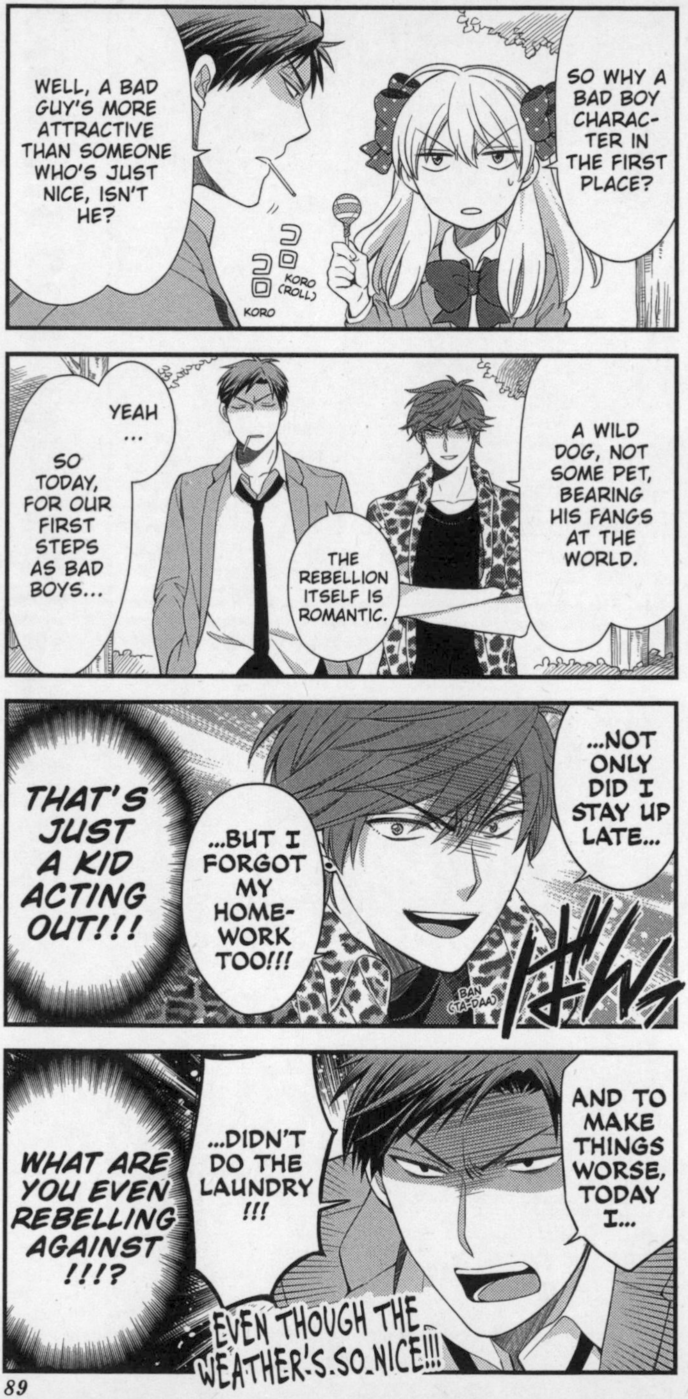
SO WHY A BAD BOY CHARACTER IN THE FIRST PLACE?
WELL, A BAD GUY'S MORE ATTRACTIVE THAN SOMEONE WHO'S JUST NICE, ISN'T HE?
コロ KORO (ROLL)
コロ KORO
A WILD DOG, NOT SOME PET, BEARING HIS FANGS AT THE WORLD.
THE REBELLION ITSELF IS ROMANTIC.
YEAH ...
SO TODAY, FOR OUR FIRST STEPS AS BAD BOYS...
...NOT ONLY DID I STAY UP LATE...
...BUT I FORGOT MY HOME-WORK TOO!!!
ばん BAN (TA-DAA)
THAT'S JUST A KID ACTING OUT!!!
AND TO MAKE THINGS WORSE, TODAY I...
...DIDN'T DO THE LAUNDRY !!!
EVEN THOUGH THE WEATHER'S SO NICE!!!
WHAT ARE YOU EVEN REBELLING AGAINST !!!?

EVEN BIGGER AND MORE DARING

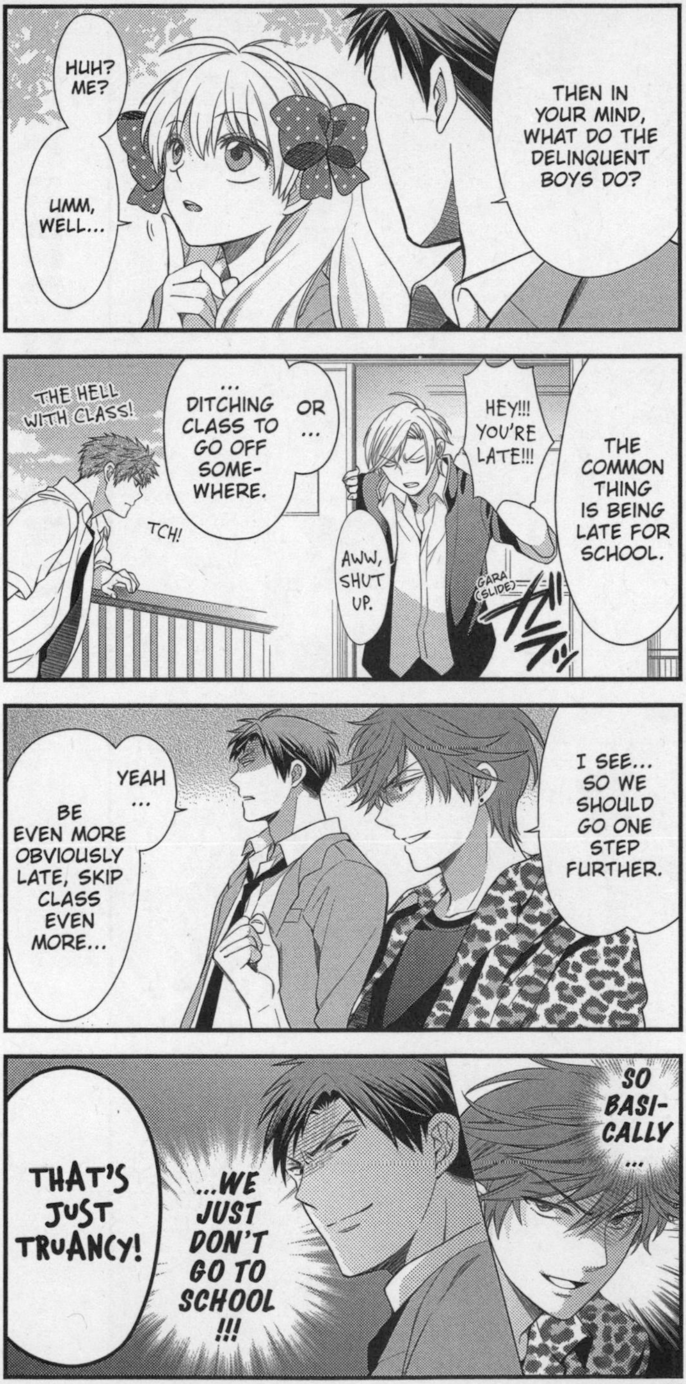

THEN IN YOUR MIND, WHAT DO THE DELINQUENT BOYS DO?
HUH? ME?
UMM, WELL...
THE COMMON THING IS BEING LATE FOR SCHOOL.
GARA (SLIDE)
HEY!!! YOU'RE LATE!!!
AWW, SHUT UP.
OR ...
... DITCHING CLASS TO GO OFF SOME-WHERE.
THE HELL WITH CLASS!
TCH!
I SEE... SO WE SHOULD GO ONE STEP FURTHER.
YEAH ...
BE EVEN MORE OBVIOUSLY LATE, SKIP CLASS EVEN MORE...
SO BASI-CALLY ...
...WE JUST DON'T GO TO SCHOOL !!!
THAT'S JUST TRUANCY!

A BAD BOY

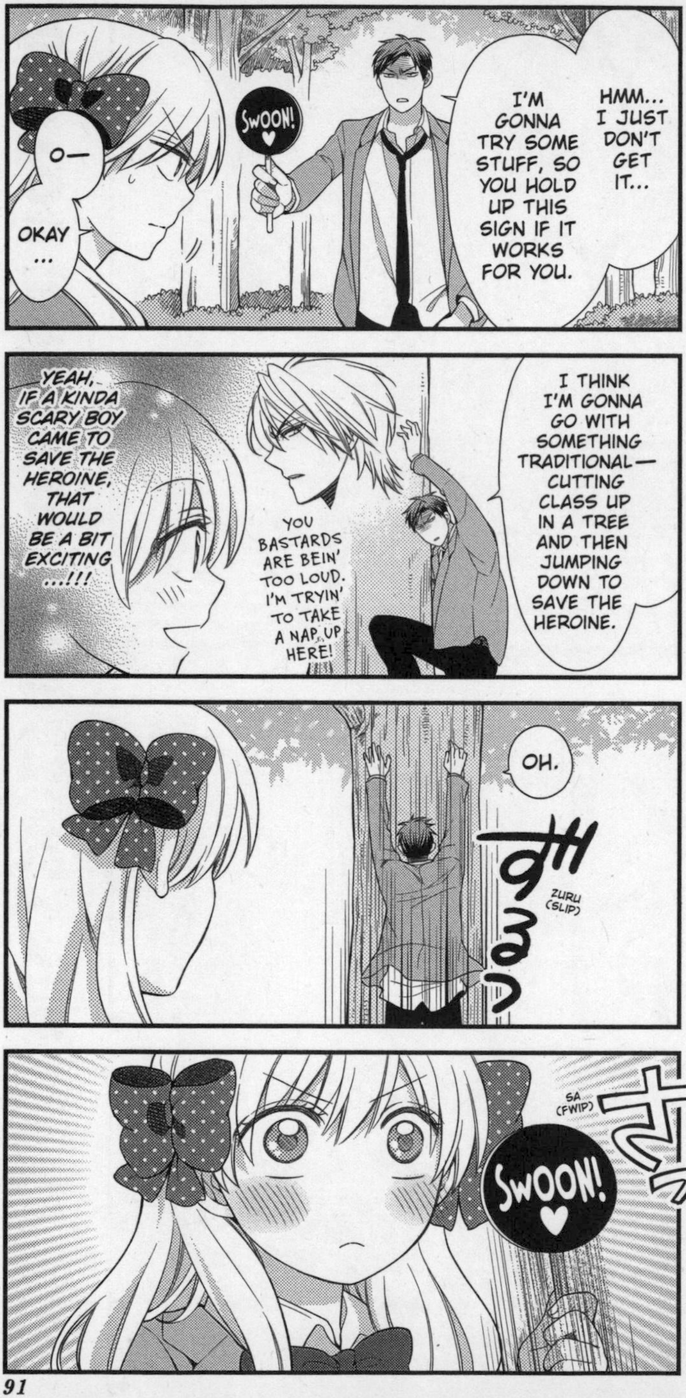
HMM... I JUST DON'T GET IT...
I'M GONNA TRY SOME STUFF, SO YOU HOLD UP THIS SIGN IF IT WORKS FOR YOU.
SWOON! ♥
O—
OKAY ...
I THINK I'M GONNA GO WITH SOMETHING TRADITIONAL—CUTTING CLASS UP IN A TREE AND THEN JUMPING DOWN TO SAVE THE HEROINE.
YOU BASTARDS ARE BEIN' TOO LOUD. I'M TRYIN' TO TAKE A NAP UP HERE!
YEAH, IF A KINDA SCARY BOY CAME TO SAVE THE HEROINE, THAT WOULD BE A BIT EXCITING ...!!!
OH.
ずるっ
ZURU (SLIP)
さっ
SA (FWIP)
SWOON! ♥

JUST YOU WATCH HOW AMAZING I AM!

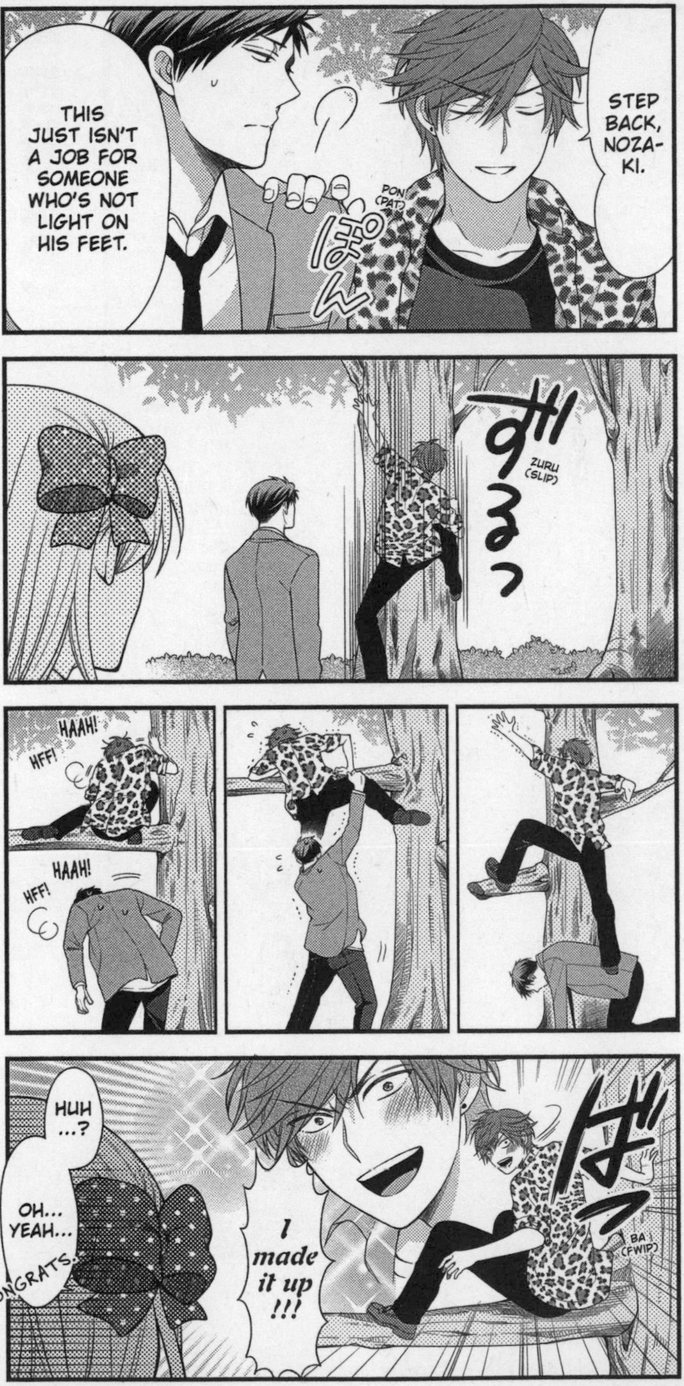
STEP BACK, NOZA-KI.
ぽん
PON (PAT)
THIS JUST ISN'T A JOB FOR SOMEONE WHO'S NOT LIGHT ON HIS FEET.
ずるっ
ZURU (SLIP)
HAAH!
HFF!
HAAH!
HFF!
ばっ
BA (FWIP)
I made it up !!!
HUH ...?
OH... YEAH...
CONGRATS.

MIKORIN IN A TREE

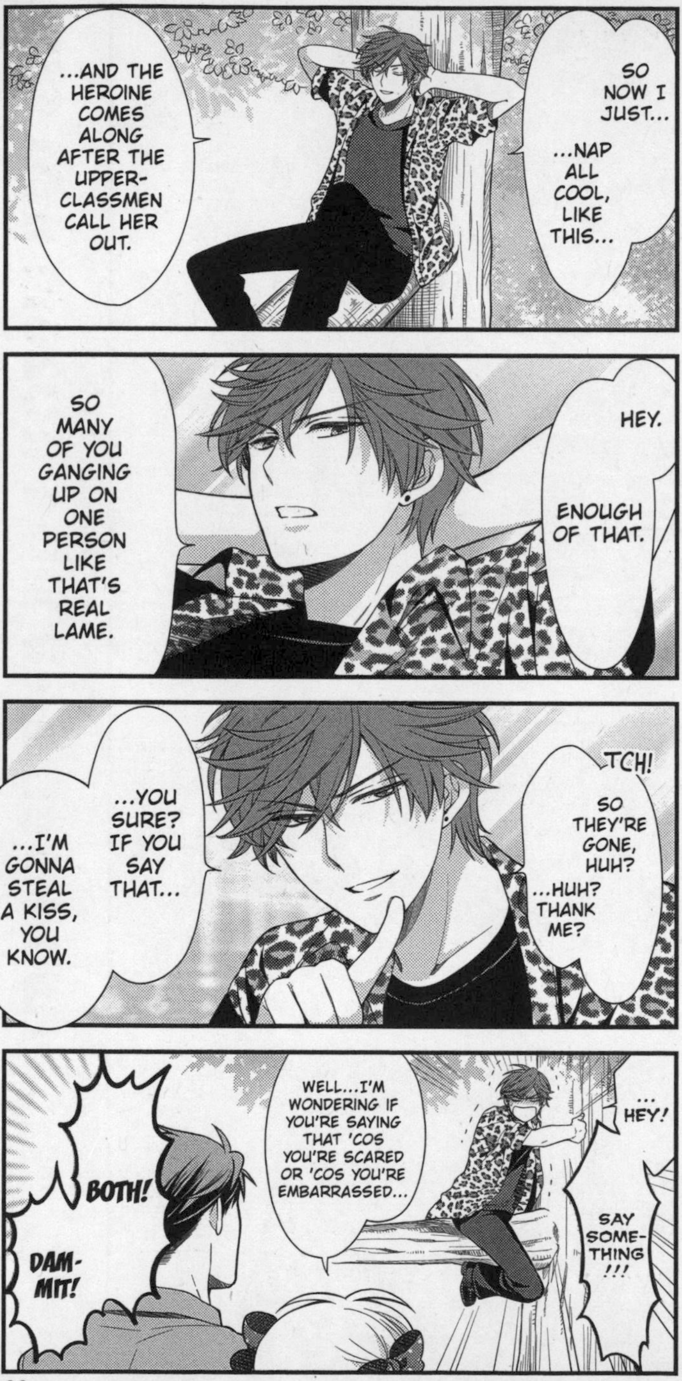
SO NOW I JUST...
...NAP ALL COOL, LIKE THIS...
...AND THE HEROINE COMES ALONG AFTER THE UPPER-CLASSMEN CALL HER OUT.
HEY.
ENOUGH OF THAT.
SO MANY OF YOU GANGING UP ON ONE PERSON LIKE THAT'S REAL LAME.
TCH!
SO THEY'RE GONE, HUH?
...HUH? THANK ME?
...YOU SURE? IF YOU SAY THAT...
...I'M GONNA STEAL A KISS, YOU KNOW.
... HEY!
SAY SOME-THING!!!
WELL...I'M WONDERING IF YOU'RE SAYING THAT 'COS YOU'RE SCARED OR 'COS YOU'RE EMBARRASSED...
BOTH!
DAM-MIT!

BAD US

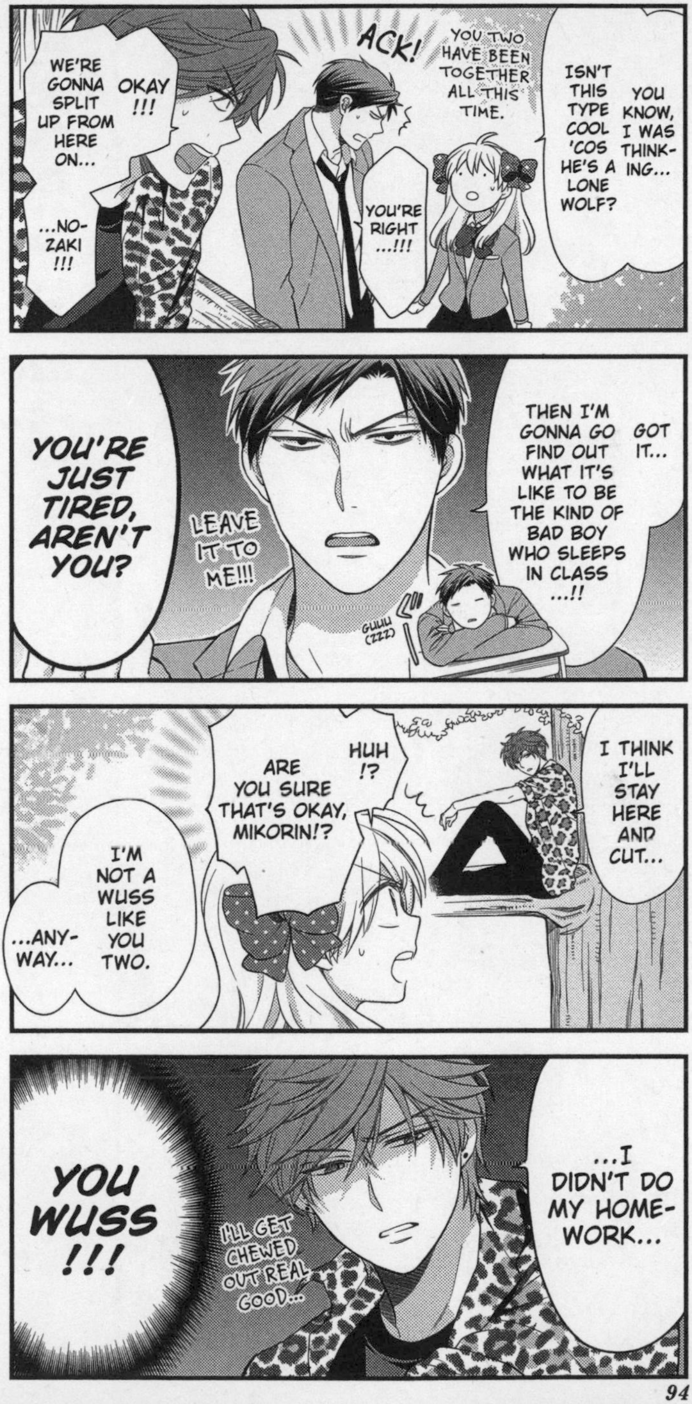
YOU KNOW, I WAS THINKING... ISN'T THIS TYPE COOL 'COS HE'S A LONE WOLF?
YOU TWO HAVE BEEN TOGETHER ALL THIS TIME.
ACK!
YOU'RE RIGHT ...!!!
OKAY !!!
WE'RE GONNA SPLIT UP FROM HERE ON... ...NOZAKI !!!
GOT IT... THEN I'M GONNA GO FIND OUT WHAT IT'S LIKE TO BE THE KIND OF BAD BOY WHO SLEEPS IN CLASS ...!!
GUUU (ZZZ)
LEAVE IT TO ME!!!
YOU'RE JUST TIRED, AREN'T YOU?
I THINK I'LL STAY HERE AND CUT...
HUH !?
ARE YOU SURE THAT'S OKAY, MIKORIN!?
I'M NOT A WUSS LIKE YOU TWO. ...ANYWAY...
...I DIDN'T DO MY HOMEWORK...
I'LL GET CHEWED OUT REAL GOOD...
YOU WUSS !!!

SHOULD HAVE GIVEN UP

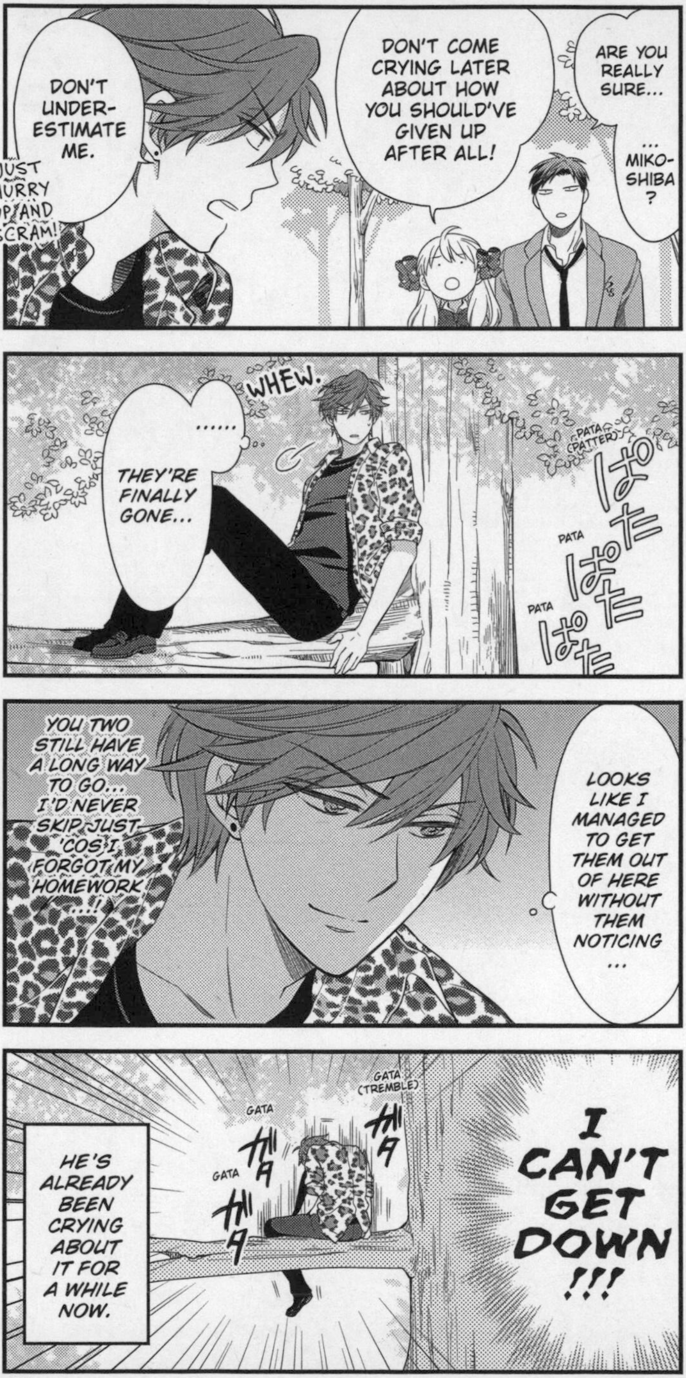

ARE YOU REALLY SURE...
...MIKO-SHIBA?
DON'T COME CRYING LATER ABOUT HOW YOU SHOULD'VE GIVEN UP AFTER ALL!
DON'T UNDER-ESTIMATE ME.
JUST HURRY UP AND SCRAM!
ぱたぱたぱた
PATA (PATTER)
PATA
PATA
WHEW.
......
THEY'RE FINALLY GONE...
LOOKS LIKE I MANAGED TO GET THEM OUT OF HERE WITHOUT THEM NOTICING...
YOU TWO STILL HAVE A LONG WAY TO GO... I'D NEVER SKIP JUST 'COS I FORGOT MY HOMEWORK...!!
I CAN'T GET DOWN!!!
ガタ
GATA (TREMBLE)
ガタ
GATA
ガタ
GATA
HE'S ALREADY BEEN CRYING ABOUT IT FOR A WHILE NOW.

A SHOUJO MANGA TURN OF EVENTS ①

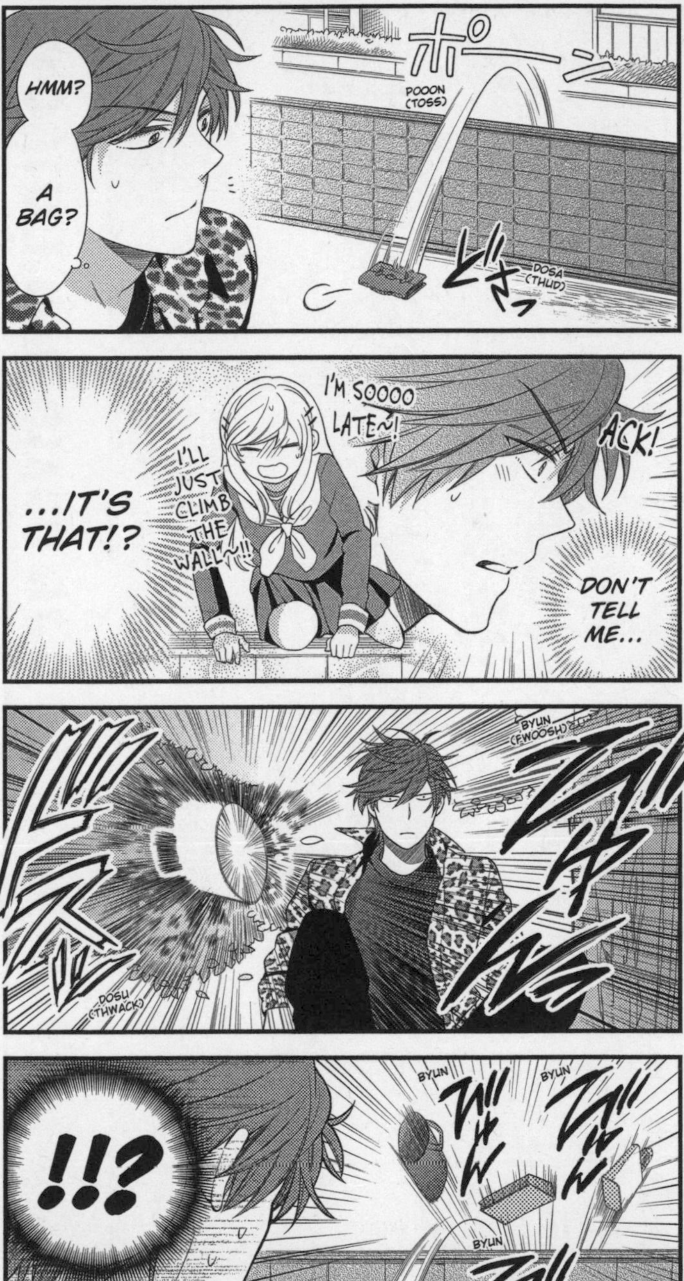
POOON (TOSS)
DOSA (THUD)
HMM?
A BAG?
ACK!
DON'T TELL ME...
I'M SOOOO LATE~!
I'LL JUST CLIMB THE WALL~!!
...IT'S THAT!?
BYUN (FWOOSH)
DOSU (THWACK)
BYUN
BYUN
BYUN
!!?

ASSESSING THE SITUATION AND MAKING A DECISION

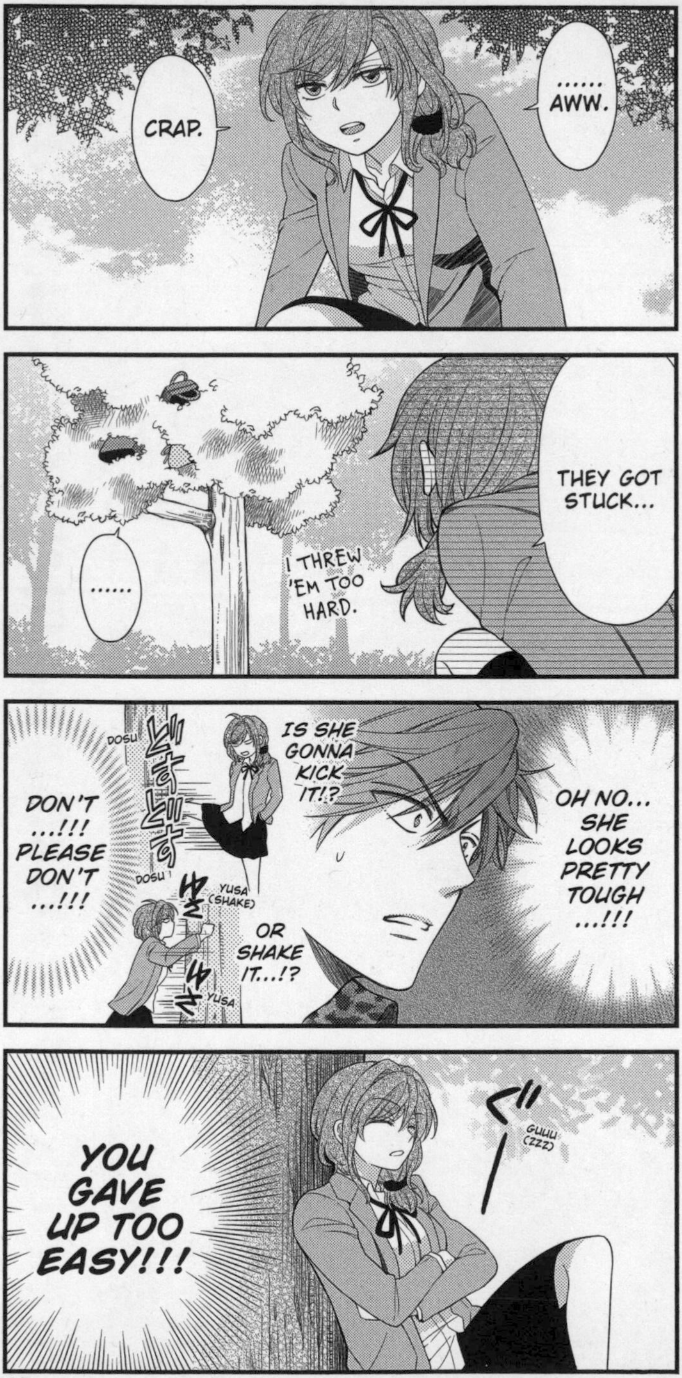

......AWW.
CRAP.
THEY GOT STUCK...
I THREW 'EM TOO HARD.
......
OH NO... SHE LOOKS PRETTY TOUGH ...!!!
IS SHE GONNA KICK IT!?
どすどす
DOSU
DOSU
DON'T ...!!! PLEASE DON'T ...!!!
ゆさゆさ
YUSA (SHAKE)
OR SHAKE IT...!?
YUSA
ぐー
GUUU (ZZZ)
YOU GAVE UP TOO EASY!!!

OFFENSE AND DEFENSE FROM ABOVE AND BELOW

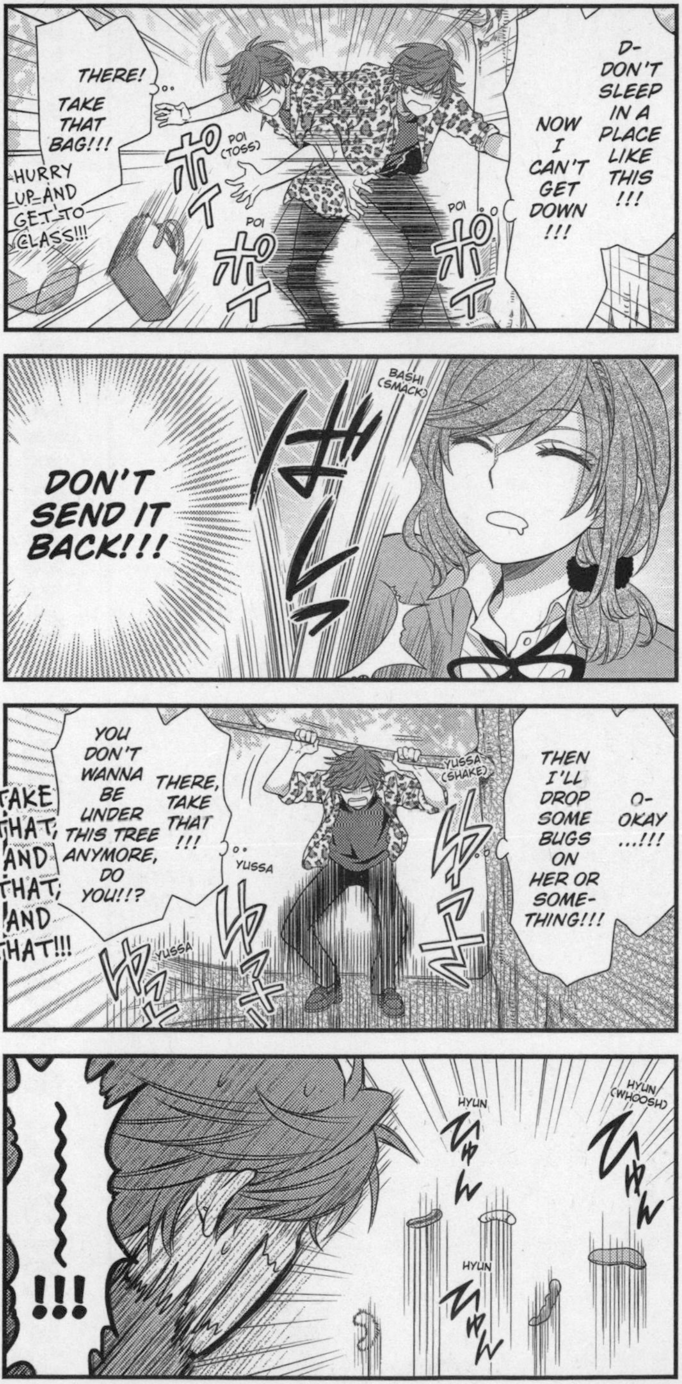
D-DON'T SLEEP IN A PLACE LIKE THIS!!!
NOW I CAN'T GET DOWN!!!
POI
POI
POI (TOSS)
THERE!
TAKE THAT BAG!!!
HURRY UP AND GET TO CLASS!!!
BASHI (SMACK)
DON'T SEND IT BACK!!!
O-OKAY...!!!
THEN I'LL DROP SOME BUGS ON HER OR SOMETHING!!!
YUSSA (SHAKE)
THERE, TAKE THAT!!!
YOU DON'T WANNA BE UNDER THIS TREE ANYMORE, DO YOU!!?
YUSSA
YUSSA
TAKE THAT, AND THAT, AND THAT!!!
HYUN (WHOOSH)
HYUN
HYUN
~~~~!!!
~~~~

A SHOUJO MANGA TURN OF EVENTS ②

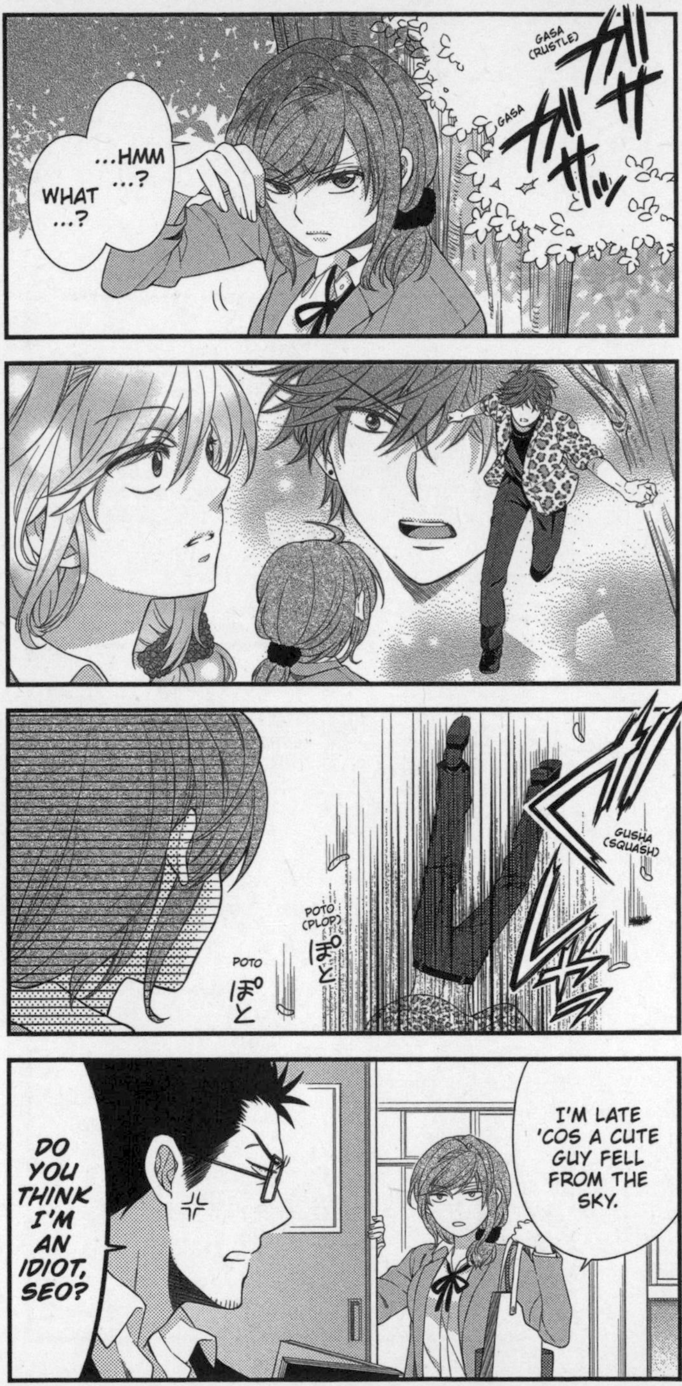
GASA (RUSTLE)
GASA
...HMM ...? WHAT ...?
GUSHA (SQUASH)
POTO (PLOP)
POTO
I'M LATE 'COS A CUTE GUY FELL FROM THE SKY.
DO YOU THINK I'M AN IDIOT, SEO?

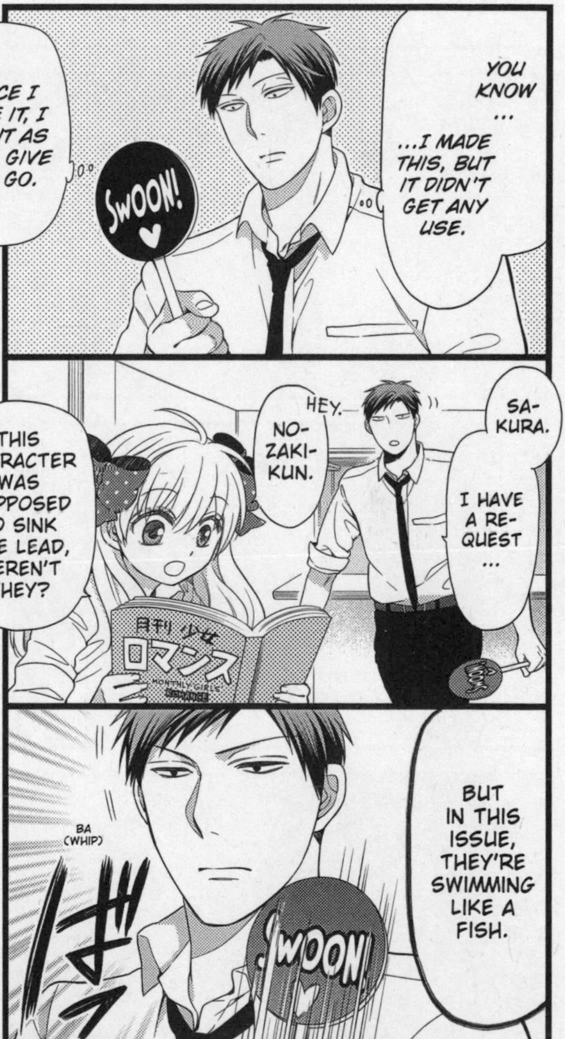
YOU KNOW ...
...I MADE THIS, BUT IT DIDN'T GET ANY USE.
SWOON!
SINCE I HAVE IT, I MIGHT AS WELL GIVE IT A GO.
SA-KURA.
I HAVE A RE-QUEST ...
HEY.
NO-ZAKI-KUN.
THIS CHARACTER WAS SUPPOSED TO SINK LIKE LEAD, WEREN'T THEY?
月刊 少女 ロマンス
MONTHLY GIRLS' ROMANCE
BUT IN THIS ISSUE, THEY'RE SWIMMING LIKE A FISH.
BA (WHIP)
SWOON!

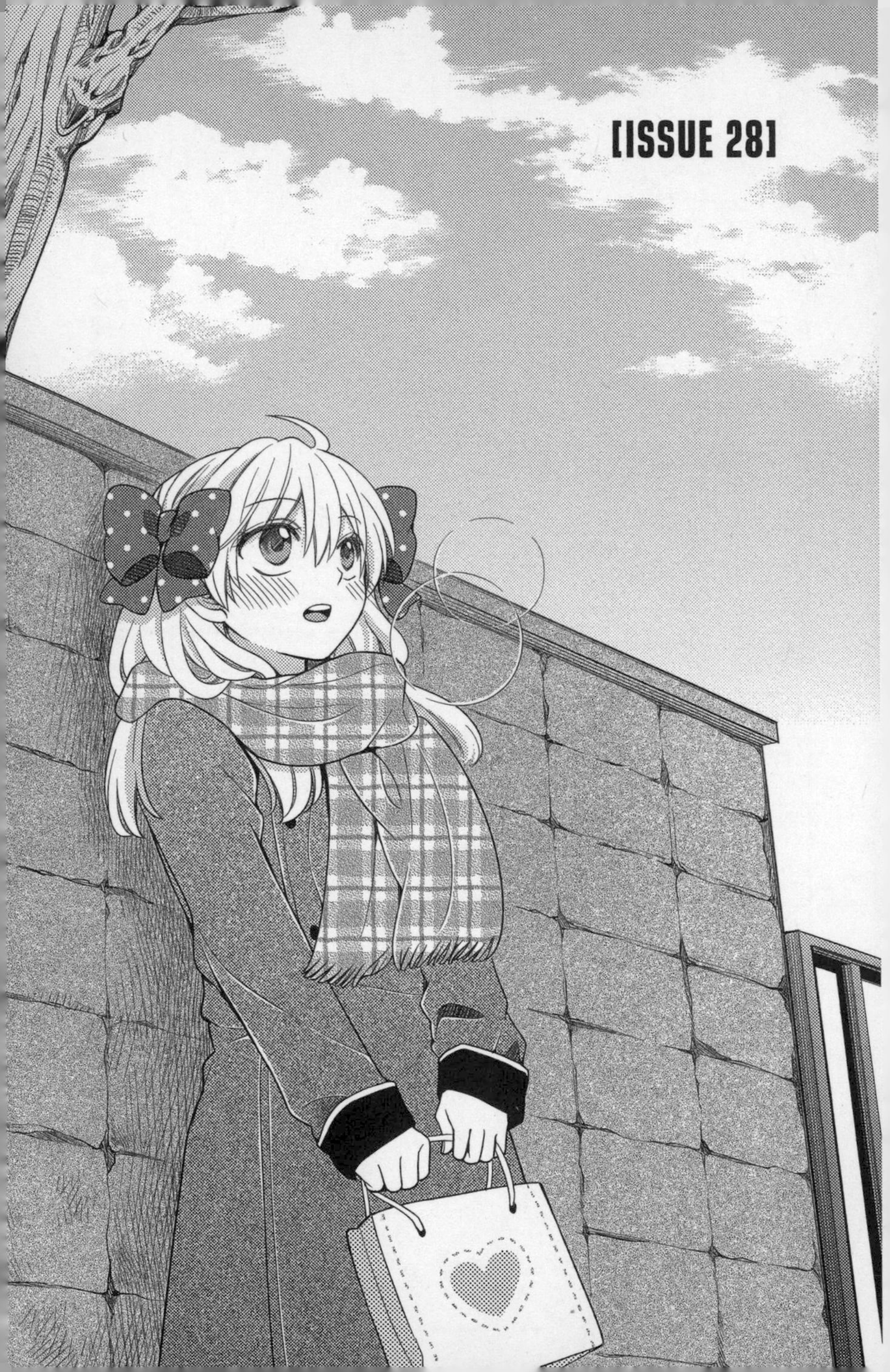
[ISSUE 28]

FOUR MONTHS AFTER PURCHASE

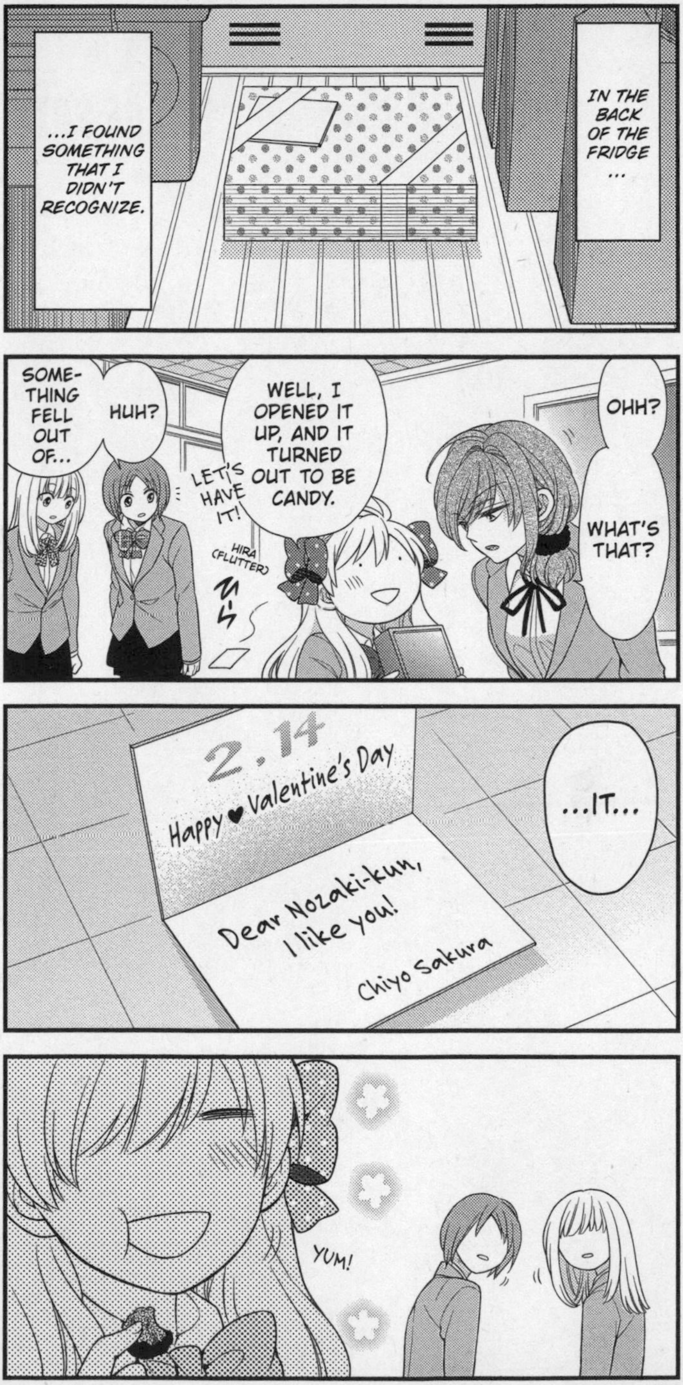
IN THE BACK OF THE FRIDGE ...
...I FOUND SOMETHING THAT I DIDN'T RECOGNIZE.
OHH?
WHAT'S THAT?
WELL, I OPENED IT UP, AND IT TURNED OUT TO BE CANDY.
LET'S HAVE IT!
HIRA (FLUTTER)
HUH?
SOME-THING FELL OUT OF...
...IT...
2.14
Happy ♥ Valentine's Day
Dear Nozaki-kun, I like you!
Chiyo Sakura
YUM!

A DAY RUNNING ALL AROUND THE SCHOOL

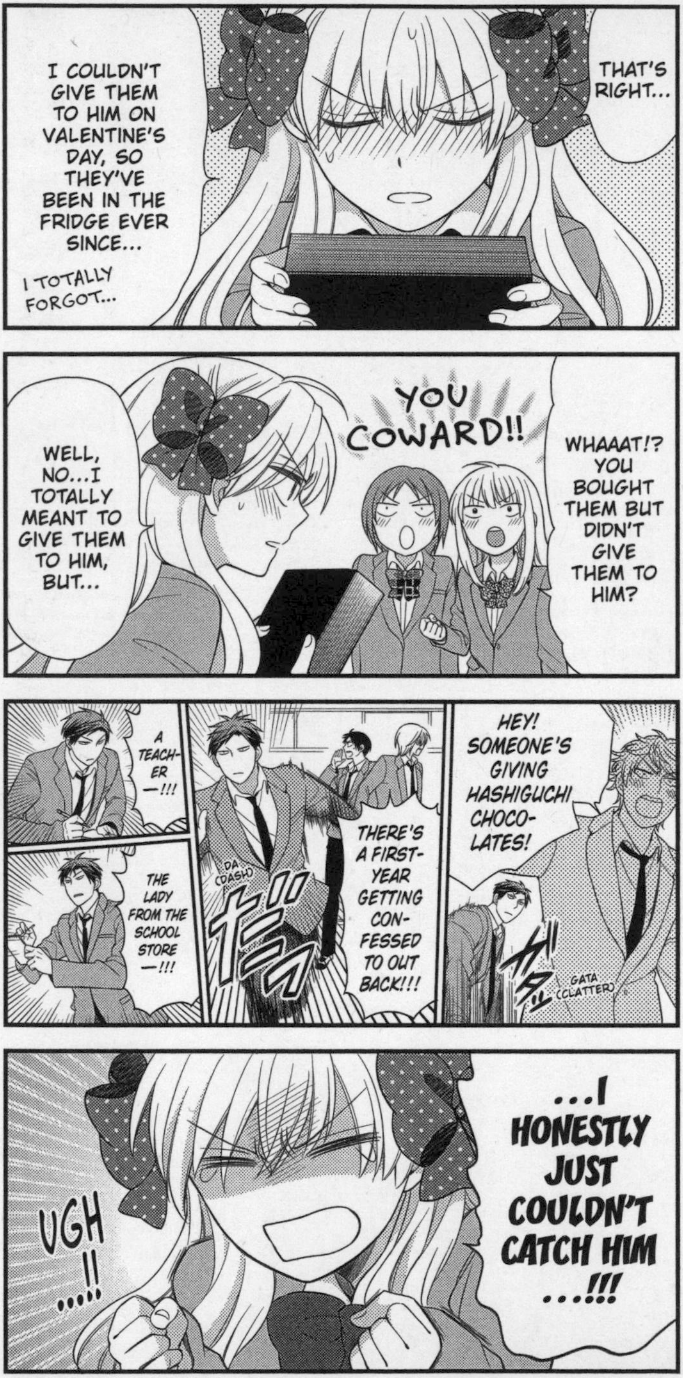
THAT'S RIGHT...
I COULDN'T GIVE THEM TO HIM ON VALENTINE'S DAY, SO THEY'VE BEEN IN THE FRIDGE EVER SINCE...
I TOTALLY FORGOT...
WHAAAT!? YOU BOUGHT THEM BUT DIDN'T GIVE THEM TO HIM?
YOU COWARD!!
WELL, NO...I TOTALLY MEANT TO GIVE THEM TO HIM, BUT...
HEY! SOMEONE'S GIVING HASHIGUCHI CHOCO-LATES!
GATA (CLATTER)
THERE'S A FIRST-YEAR GETTING CON-FESSED TO OUT BACK!!!
DA (DASH)
A TEACH-ER —!!!
THE LADY FROM THE SCHOOL STORE —!!!
...I HONESTLY JUST COULDN'T CATCH HIM ...!!!
UGH ...!!

A FUN EVENT

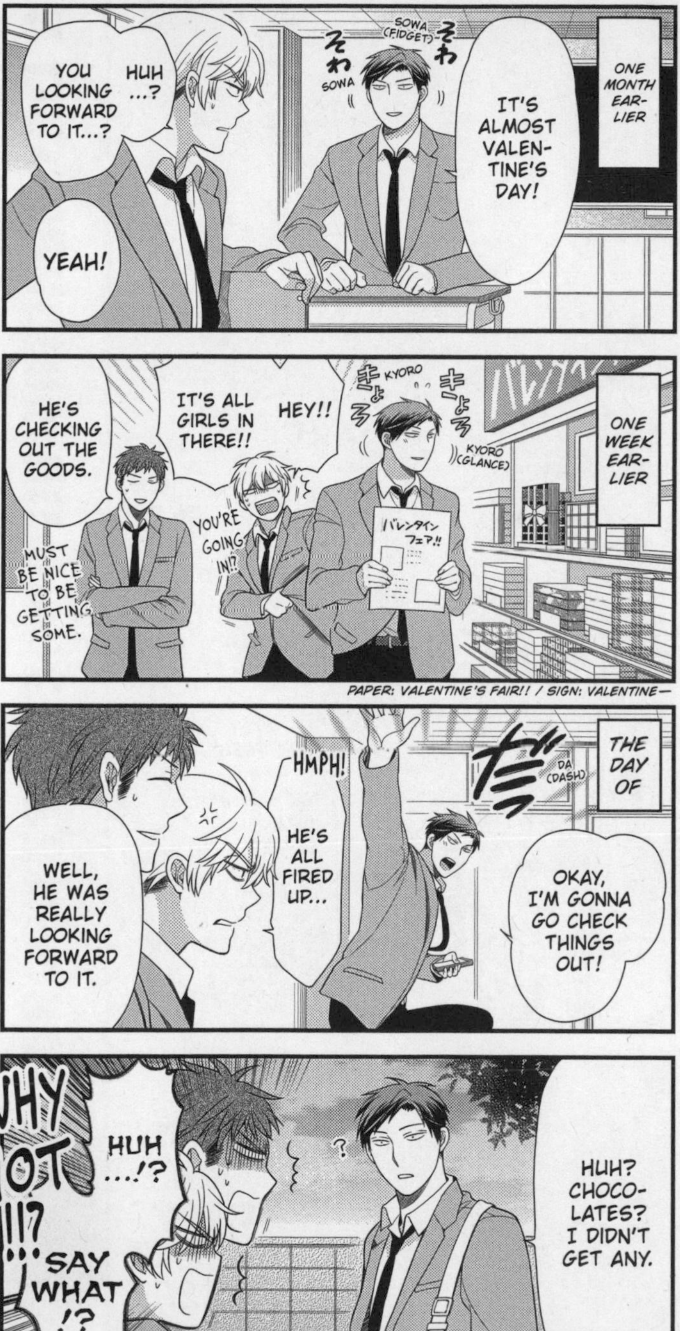
ONE MONTH EARLIER
そわ SOWA (FIDGET)
そわ SOWA
IT'S ALMOST VALENTINE'S DAY!
HUH ...?
YOU LOOKING FORWARD TO IT...?
YEAH!
ONE WEEK EARLIER
きょろ KYORO (GLANCE)
きょろ KYORO
バレンタイン フェア!!
HEY!!
IT'S ALL GIRLS IN THERE!!
YOU'RE GOING IN!?
HE'S CHECKING OUT THE GOODS.
MUST BE NICE TO BE GETTING SOME.
PAPER: VALENTINE'S FAIR!! / SIGN: VALENTINE—
THE DAY OF
DA (DASH)
OKAY, I'M GONNA GO CHECK THINGS OUT!
HMPH!
HE'S ALL FIRED UP...
WELL, HE WAS REALLY LOOKING FORWARD TO IT.
HUH? CHOCOLATES? I DIDN'T GET ANY.
?
HUH ...!?
WHY NOT!!?
SAY WHAT !?

A SPECIAL SECTION

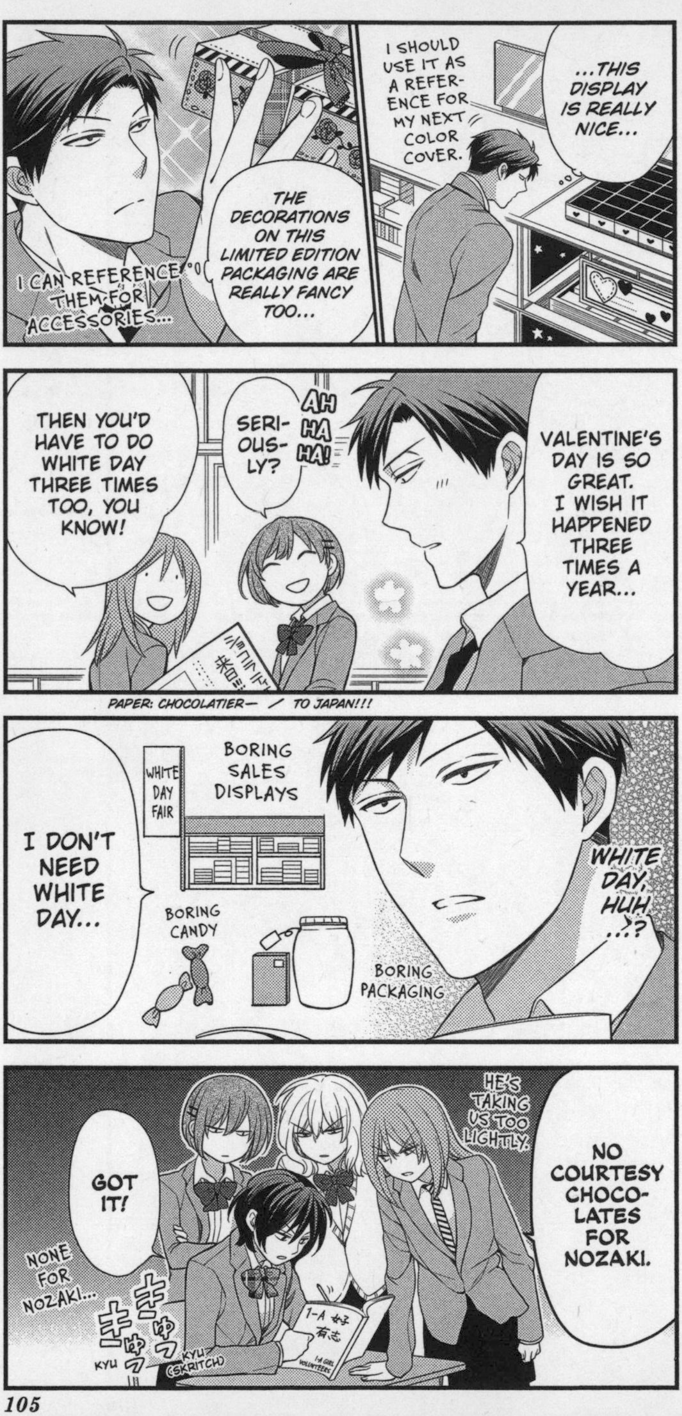
...THIS DISPLAY IS REALLY NICE...
I SHOULD USE IT AS A REFERENCE FOR MY NEXT COLOR COVER.
THE DECORATIONS ON THIS LIMITED EDITION PACKAGING ARE REALLY FANCY TOO...
I CAN REFERENCE THEM FOR ACCESSORIES...
VALENTINE'S DAY IS SO GREAT. I WISH IT HAPPENED THREE TIMES A YEAR...
AH HA HA!
SERIOUSLY?
THEN YOU'D HAVE TO DO WHITE DAY THREE TIMES TOO, YOU KNOW!
PAPER: CHOCOLATIER— / TO JAPAN!!!
WHITE DAY, HUH...?
BORING SALES DISPLAYS
WHITE DAY FAIR
I DON'T NEED WHITE DAY...
BORING CANDY
BORING PACKAGING
NO COURTESY CHOCOLATES FOR NOZAKI.
HE'S TAKING US TOO LIGHTLY.
GOT IT!
1-A 女子 有志
1-A GIRL VOLUNTEERS
NONE FOR NOZAKI...
キュッ キュッ
KYU KYU (SKRITCH)

GOOD FRIENDS

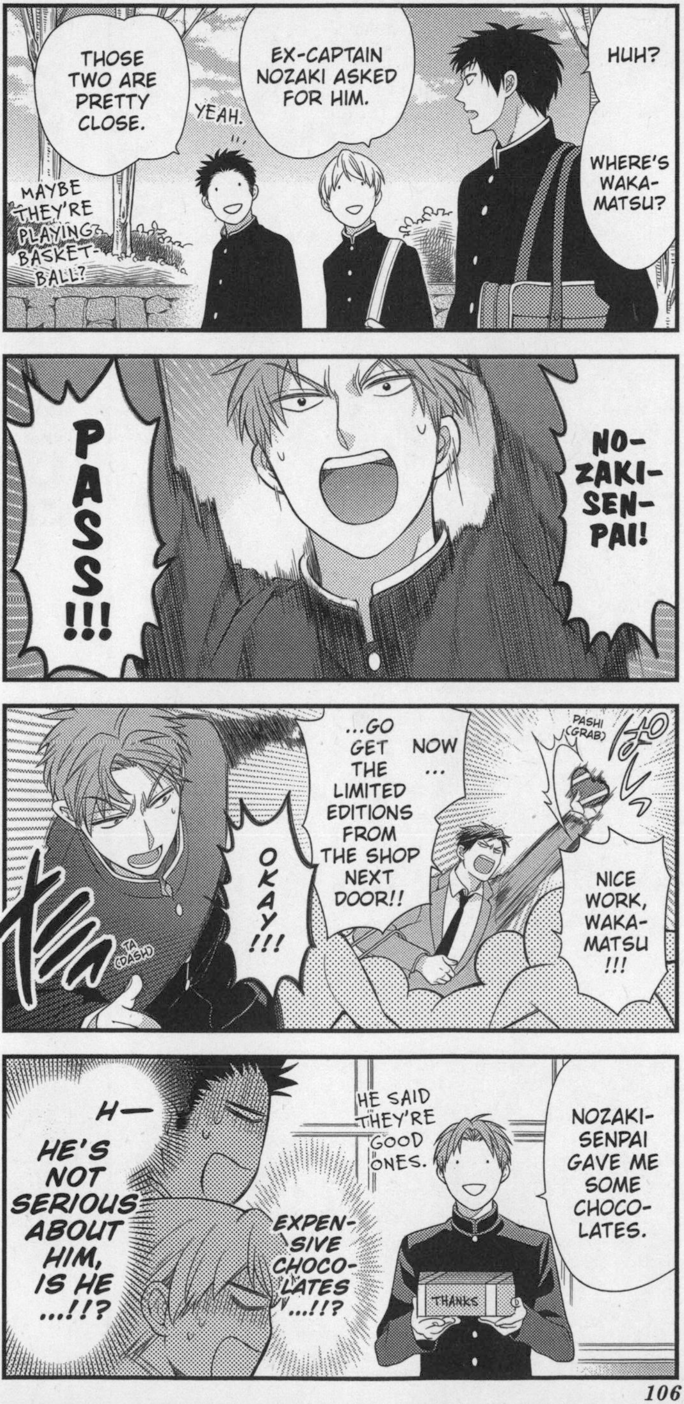
HUH?
WHERE'S WAKA-MATSU?
EX-CAPTAIN NOZAKI ASKED FOR HIM.
YEAH.
THOSE TWO ARE PRETTY CLOSE.
MAYBE THEY'RE PLAYING BASKET-BALL?
NO-ZAKI-SEN-PAI!
PASS!!!
PASHI (GRAB)
NICE WORK, WAKA-MATSU!!!
NOW...
...GO GET THE LIMITED EDITIONS FROM THE SHOP NEXT DOOR!!
OKAY!!!
TA (DASH)
NOZAKI-SENPAI GAVE ME SOME CHOCO-LATES.
HE SAID THEY'RE GOOD ONES.
THANKS
EXPEN-SIVE CHOCO-LATES ...!!?
H— HE'S NOT SERIOUS ABOUT HIM, IS HE ...!!?

A BOY FROM THE PAST WHO WAS ON HER MIND

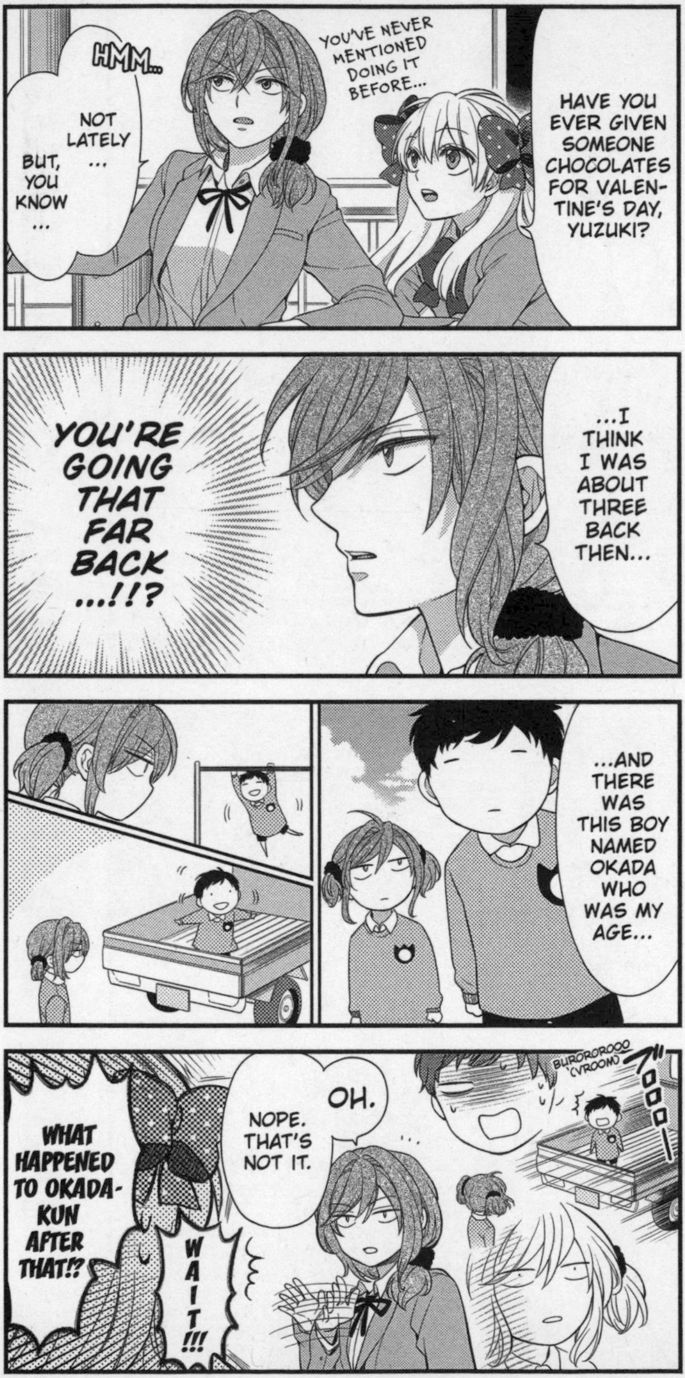
HAVE YOU EVER GIVEN SOMEONE CHOCOLATES FOR VALEN-TINE'S DAY, YUZUKI?
YOU'VE NEVER MENTIONED DOING IT BEFORE...
HMM...
NOT LATELY ... BUT, YOU KNOW ...
...I THINK I WAS ABOUT THREE BACK THEN...
YOU'RE GOING THAT FAR BACK ...!!?
...AND THERE WAS THIS BOY NAMED OKADA WHO WAS MY AGE...
BUROROROOO (VROOM)
OH.
NOPE. THAT'S NOT IT.
WHAT HAPPENED TO OKADA-KUN AFTER THAT!?
WAIT!!!

PUTTING A LOT OF TIME AND EFFORT INTO IT

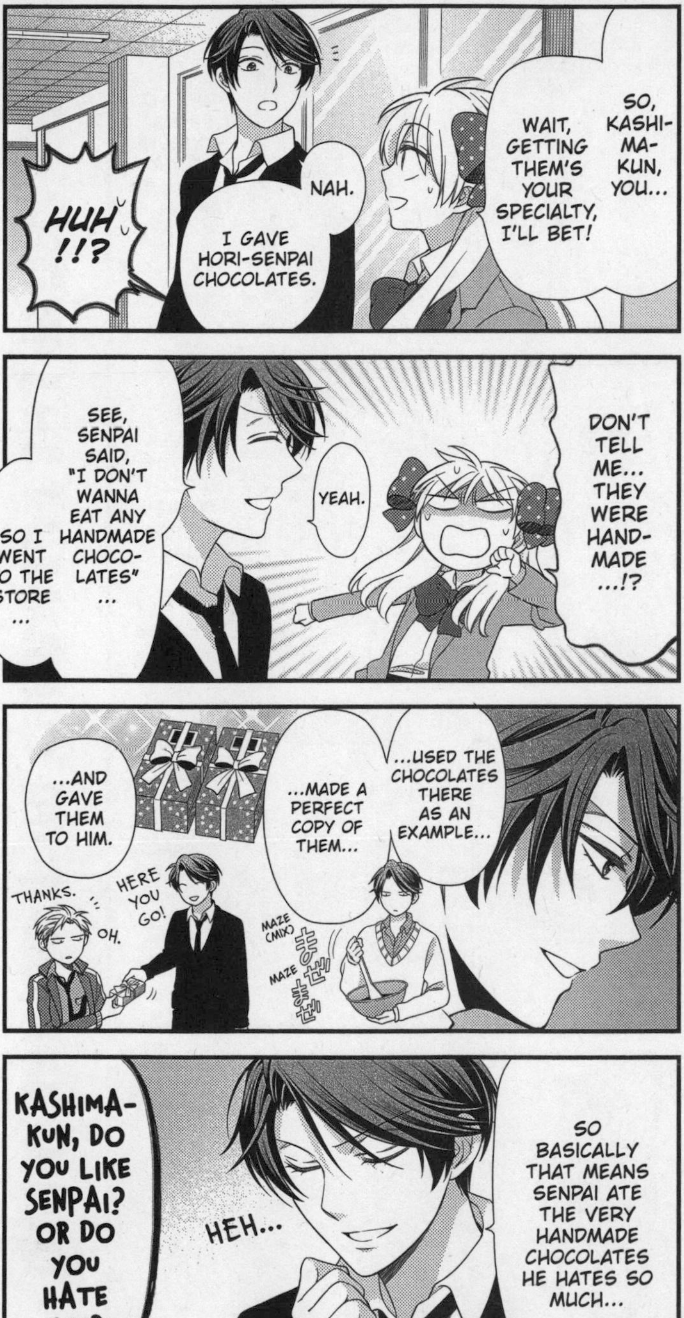
SO, KASHIMA-KUN, YOU...
WAIT, GETTING THEM'S YOUR SPECIALTY, I'LL BET!
NAH.
I GAVE HORI-SENPAI CHOCOLATES.
HUH!!?
DON'T TELL ME... THEY WERE HANDMADE...!?
YEAH.
SEE, SENPAI SAID, "I DON'T WANNA EAT ANY HANDMADE CHOCOLATES"...
SO I WENT TO THE STORE...
...USED THE CHOCOLATES THERE AS AN EXAMPLE...
...MADE A PERFECT COPY OF THEM...
MAZE (MIX)
MAZE
...AND GAVE THEM TO HIM.
HERE YOU GO!
OH.
THANKS.
SO BASICALLY THAT MEANS SENPAI ATE THE VERY HANDMADE CHOCOLATES HE HATES SO MUCH...
HEH...
KASHIMA-KUN, DO YOU LIKE SENPAI? OR DO YOU HATE HIM?

THE MEASURE OF KASHIMA-KUN'S SENTIMENT

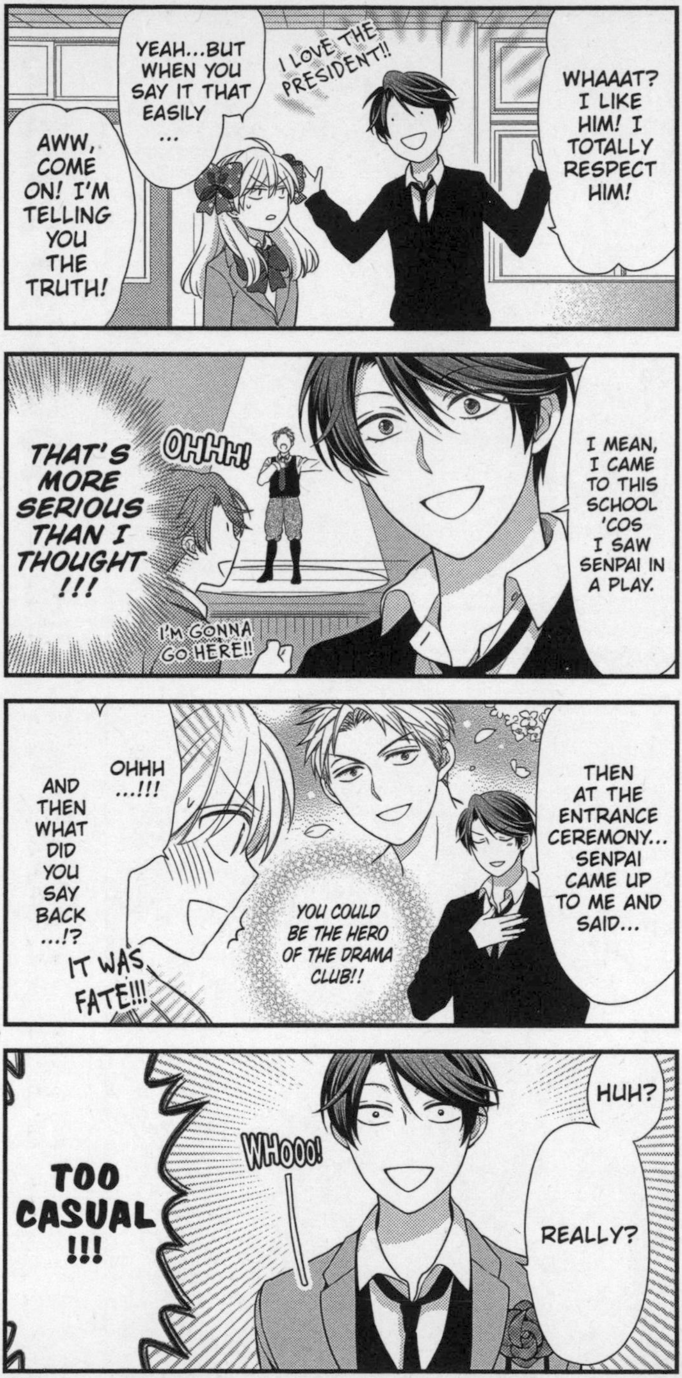
WHAAAT? I LIKE HIM! I TOTALLY RESPECT HIM!
I LOVE THE PRESIDENT!!
YEAH...BUT WHEN YOU SAY IT THAT EASILY ...
AWW, COME ON! I'M TELLING YOU THE TRUTH!
I MEAN, I CAME TO THIS SCHOOL 'COS I SAW SENPAI IN A PLAY.
OHHH!
I'M GONNA GO HERE!!
THAT'S MORE SERIOUS THAN I THOUGHT!!!
THEN AT THE ENTRANCE CEREMONY... SENPAI CAME UP TO ME AND SAID...
YOU COULD BE THE HERO OF THE DRAMA CLUB!!
OHHH ...!!!
AND THEN WHAT DID YOU SAY BACK ...!?
IT WAS FATE!!!
HUH?
REALLY?
WHOOO!
TOO CASUAL!!!

CHIYO'S FEELINGS

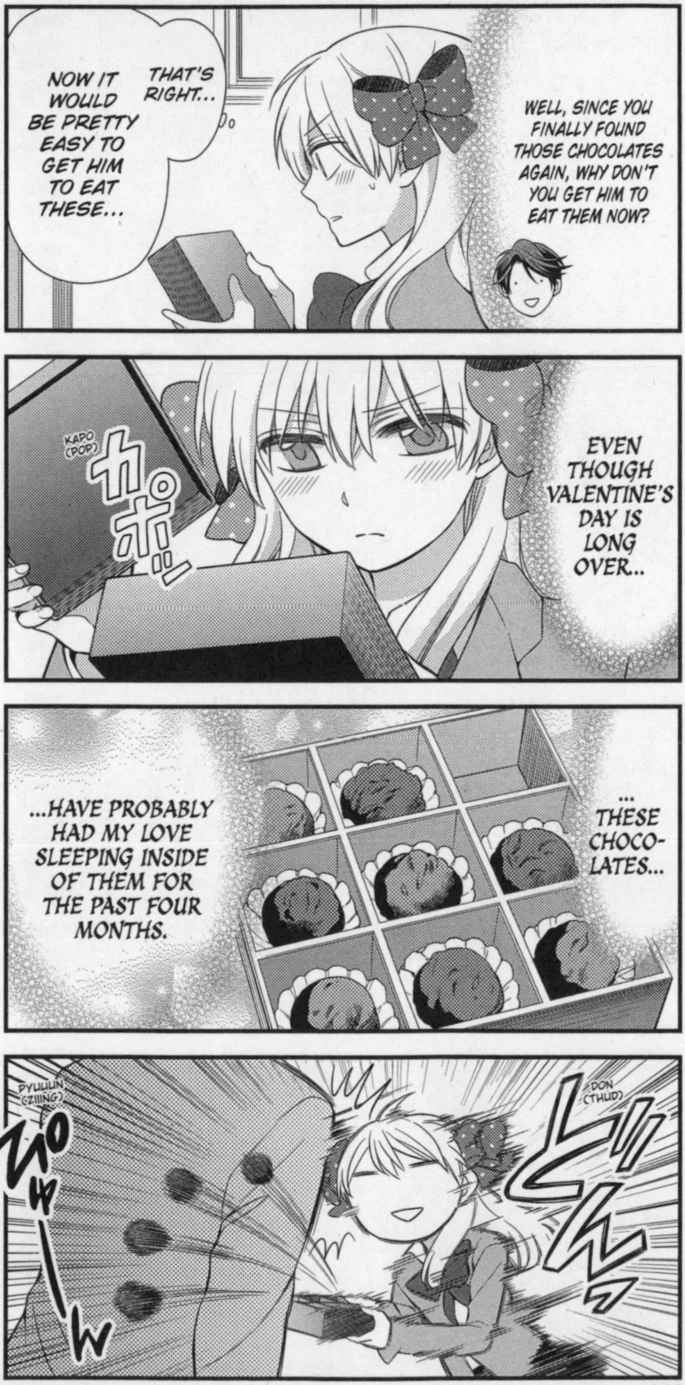
WELL, SINCE YOU FINALLY FOUND THOSE CHOCOLATES AGAIN, WHY DON'T YOU GET HIM TO EAT THEM NOW?
THAT'S RIGHT...
NOW IT WOULD BE PRETTY EASY TO GET HIM TO EAT THESE...
EVEN THOUGH VALENTINE'S DAY IS LONG OVER..
KAPO (POP)
... THESE CHOCO-LATES...
...HAVE PROBABLY HAD MY LOVE SLEEPING INSIDE OF THEM FOR THE PAST FOUR MONTHS.
DON (THUD)
PYUUUN (ZIIING)

THE WHEREABOUTS OF HER LOVE

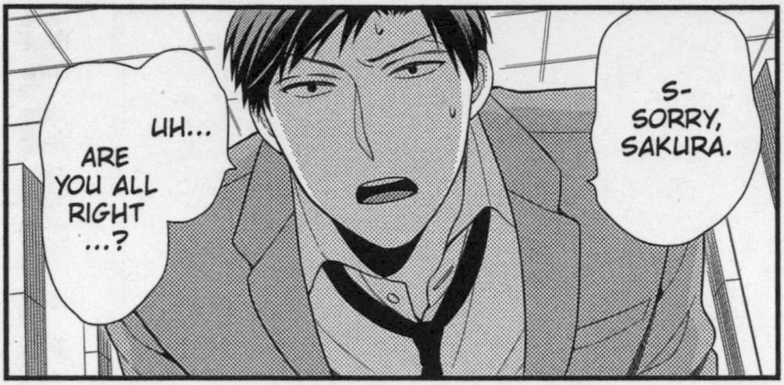
S-SORRY, SAKURA.
UH... ARE YOU ALL RIGHT ...?

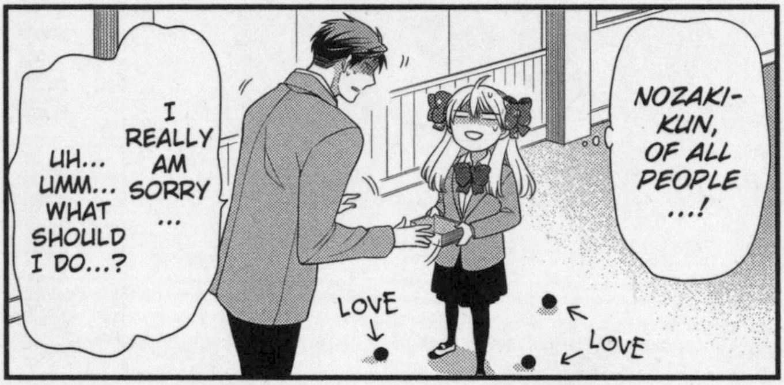
NOZAKI-KUN, OF ALL PEOPLE ...!
I REALLY AM SORRY ...
UH... UMM... WHAT SHOULD I DO...?
LOVE
LOVE

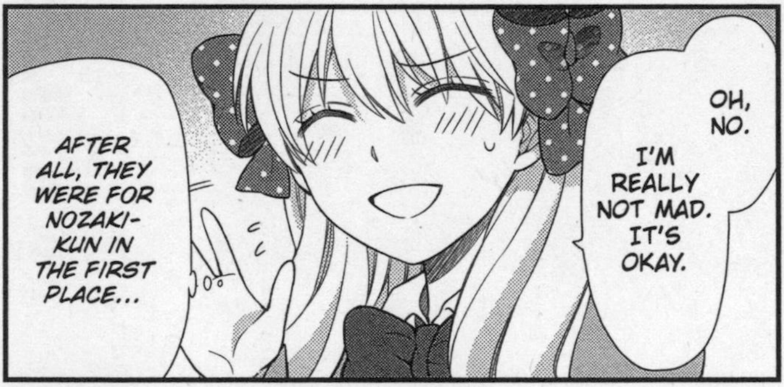
OH, NO. I'M REALLY NOT MAD. IT'S OKAY.
AFTER ALL, THEY WERE FOR NOZAKI-KUN IN THE FIRST PLACE...

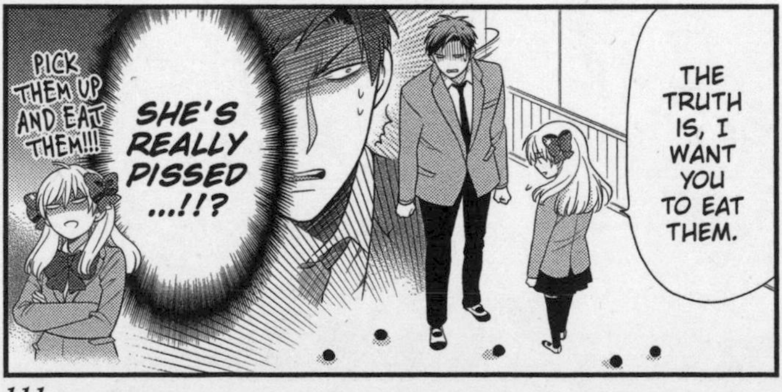
THE TRUTH IS, I WANT YOU TO EAT THEM.
SHE'S REALLY PISSED ...!!?
PICK THEM UP AND EAT THEM!!!

HE WON'T GET IT TODAY EITHER ①

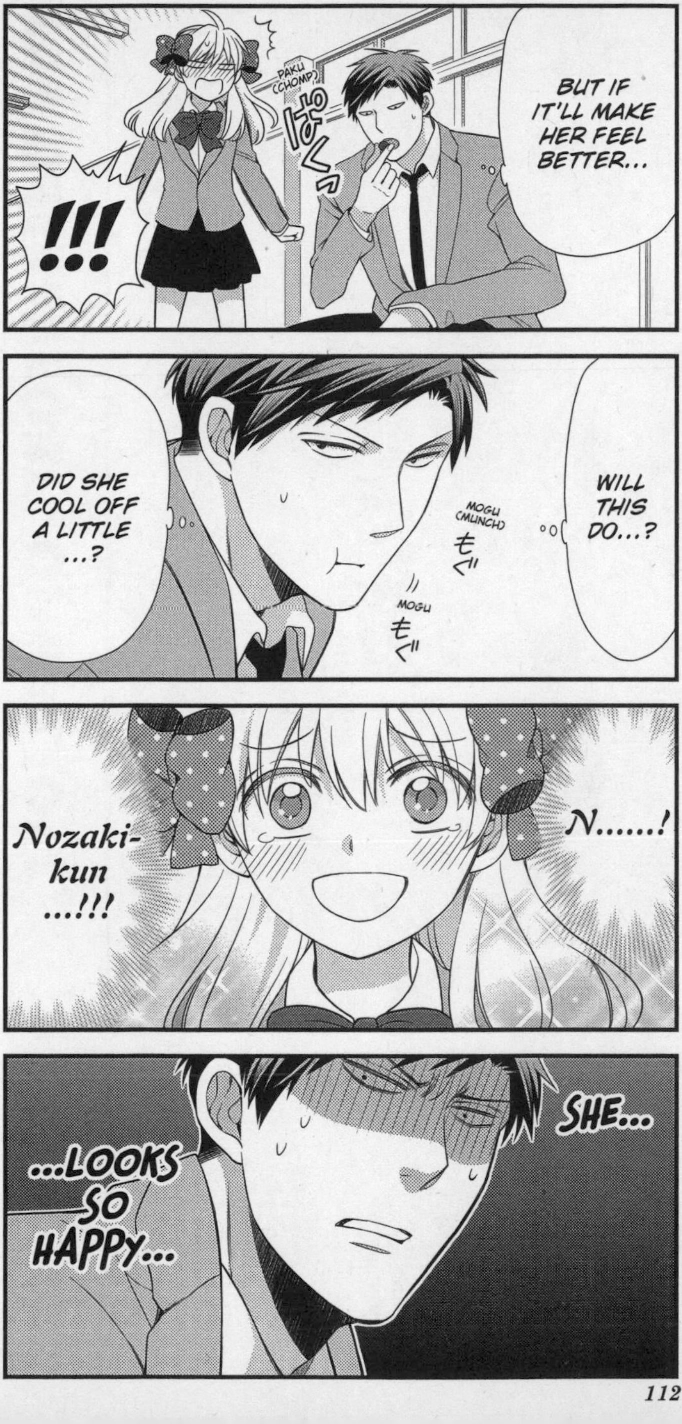

BUT IF IT'LL MAKE HER FEEL BETTER...
PAKU (CHOMP)
!!!
WILL THIS DO...?
MOGU (MUNCH)
MOGU
DID SHE COOL OFF A LITTLE ...?
N......!
Nozaki-kun ...!!!
SHE...
...LOOKS SO HAPPY...

HE WON'T GET IT TODAY EITHER ②

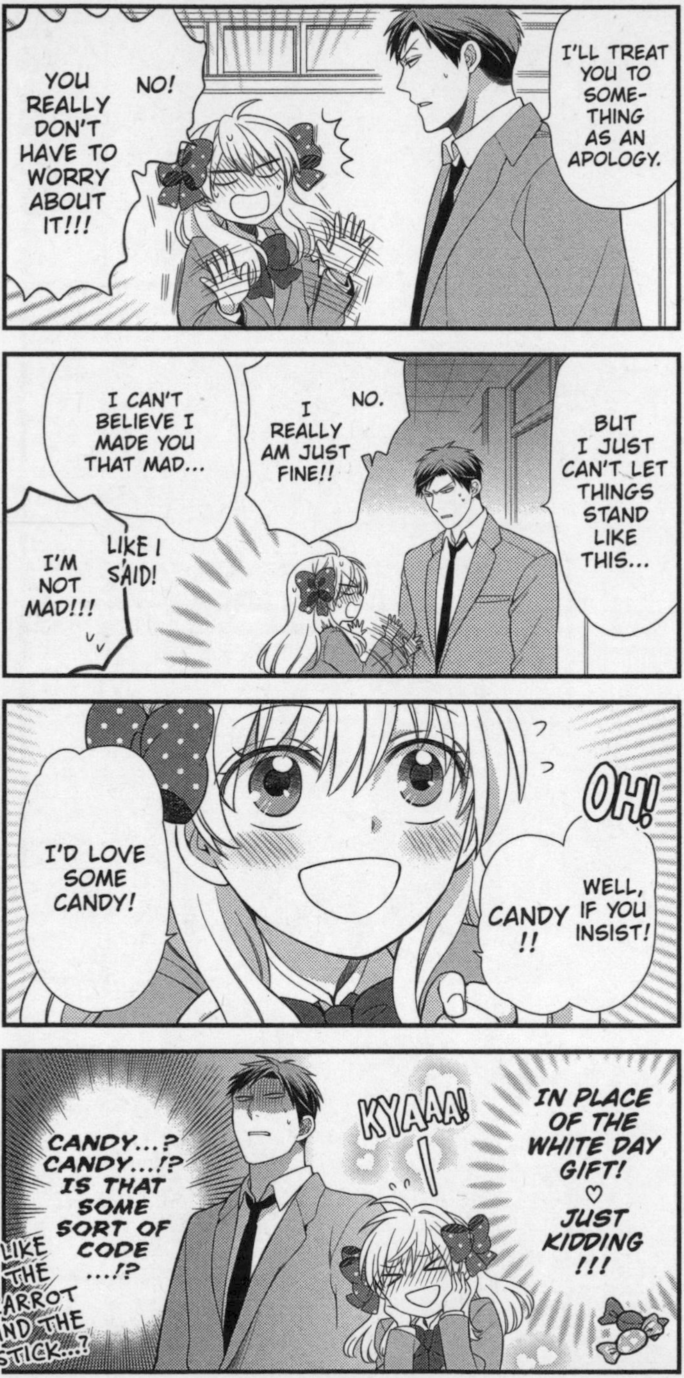

I'LL TREAT YOU TO SOME-THING AS AN APOLOGY.
NO!
YOU REALLY DON'T HAVE TO WORRY ABOUT IT!!!
BUT I JUST CAN'T LET THINGS STAND LIKE THIS...
NO.
I REALLY AM JUST FINE!!
I CAN'T BELIEVE I MADE YOU THAT MAD...
LIKE I SAID!
I'M NOT MAD!!!
OH!
WELL, IF YOU INSIST!
CANDY !!
I'D LOVE SOME CANDY!
IN PLACE OF THE WHITE DAY GIFT! ♡ JUST KIDDING !!!
KYAAA!
CANDY...? CANDY...!? IS THAT SOME SORT OF CODE ...!?
LIKE THE CARROT AND THE STICK...?

VALENTINES FOR MIKOSHIBA-KUN

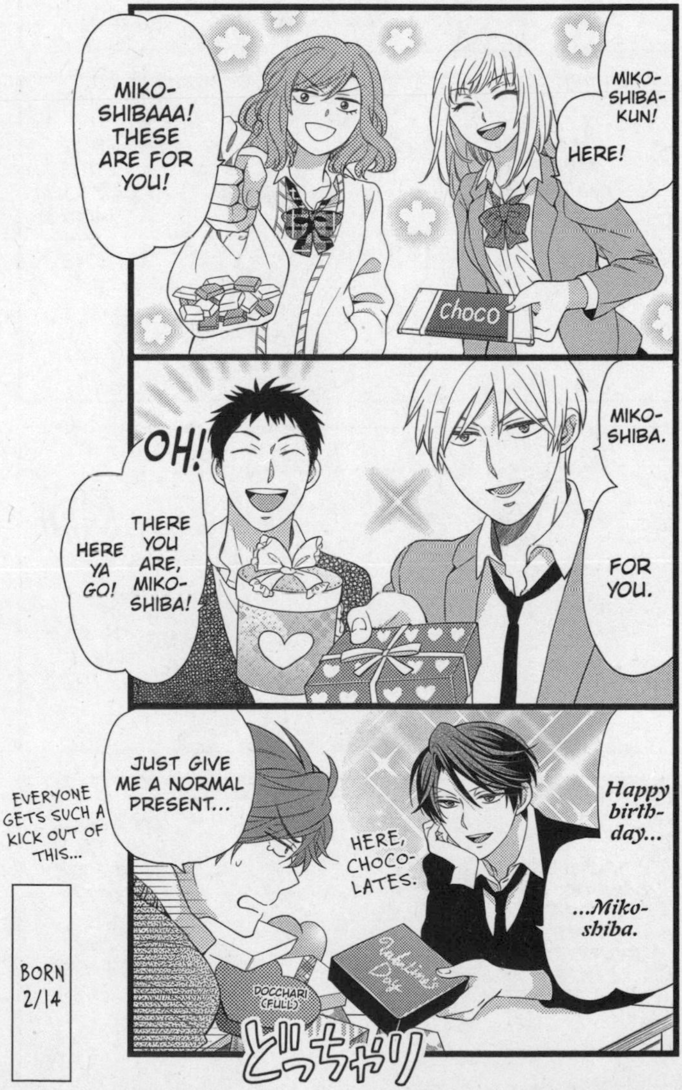
MIKO-SHIBA-KUN!
HERE!
MIKO-SHIBAAA! THESE ARE FOR YOU!
choco
MIKO-SHIBA.
FOR YOU.
OH!
THERE YOU ARE, MIKO-SHIBA!
HERE YA GO!
Happy birth-day...
...Miko-shiba.
HERE, CHOCO-LATES.
JUST GIVE ME A NORMAL PRESENT...
EVERYONE GETS SUCH A KICK OUT OF THIS...
DOCCHARI (FULL)
どっちゃり
BORN 2/14

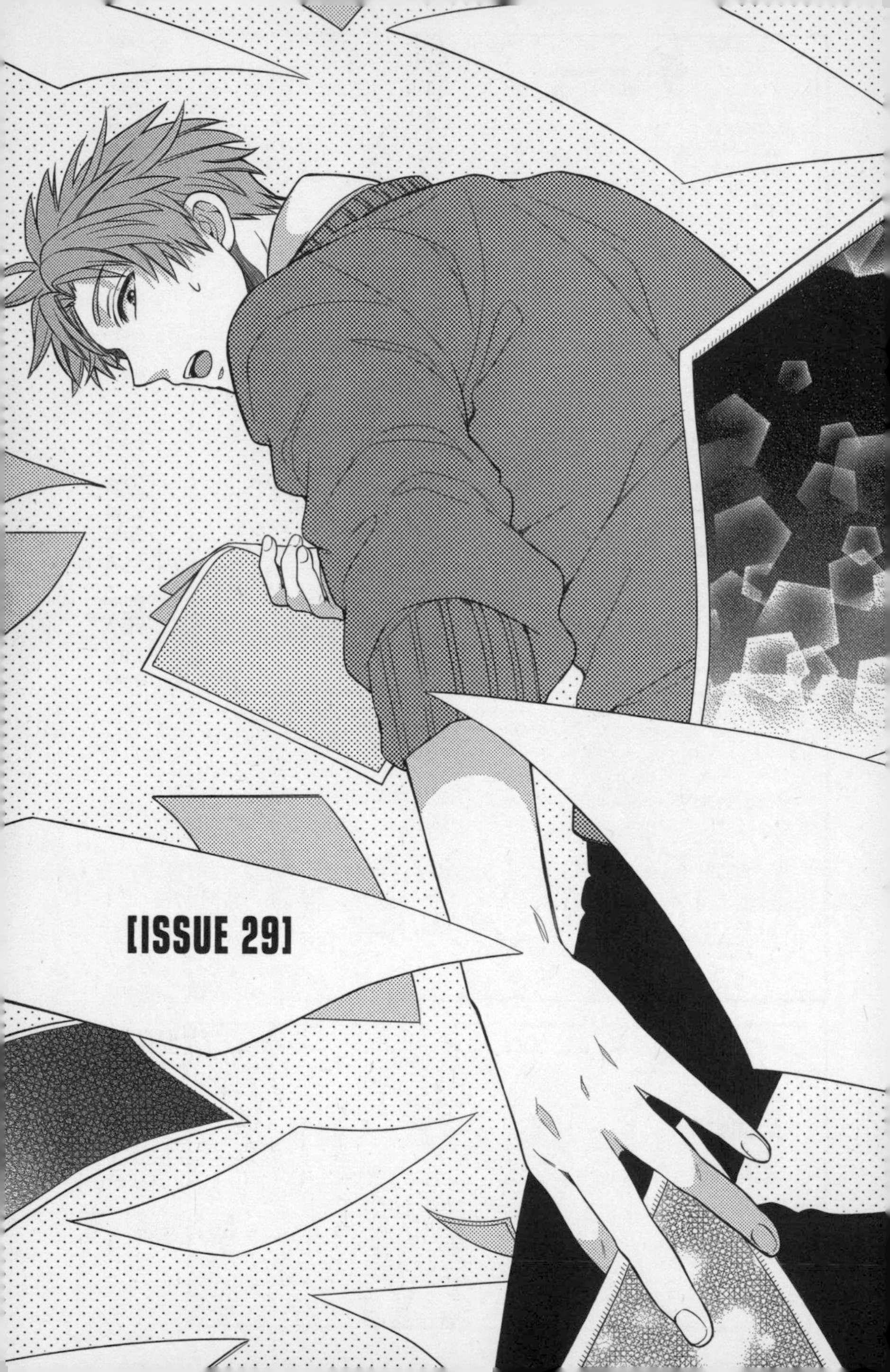
[ISSUE 29]

LOOK, LOOK! PRAISE ME!

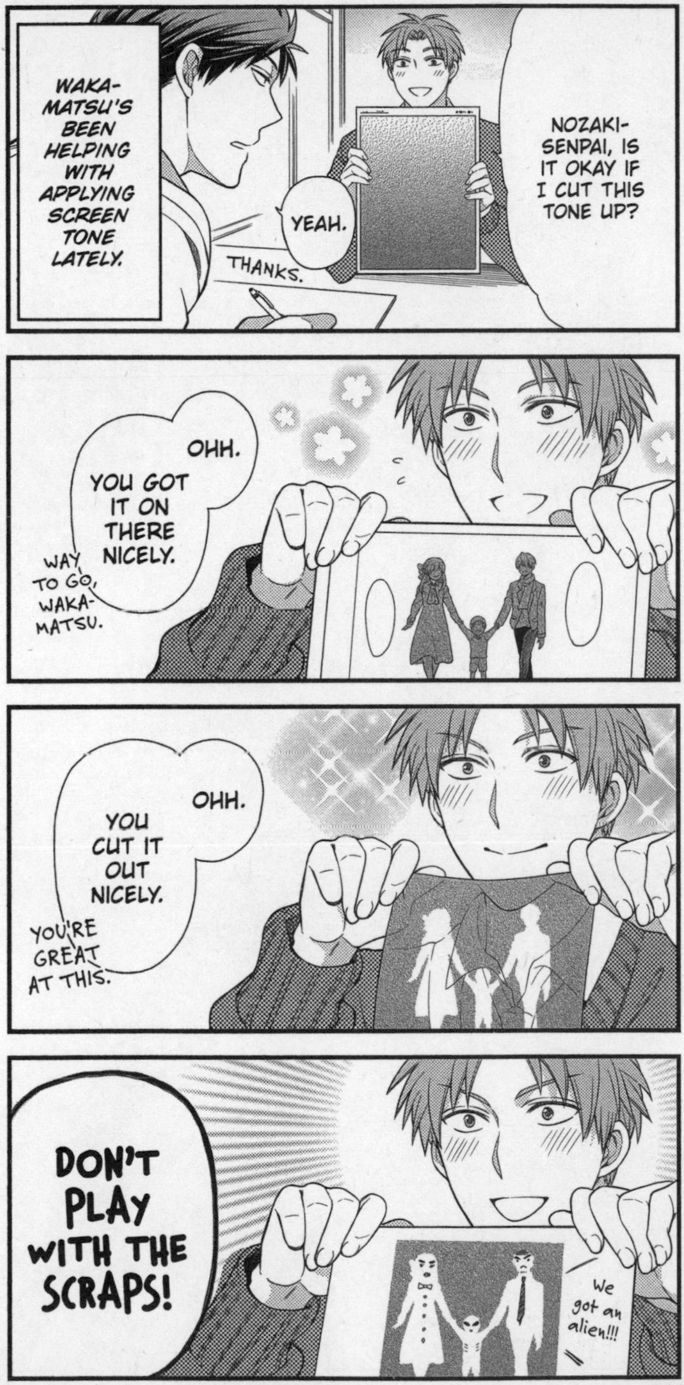

NOZAKI-SENPAI, IS IT OKAY IF I CUT THIS TONE UP?
YEAH.
THANKS.
WAKA-MATSU'S BEEN HELPING WITH APPLYING SCREEN TONE LATELY.
OHH. YOU GOT IT ON THERE NICELY.
WAY TO GO, WAKA-MATSU.
OHH. YOU CUT IT OUT NICELY.
YOU'RE GREAT AT THIS.
We got an alien!!!
DON'T PLAY WITH THE SCRAPS!

IT JUST HAPPENS WITH TONE

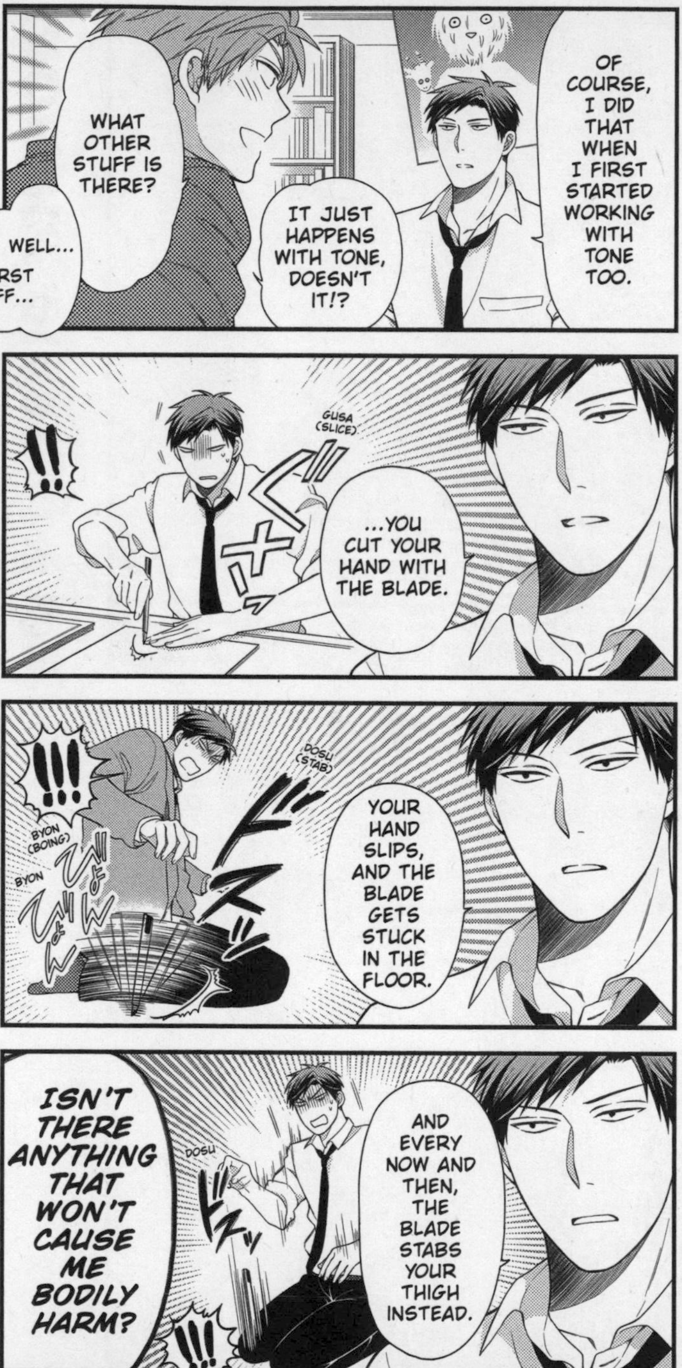
OF COURSE, I DID THAT WHEN I FIRST STARTED WORKING WITH TONE TOO.
IT JUST HAPPENS WITH TONE, DOESN'T IT!?
WHAT OTHER STUFF IS THERE?
WELL... FIRST OFF...
...YOU CUT YOUR HAND WITH THE BLADE.
GUSA (SLICE)
!!
YOUR HAND SLIPS, AND THE BLADE GETS STUCK IN THE FLOOR.
DOSU (STAB)
!!!
BYON (BOING)
BYON
AND EVERY NOW AND THEN, THE BLADE STABS YOUR THIGH INSTEAD.
DOSU
ISN'T THERE ANYTHING THAT WON'T CAUSE ME BODILY HARM?
!!!

SHOPPING PLANS

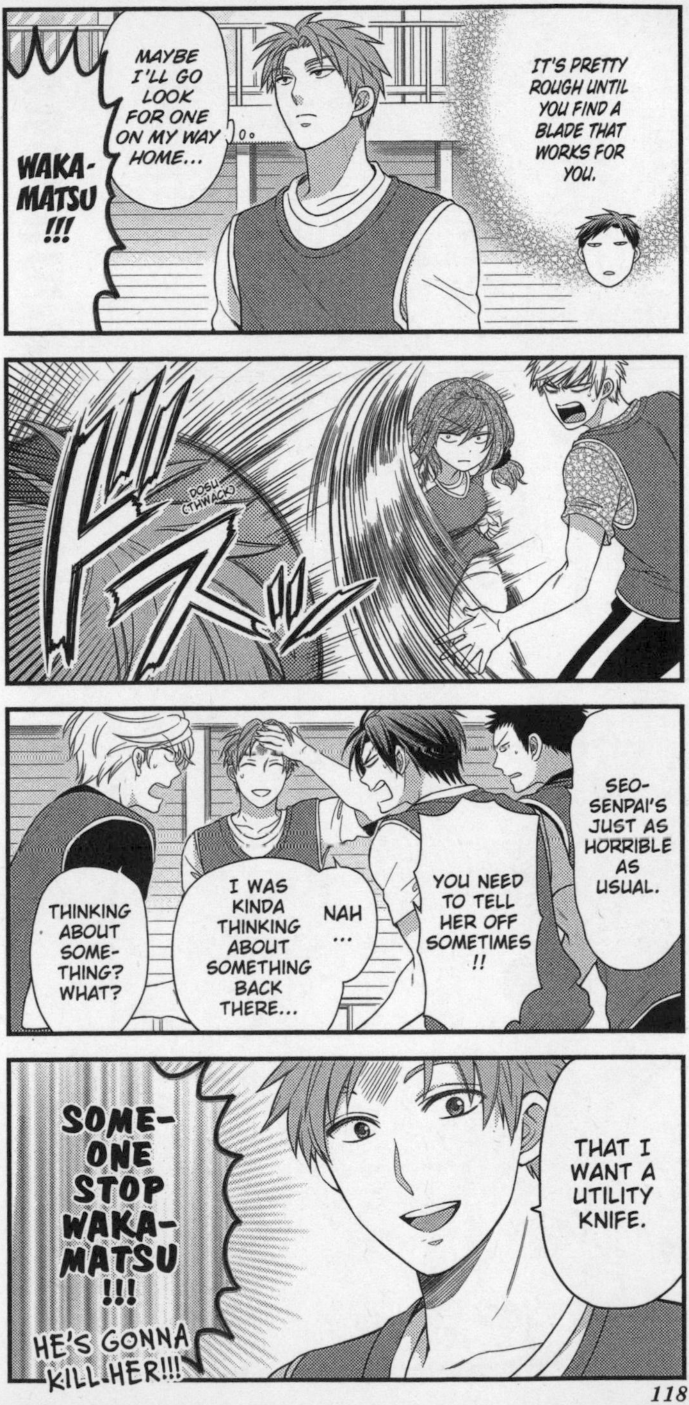

IT'S PRETTY ROUGH UNTIL YOU FIND A BLADE THAT WORKS FOR YOU.
MAYBE I'LL GO LOOK FOR ONE ON MY WAY HOME...
WAKA-MATSU!!!
DOSU (THWACK)
SEO-SENPAI'S JUST AS HORRIBLE AS USUAL.
YOU NEED TO TELL HER OFF SOMETIMES!!
NAH ...
I WAS KINDA THINKING ABOUT SOMETHING BACK THERE...
THINKING ABOUT SOME-THING? WHAT?
THAT I WANT A UTILITY KNIFE.
SOME-ONE STOP WAKA-MATSU!!!
HE'S GONNA KILL HER!!!

HOW HE SEES THINGS

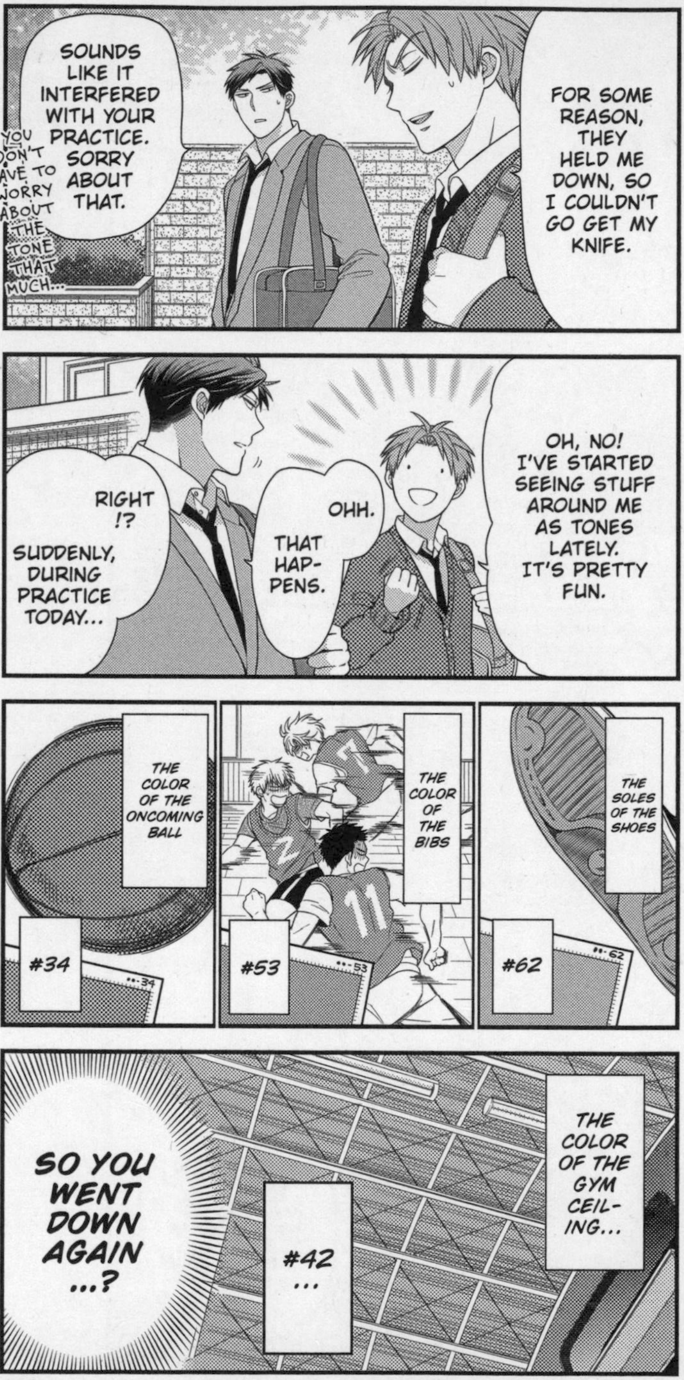
FOR SOME REASON, THEY HELD ME DOWN, SO I COULDN'T GO GET MY KNIFE.
SOUNDS LIKE IT INTERFERED WITH YOUR PRACTICE. SORRY ABOUT THAT.
YOU DON'T HAVE TO WORRY ABOUT THE TONE THAT MUCH...
OH, NO! I'VE STARTED SEEING STUFF AROUND ME AS TONES LATELY. IT'S PRETTY FUN.
OHH.
THAT HAP-PENS.
RIGHT!?
SUDDENLY, DURING PRACTICE TODAY...
THE SOLES OF THE SHOES
#62
THE COLOR OF THE BIBS
#53
THE COLOR OF THE ONCOMING BALL
#34
THE COLOR OF THE GYM CEIL-ING...
#42 ...
SO YOU WENT DOWN AGAIN ...?

NEAR MISS

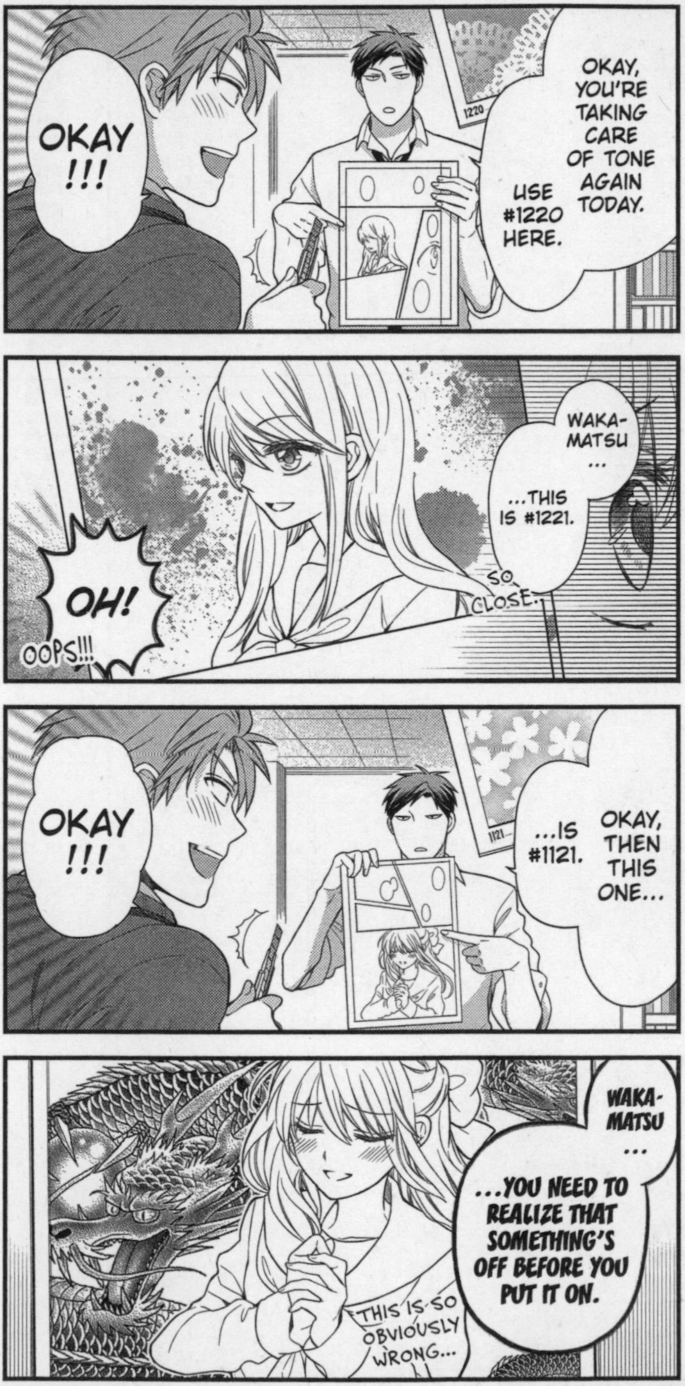
1220
OKAY, YOU'RE TAKING CARE OF TONE AGAIN TODAY.
USE #1220 HERE.
OKAY!!!
WAKA-MATSU...
...THIS IS #1221.
SO CLOSE.
OH!
OOPS!!!
1121
OKAY, THEN THIS ONE...
...IS #1121.
OKAY!!!
WAKA-MATSU...
...YOU NEED TO REALIZE THAT SOMETHING'S OFF BEFORE YOU PUT IT ON.
THIS IS SO OBVIOUSLY WRONG...

UNOFFICIAL NAMES

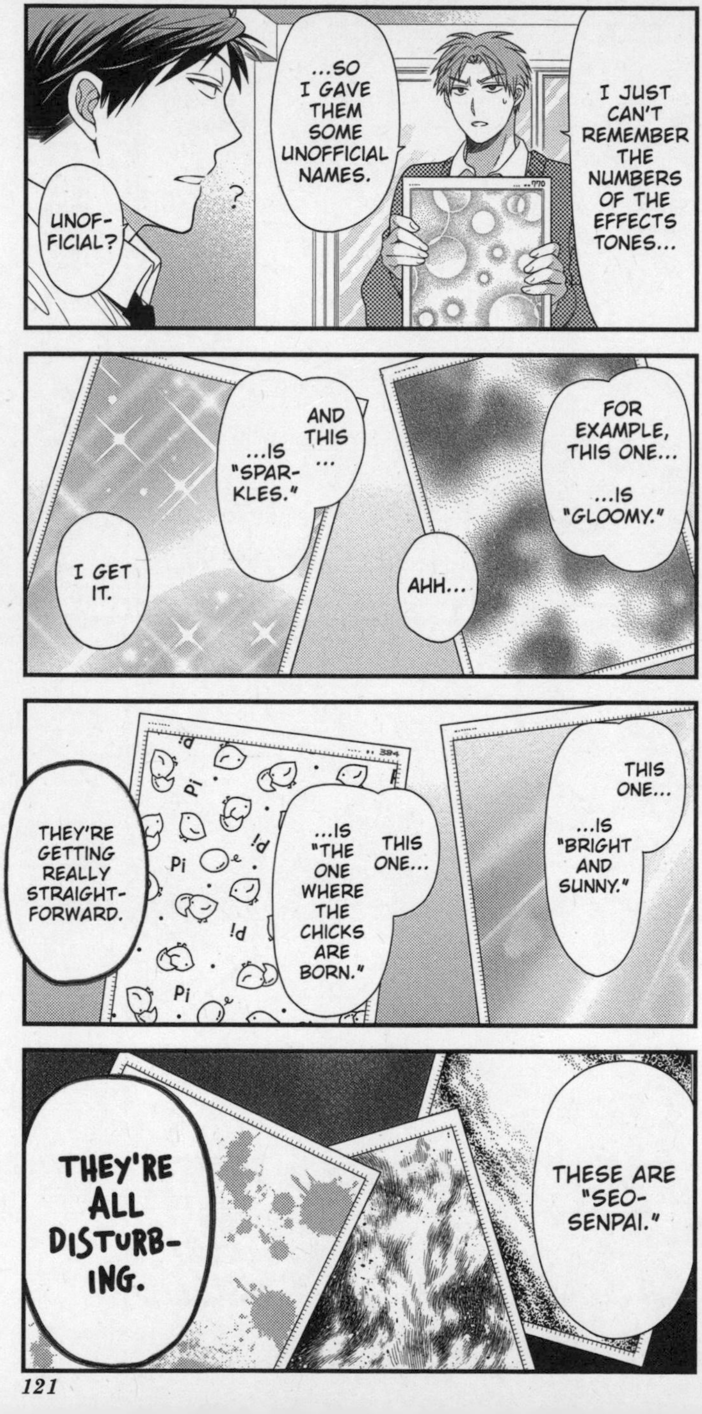

I JUST CAN'T REMEMBER THE NUMBERS OF THE EFFECTS TONES...
...SO I GAVE THEM SOME UNOFFICIAL NAMES.
?
UNOF-FICIAL?
FOR EXAMPLE, THIS ONE... ...IS "GLOOMY."
AHH...
AND THIS ... ...IS "SPAR-KLES."
I GET IT.
THIS ONE... ...IS "BRIGHT AND SUNNY."
THIS ONE... ...IS "THE ONE WHERE THE CHICKS ARE BORN."
THEY'RE GETTING REALLY STRAIGHT-FORWARD.
THESE ARE "SEO-SENPAI."
THEY'RE ALL DISTURB-ING.

SURPRISINGLY COMMON

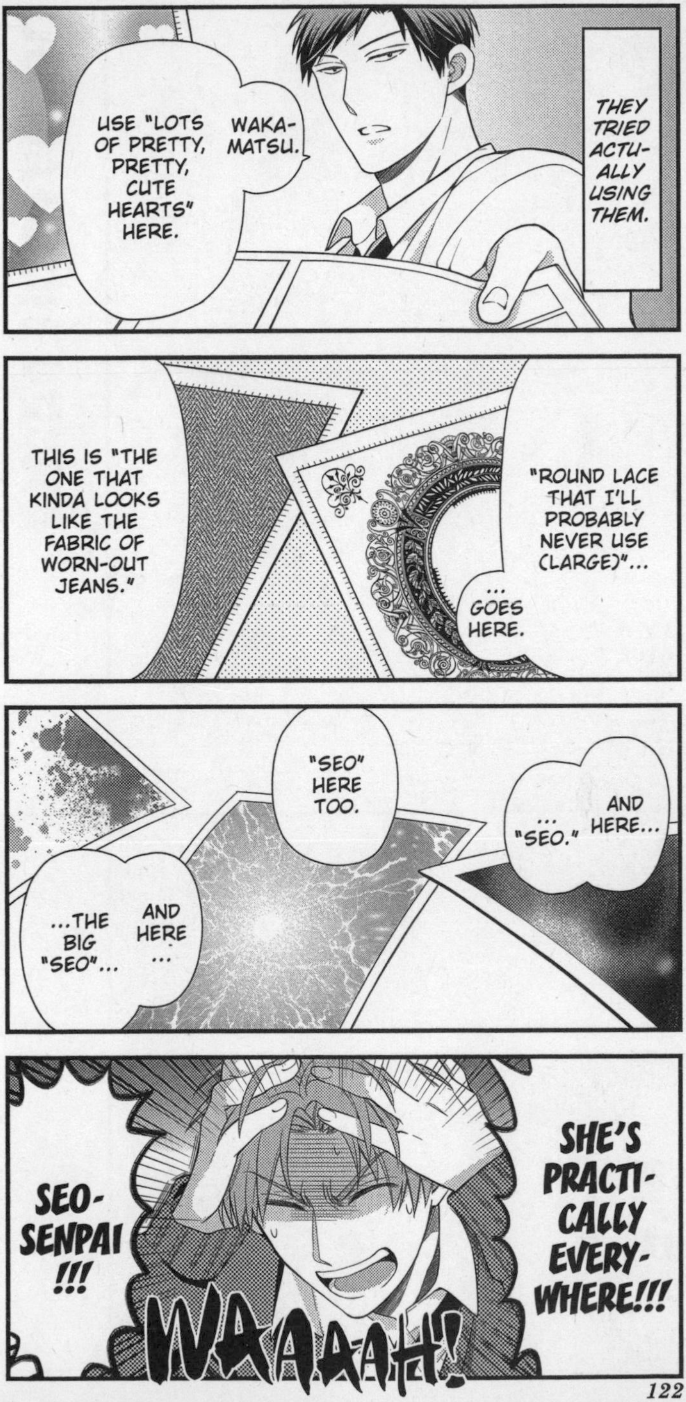

THEY TRIED ACTUALLY USING THEM.
WAKAMATSU.
USE "LOTS OF PRETTY, PRETTY, CUTE HEARTS" HERE.
"ROUND LACE THAT I'LL PROBABLY NEVER USE (LARGE)"...
... GOES HERE.
THIS IS "THE ONE THAT KINDA LOOKS LIKE THE FABRIC OF WORN-OUT JEANS."
AND HERE...
... "SEO."
"SEO" HERE TOO.
AND HERE ...
...THE BIG "SEO"...
SHE'S PRACTICALLY EVERYWHERE!!!
SEO-SENPAI!!!
WAAAAH!

"SAKURA"

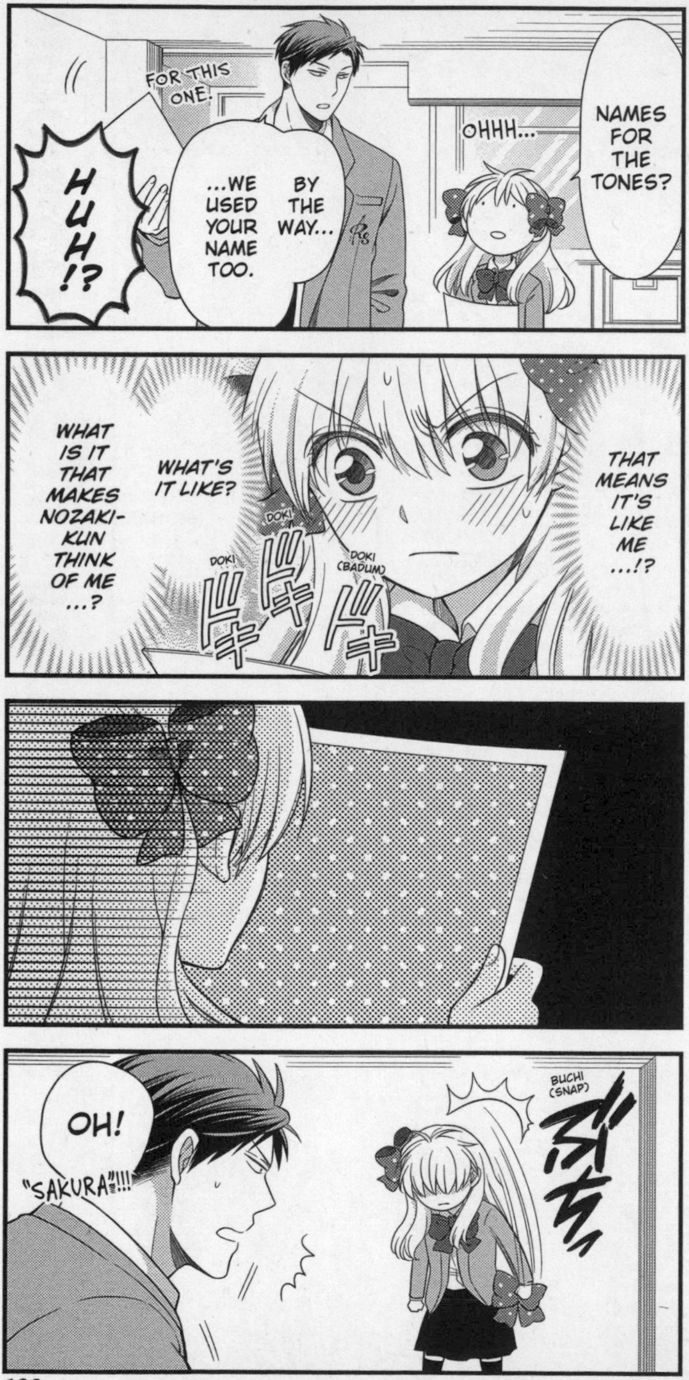
NAMES FOR THE TONES?
OHHH...
FOR THIS ONE.
BY THE WAY...
...WE USED YOUR NAME TOO.
HUH!?
THAT MEANS IT'S LIKE ME ...!?
DOKI (BADUM)
DOKI
DOKI
WHAT'S IT LIKE?
WHAT IS IT THAT MAKES NOZAKI-KUN THINK OF ME ...?
BUCHI (SNAP)
OH!
"SAKURA"!!!

WAKAMATSU ON THE BOYS' B-BALL TEAM

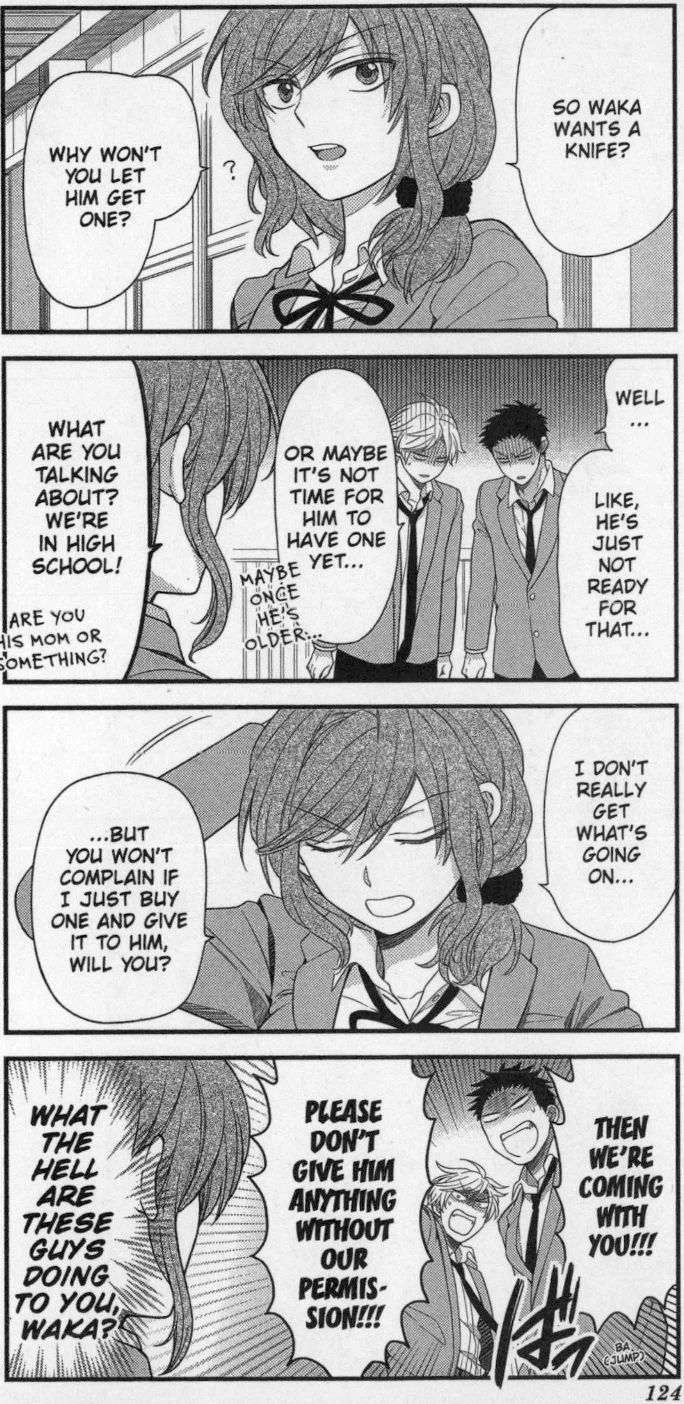
SO WAKA WANTS A KNIFE?
?
WHY WON'T YOU LET HIM GET ONE?
WELL ...
LIKE, HE'S JUST NOT READY FOR THAT...
OR MAYBE IT'S NOT TIME FOR HIM TO HAVE ONE YET...
MAYBE ONCE HE'S OLDER...
WHAT ARE YOU TALKING ABOUT? WE'RE IN HIGH SCHOOL!
ARE YOU HIS MOM OR SOMETHING?
I DON'T REALLY GET WHAT'S GOING ON...
...BUT YOU WON'T COMPLAIN IF I JUST BUY ONE AND GIVE IT TO HIM, WILL YOU?
THEN WE'RE COMING WITH YOU!!!
BA (JUMP)
PLEASE DON'T GIVE HIM ANYTHING WITHOUT OUR PERMIS-SION!!!
WHAT THE HELL ARE THESE GUYS DOING TO YOU, WAKA?

CRITERIA

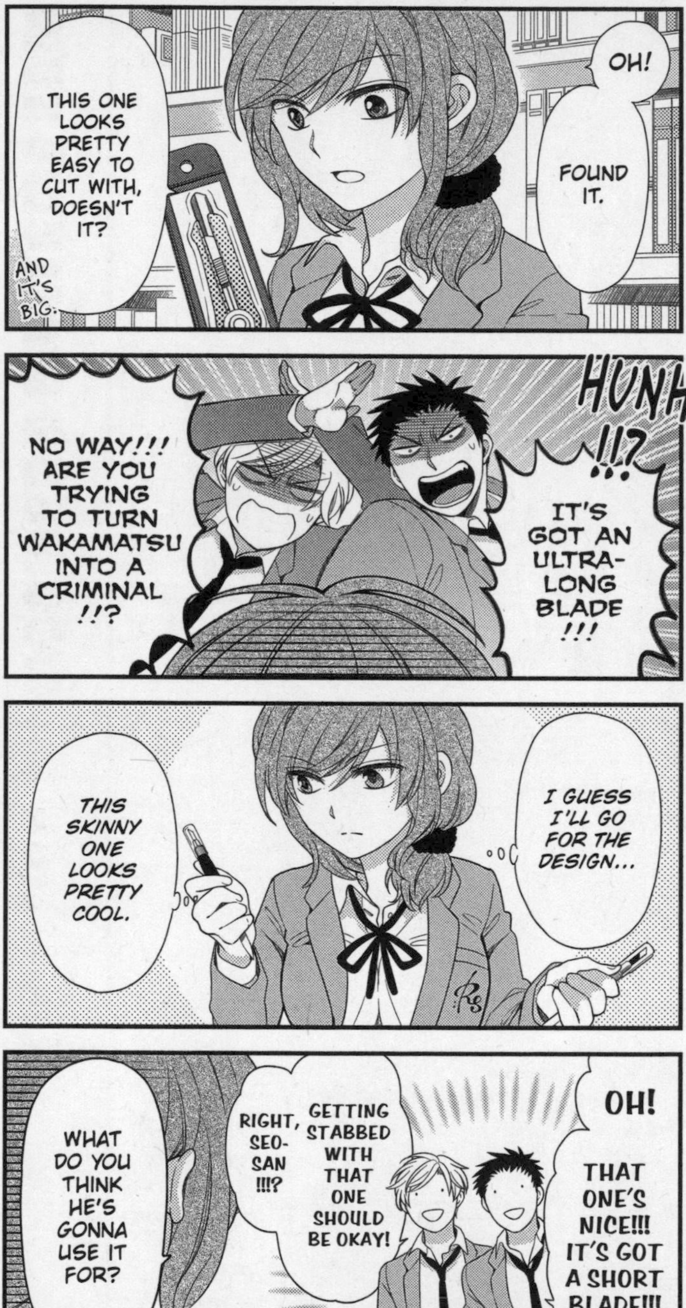

OH!
FOUND IT.
THIS ONE LOOKS PRETTY EASY TO CUT WITH, DOESN'T IT?
AND IT'S BIG.
HUNH!!?
IT'S GOT AN ULTRA-LONG BLADE!!!
NO WAY!!! ARE YOU TRYING TO TURN WAKAMATSU INTO A CRIMINAL!!?
I GUESS I'LL GO FOR THE DESIGN...
THIS SKINNY ONE LOOKS PRETTY COOL.
OH!
THAT ONE'S NICE!!! IT'S GOT A SHORT BLADE!!!
GETTING STABBED WITH THAT ONE SHOULD BE OKAY!
RIGHT, SEO-SAN!!!?
WHAT DO YOU THINK HE'S GONNA USE IT FOR?
FREAKY!

WAKAMATSU'S HAPPINESS

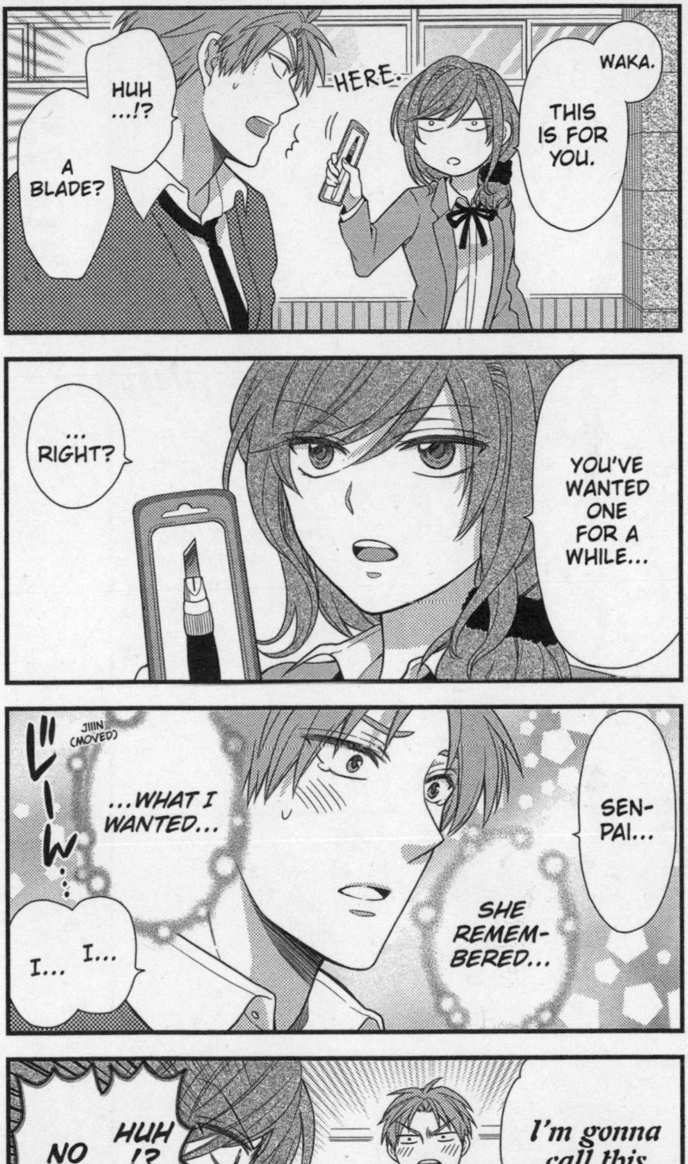
WAKA.
THIS IS FOR YOU.
HERE.
HUH ...!?
A BLADE?
YOU'VE WANTED ONE FOR A WHILE...
... RIGHT?
SEN-PAI...
SHE REMEM-BERED...
...WHAT I WANTED...
JIIIN (MOVED)
I... I...
I'm gonna call this pattern "Seo-senpai (rare)" from now on!!!
HUH !?
NO WAY!
DON'T!!!!

WHAT EXTRAORDINARY SHARPNESS!!

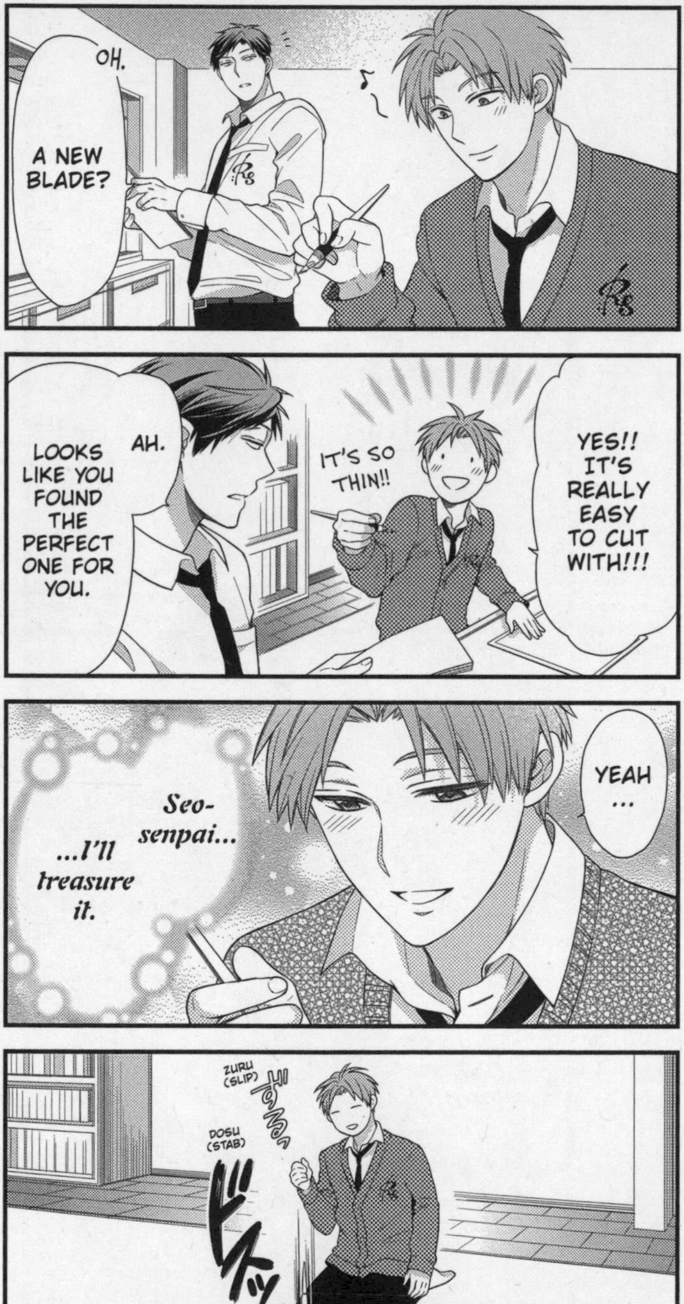
OH.
A NEW BLADE?
YES!! IT'S REALLY EASY TO CUT WITH!!!
IT'S SO THIN!!
AH.
LOOKS LIKE YOU FOUND THE PERFECT ONE FOR YOU.
YEAH ...
Seo-senpai...
...I'll treasure it.
ZURU (SLIP)
DOSU (STAB)

EYEBALLING IT

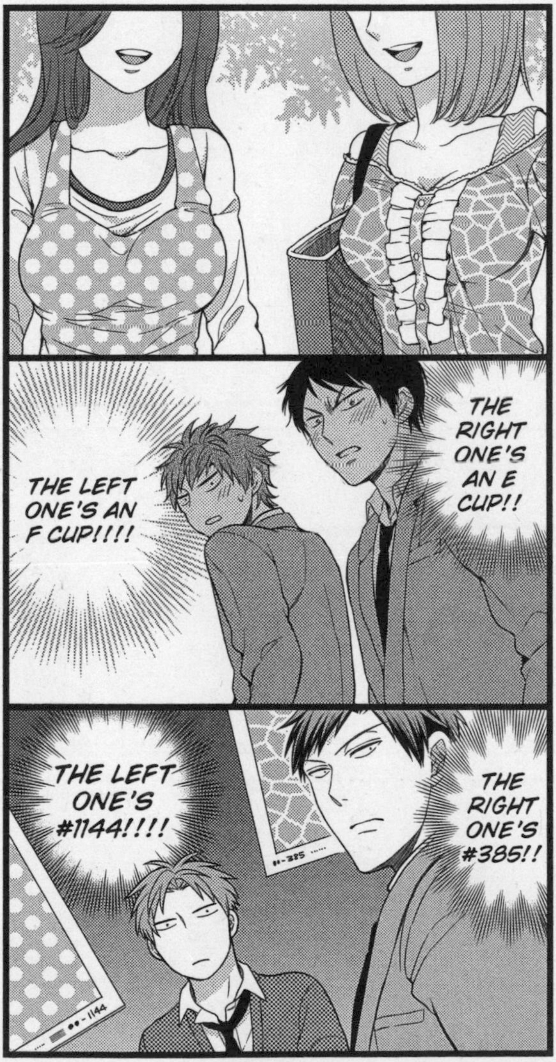
THE RIGHT ONE'S AN E CUP!!
THE LEFT ONE'S AN F CUP!!!!
THE RIGHT ONE'S #385!!
THE LEFT ONE'S #1144!!!!

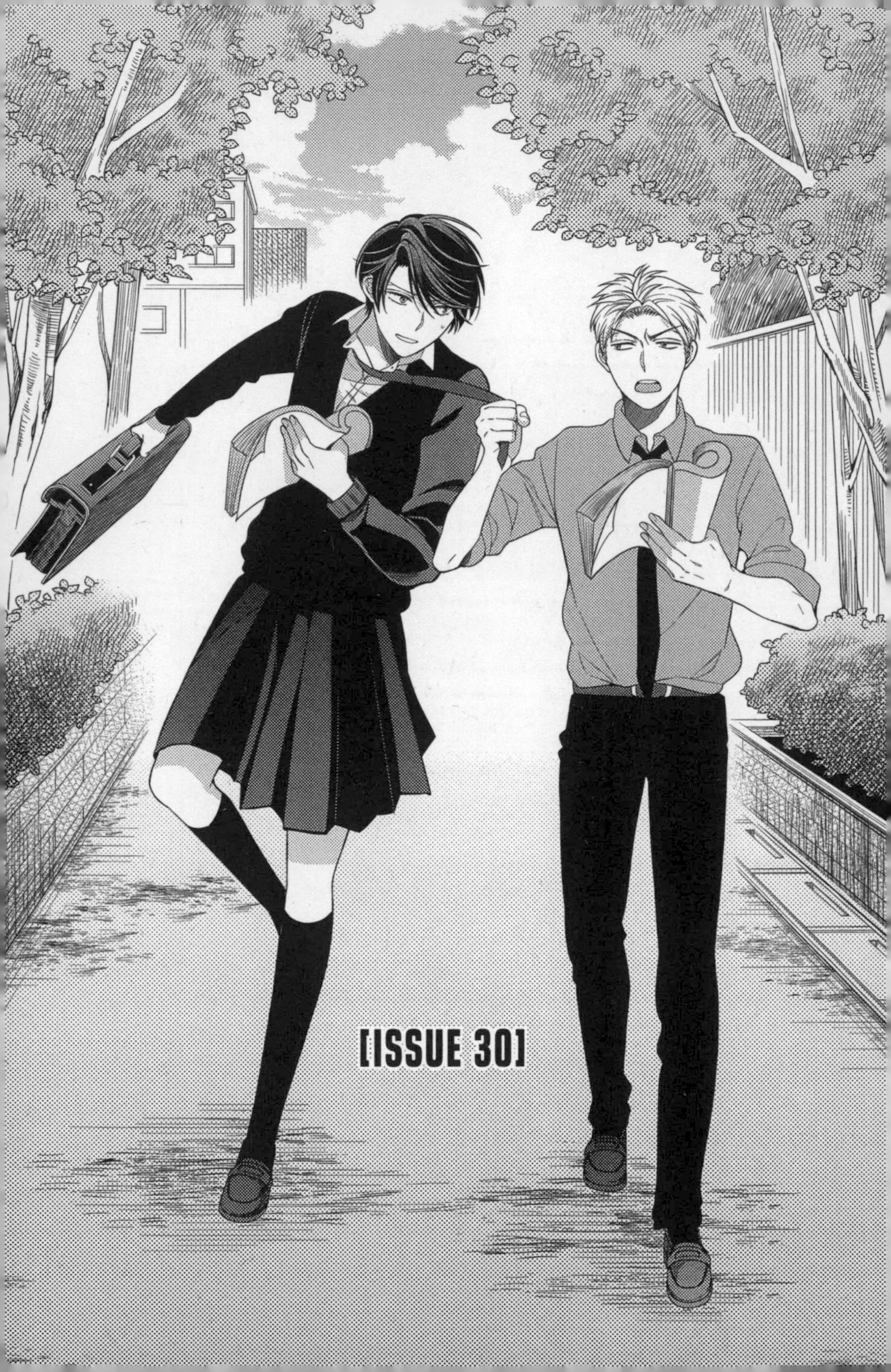
[ISSUE 30]

STAND-IN

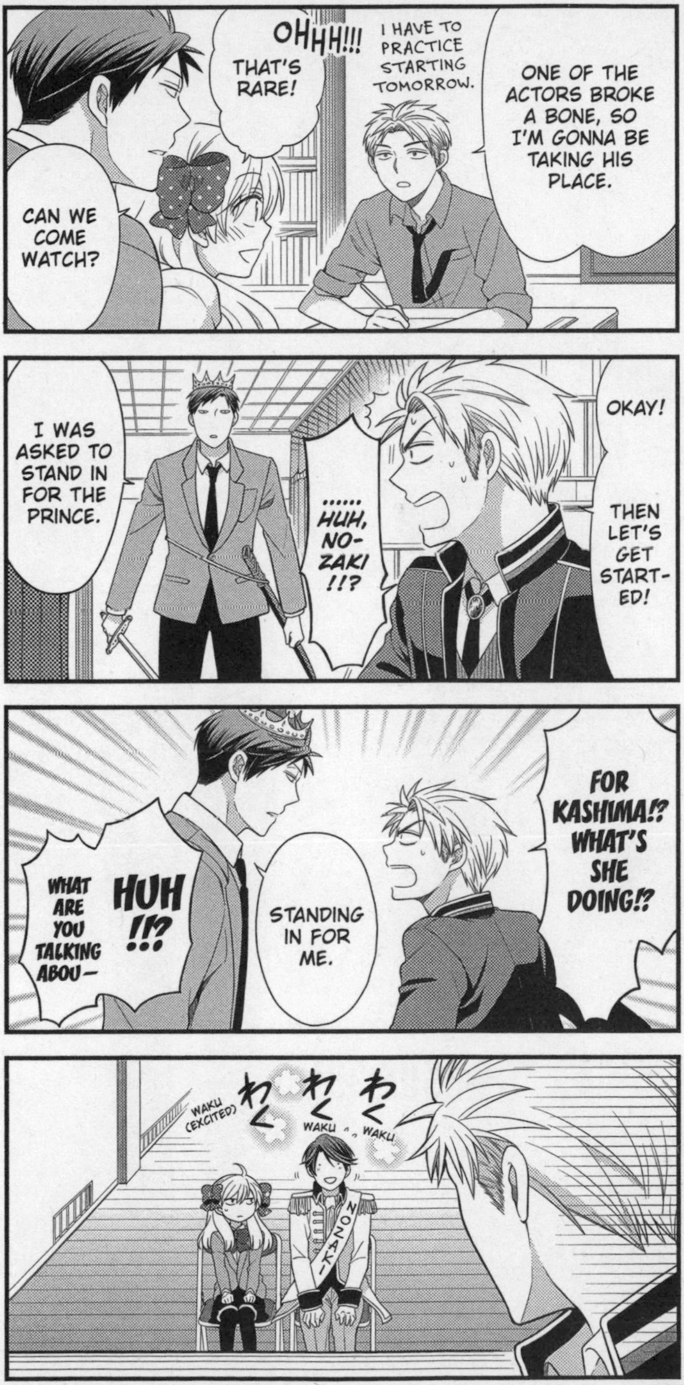
ONE OF THE ACTORS BROKE A BONE, SO I'M GONNA BE TAKING HIS PLACE.
I HAVE TO PRACTICE STARTING TOMORROW.
OHHH!!! THAT'S RARE!
CAN WE COME WATCH?
OKAY!
THEN LET'S GET START-ED!
......HUH, NO-ZAKI!!?
I WAS ASKED TO STAND IN FOR THE PRINCE.
FOR KASHIMA!? WHAT'S SHE DOING!?
STANDING IN FOR ME.
HUH!!?
WHAT ARE YOU TALKING ABOU—
わく
WAKU
わく
WAKU
わく
WAKU (EXCITED)
NOZAKI

WHEN I SEE YOUR FACE...

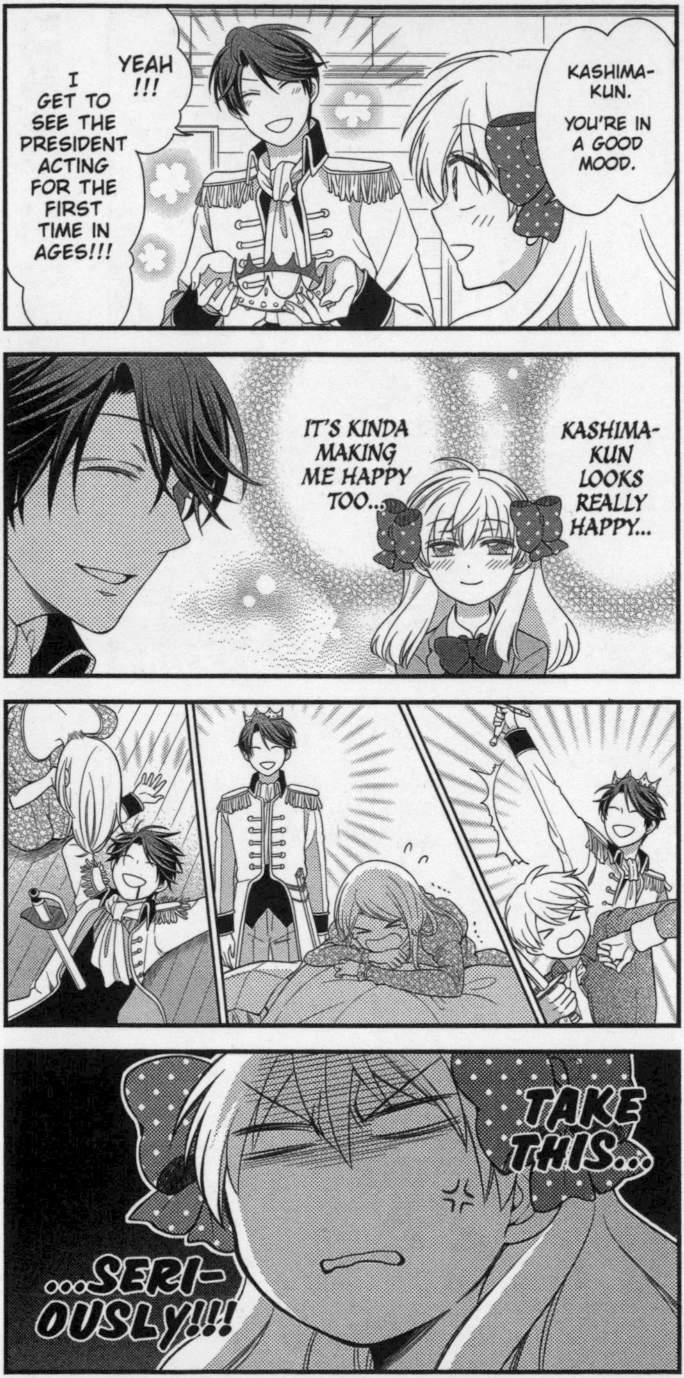
KASHIMA-KUN.
YOU'RE IN A GOOD MOOD.
YEAH!!!
I GET TO SEE THE PRESIDENT ACTING FOR THE FIRST TIME IN AGES!!!
KASHIMA-KUN LOOKS REALLY HAPPY...
IT'S KINDA MAKING ME HAPPY TOO...
TAKE THIS...
...SERI-OUSLY!!!

SHE JUST CAN'T HELP IT

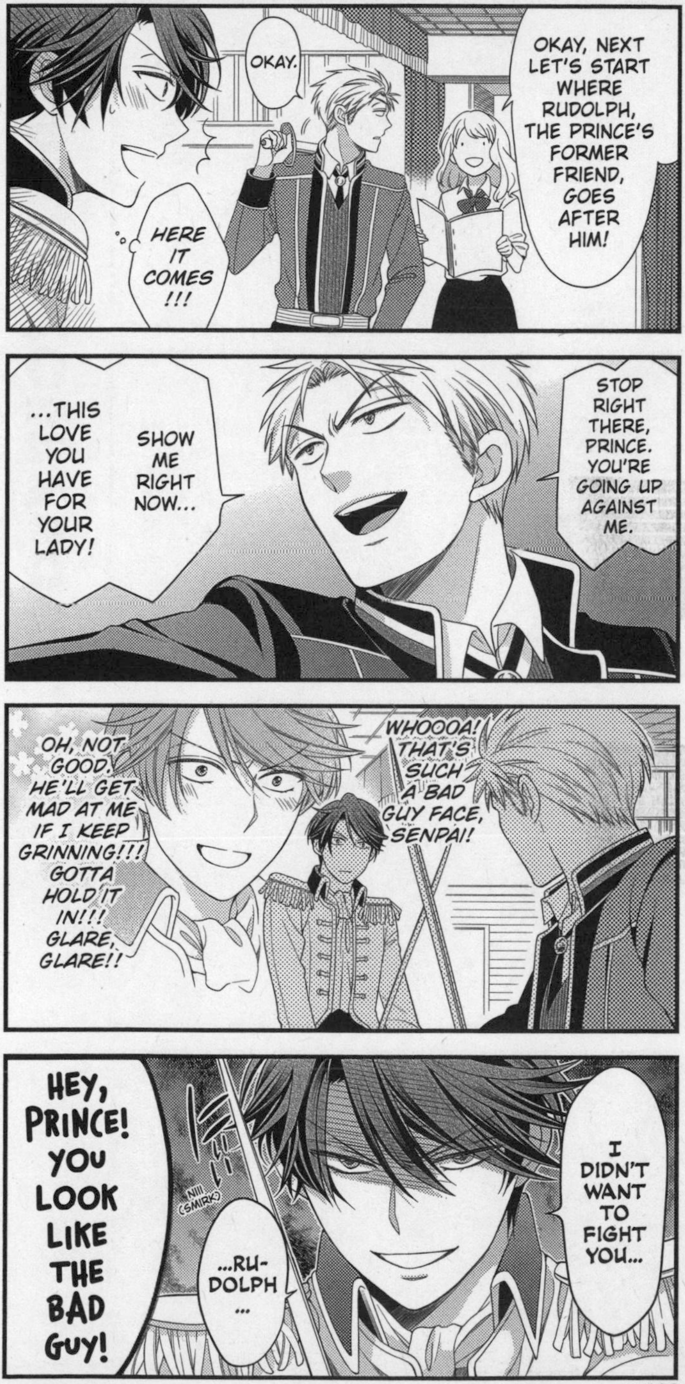
OKAY, NEXT LET'S START WHERE RUDOLPH, THE PRINCE'S FORMER FRIEND, GOES AFTER HIM!
OKAY.
HERE IT COMES!!!
STOP RIGHT THERE, PRINCE. YOU'RE GOING UP AGAINST ME.
SHOW ME RIGHT NOW...
...THIS LOVE YOU HAVE FOR YOUR LADY!
WHOOOA! THAT'S SUCH A BAD GUY FACE, SENPAI!
OH, NOT GOOD. HE'LL GET MAD AT ME IF I KEEP GRINNING!!! GOTTA HOLD IT IN!!! GLARE, GLARE!!
I DIDN'T WANT TO FIGHT YOU...
NIII (SMIRK)
...RU-DOLPH ...
HEY, PRINCE! YOU LOOK LIKE THE BAD GUY!

BECAUSE OF DAILY HABIT

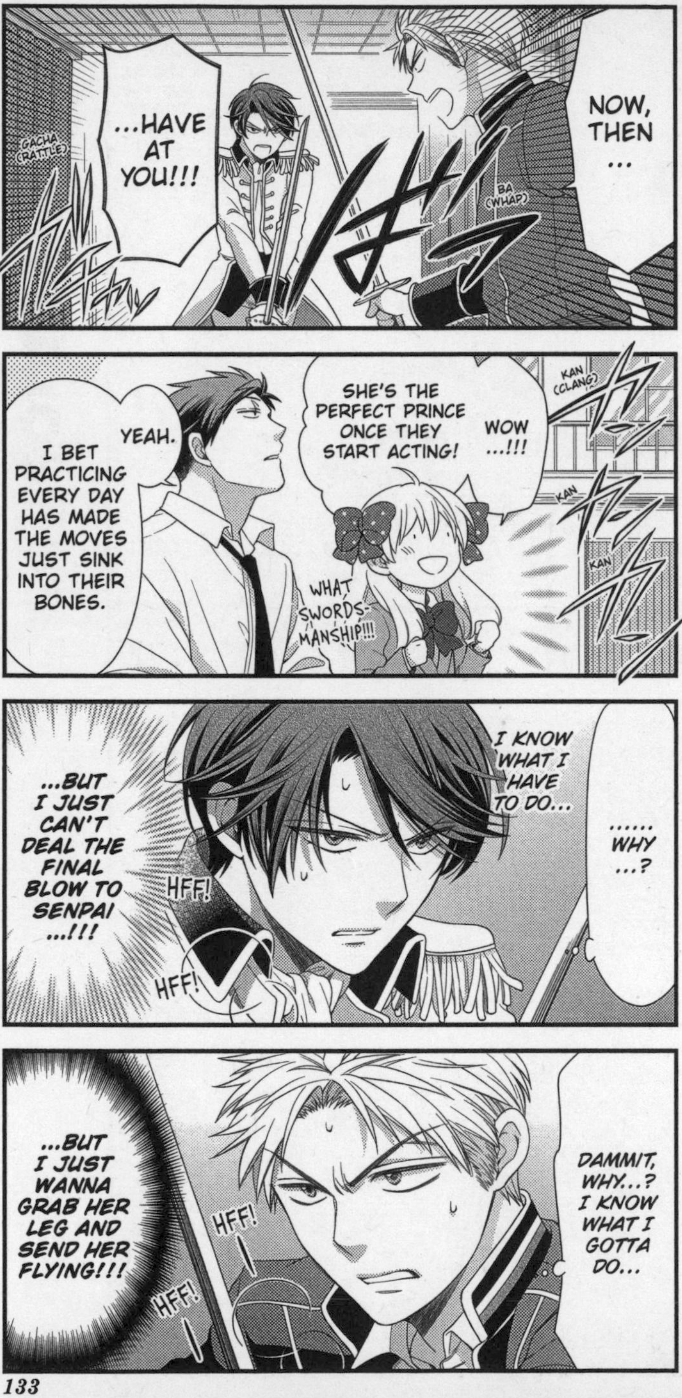
NOW, THEN ...
BA (WHAP)
...HAVE AT YOU!!!
GACHA (RATTLE)
KAN (CLANG)
KAN
KAN
WOW ...!!!
SHE'S THE PERFECT PRINCE ONCE THEY START ACTING!
WHAT SWORDS-MANSHIP!!!
YEAH.
I BET PRACTICING EVERY DAY HAS MADE THE MOVES JUST SINK INTO THEIR BONES.
...... WHY ...?
I KNOW WHAT I HAVE TO DO...
...BUT I JUST CAN'T DEAL THE FINAL BLOW TO SENPAI ...!!!
HFF!
HFF!
DAMMIT, WHY...? I KNOW WHAT I GOTTA DO...
HFF!
...BUT I JUST WANNA GRAB HER LEG AND SEND HER FLYING!!!
HFF!

COMPREHENSION

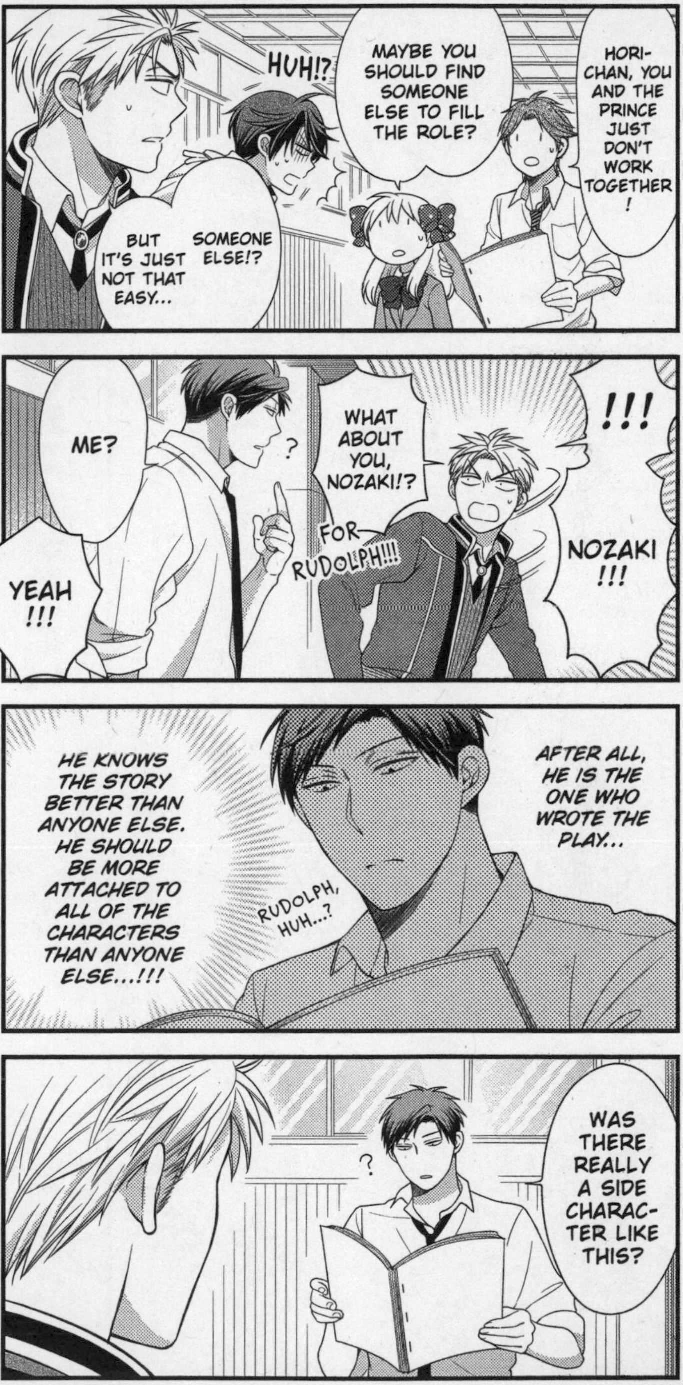
HORI-CHAN, YOU AND THE PRINCE JUST DON'T WORK TOGETHER!
MAYBE YOU SHOULD FIND SOMEONE ELSE TO FILL THE ROLE?
HUH!?
SOMEONE ELSE!?
BUT IT'S JUST NOT THAT EASY...
!!!
NOZAKI!!!
WHAT ABOUT YOU, NOZAKI!?
FOR RUDOLPH!!!
?
ME?
YEAH!!!
AFTER ALL, HE IS THE ONE WHO WROTE THE PLAY...
RUDOLPH, HUH...?
HE KNOWS THE STORY BETTER THAN ANYONE ELSE. HE SHOULD BE MORE ATTACHED TO ALL OF THE CHARACTERS THAN ANYONE ELSE...!!!
WAS THERE REALLY A SIDE CHARACTER LIKE THIS?
?

HE'S A MANGA-KA AFTER ALL

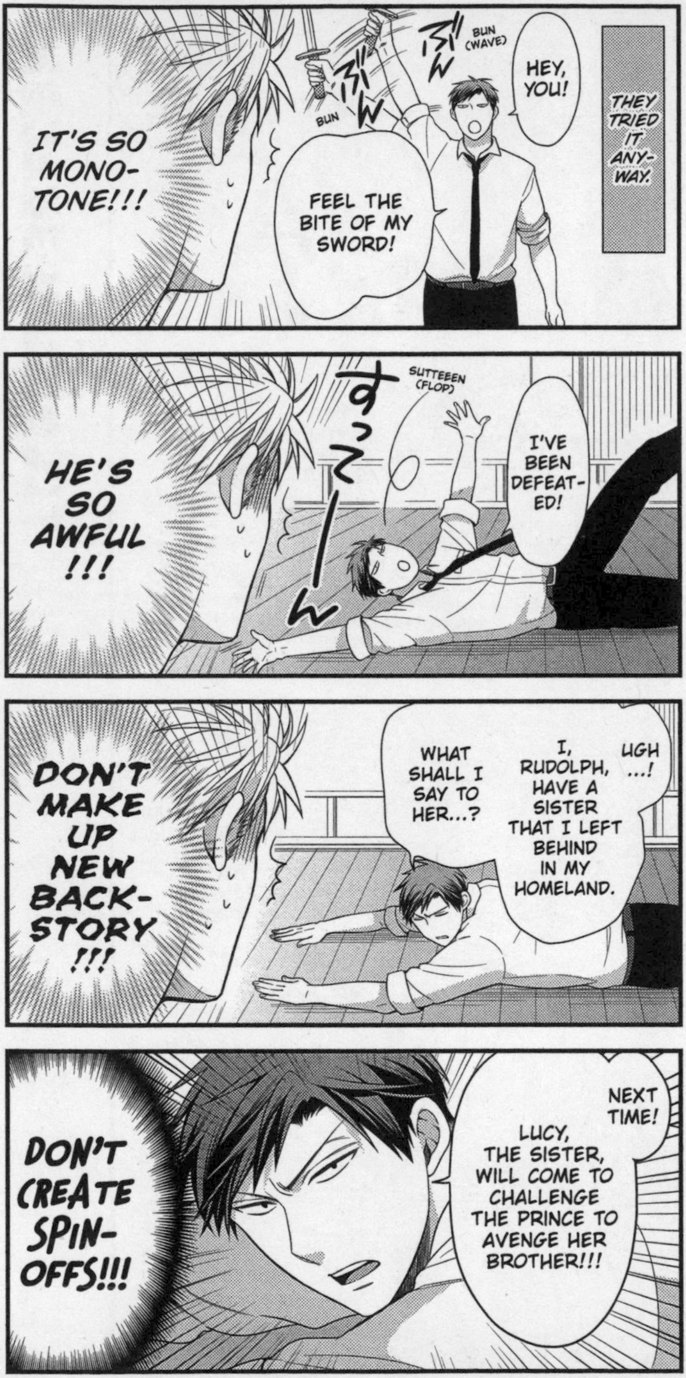
THEY TRIED IT ANYWAY.
HEY, YOU!
BUN (WAVE)
ぶん
ぶん
BUN
FEEL THE BITE OF MY SWORD!
IT'S SO MONOTONE!!!
I'VE BEEN DEFEATED!
SUTTEEEN (FLOP)
すってーん
HE'S SO AWFUL!!!
UGH ...!
I, RUDOLPH, HAVE A SISTER THAT I LEFT BEHIND IN MY HOMELAND.
WHAT SHALL I SAY TO HER...?
DON'T MAKE UP NEW BACK-STORY!!!
NEXT TIME!
LUCY, THE SISTER, WILL COME TO CHALLENGE THE PRINCE TO AVENGE HER BROTHER!!!
DON'T CREATE SPIN-OFFS!!!

THE TYPE HE WANTS

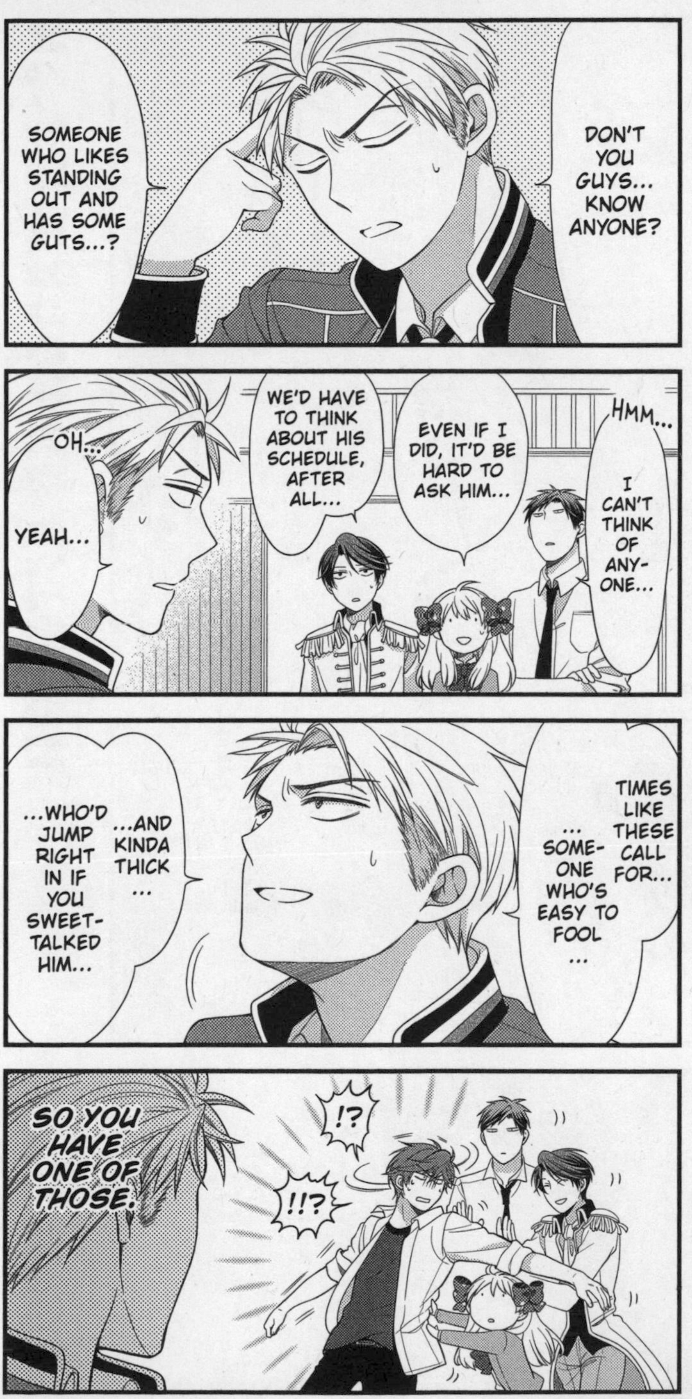
DON'T YOU GUYS... KNOW ANYONE?
SOMEONE WHO LIKES STANDING OUT AND HAS SOME GUTS...?
HMM...
I CAN'T THINK OF ANY-ONE...
EVEN IF I DID, IT'D BE HARD TO ASK HIM...
WE'D HAVE TO THINK ABOUT HIS SCHEDULE, AFTER ALL...
OH...
YEAH...
TIMES LIKE THESE CALL FOR...
...SOME-ONE WHO'S EASY TO FOOL...
...AND KINDA THICK...
...WHO'D JUMP RIGHT IN IF YOU SWEET-TALKED HIM...
!?
!!?
SO YOU HAVE ONE OF THOSE.

HOW TO DEAL WITH MIKOSHIBA

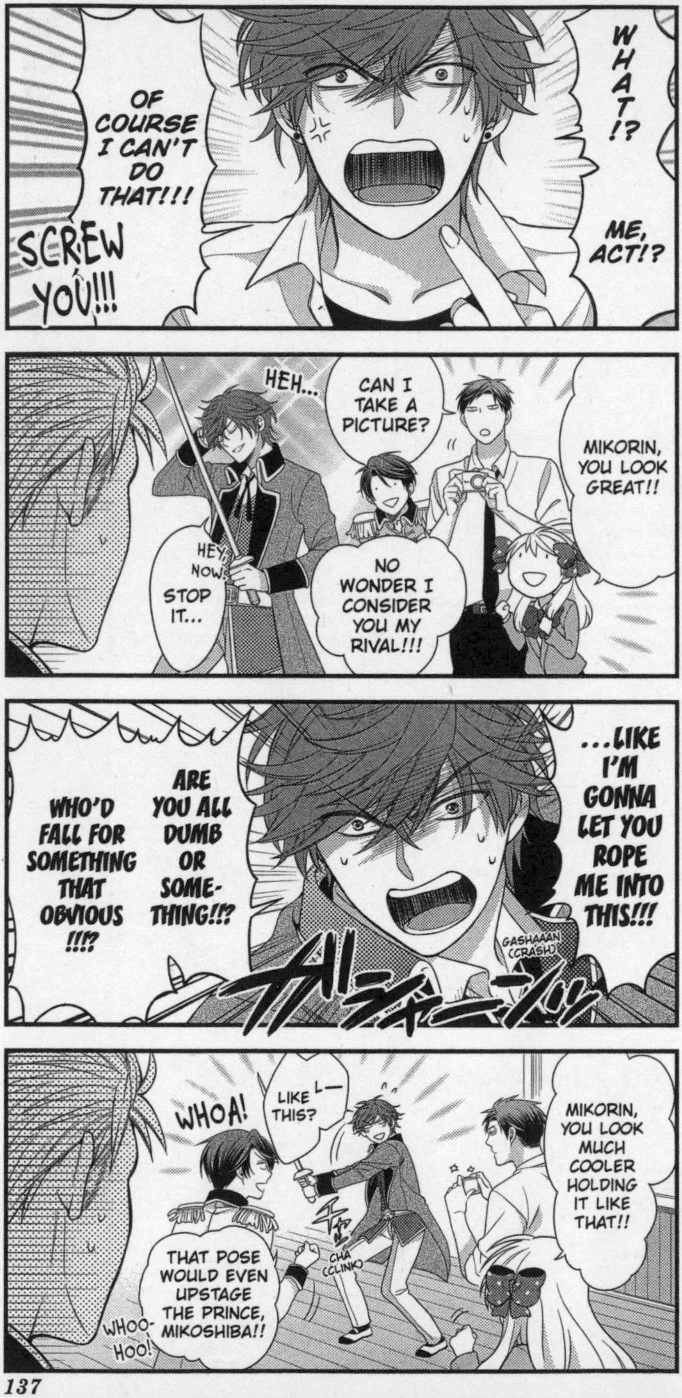

WHAT!?
ME, ACT!?
OF COURSE I CAN'T DO THAT!!!
SCREW YOU!!!
MIKORIN, YOU LOOK GREAT!!
CAN I TAKE A PICTURE?
HEH...
NO WONDER I CONSIDER YOU MY RIVAL!!!
HEY, NOW. STOP IT...
...LIKE I'M GONNA LET YOU ROPE ME INTO THIS!!!
GASHAAAN (CRASH)
ARE YOU ALL DUMB OR SOME-THING!!?
WHO'D FALL FOR SOMETHING THAT OBVIOUS!!!?
MIKORIN, YOU LOOK MUCH COOLER HOLDING IT LIKE THAT!!
L— LIKE THIS?
WHOA!
CHA (CLINK)
THAT POSE WOULD EVEN UPSTAGE THE PRINCE, MIKOSHIBA!!
WHOO-HOO!

A VERY FAMILIAR PERSON

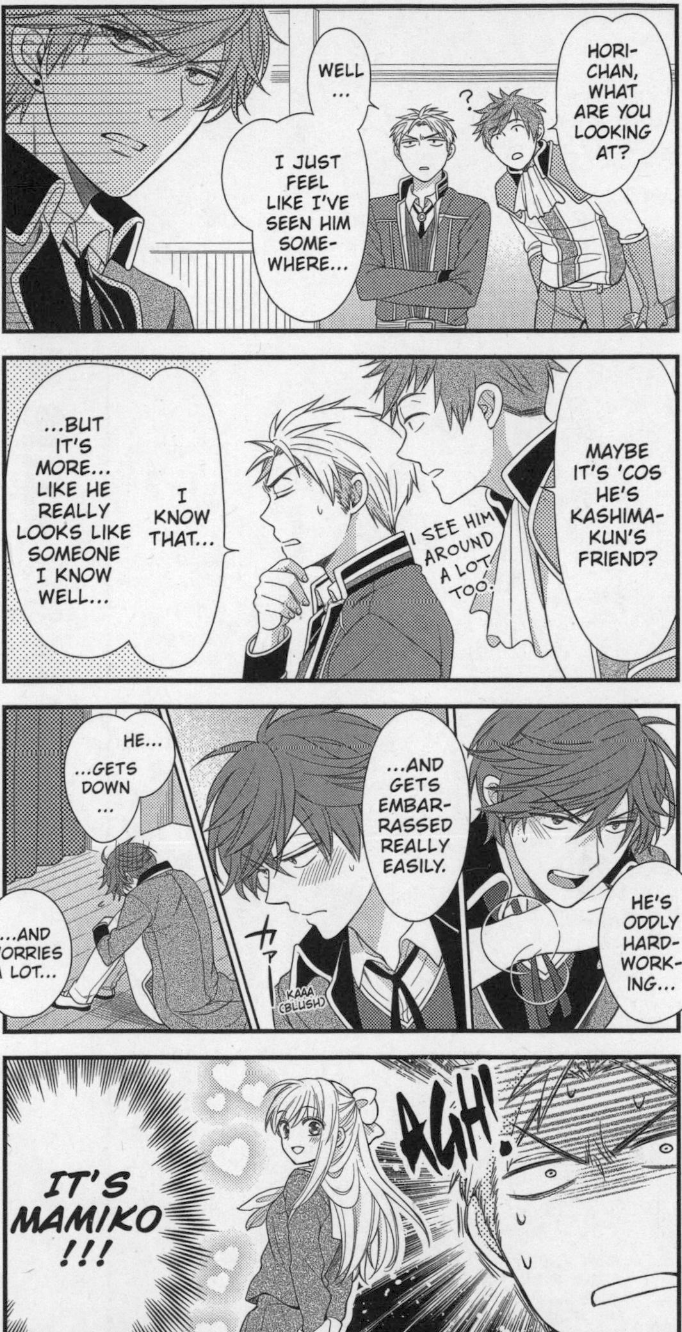

HORI-CHAN, WHAT ARE YOU LOOKING AT?
?
WELL ...
I JUST FEEL LIKE I'VE SEEN HIM SOME-WHERE...
MAYBE IT'S 'COS HE'S KASHIMA-KUN'S FRIEND?
I SEE HIM AROUND A LOT TOO.
I KNOW THAT...
...BUT IT'S MORE... LIKE HE REALLY LOOKS LIKE SOMEONE I KNOW WELL...
HE'S ODDLY HARD-WORK-ING...
...AND GETS EMBAR-RASSED REALLY EASILY.
KAAA (BLUSH)
HE... ...GETS DOWN ...
...AND WORRIES A LOT...
AGH!
IT'S MAMIKO !!!

JUST COULDN'T HELP BUT SAY IT

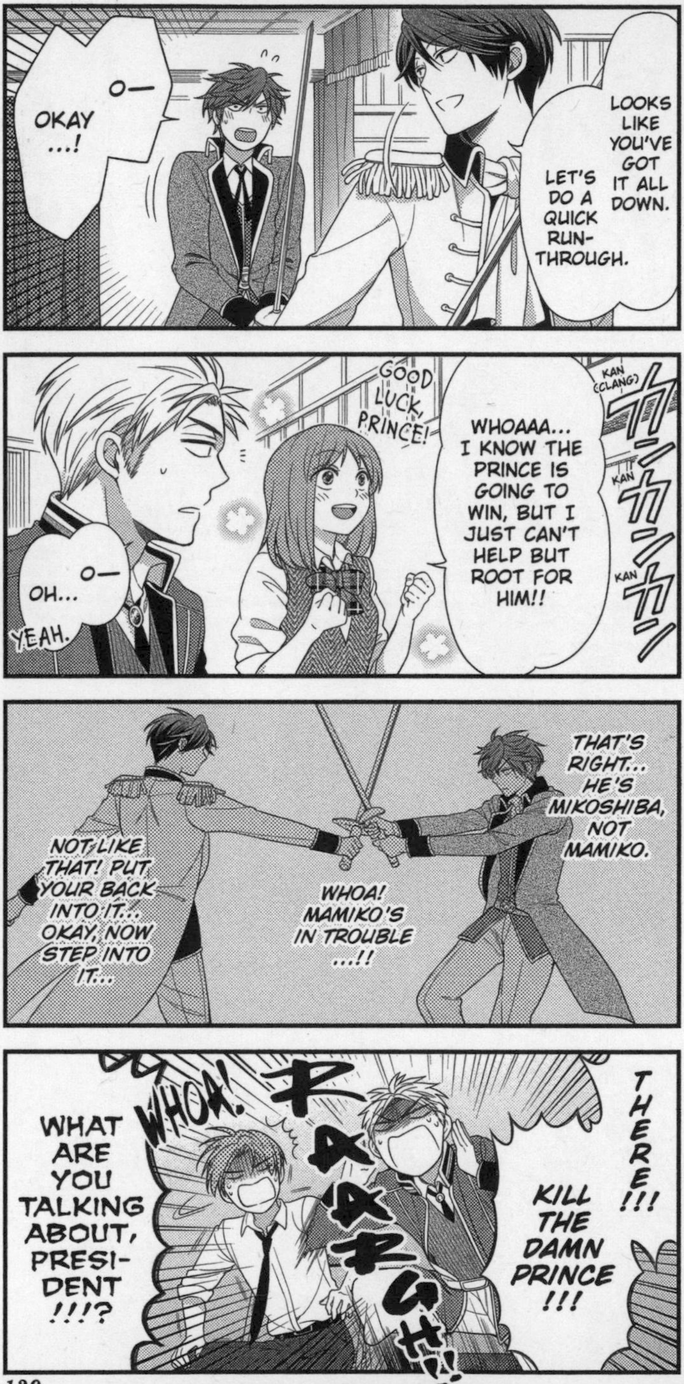

LOOKS LIKE YOU'VE GOT IT ALL DOWN.
LET'S DO A QUICK RUN-THROUGH.
O— OKAY ...!
KAN (CLANG)
カン
KAN
カン
KAN
カン
WHOAAA... I KNOW THE PRINCE IS GOING TO WIN, BUT I JUST CAN'T HELP BUT ROOT FOR HIM!!
GOOD LUCK, PRINCE!
O— OH... YEAH.
THAT'S RIGHT... HE'S MIKOSHIBA, NOT MAMIKO.
WHOA! MAMIKO'S IN TROUBLE ...!!
NOT LIKE THAT! PUT YOUR BACK INTO IT... OKAY, NOW STEP INTO IT...
THERE!!!
KILL THE DAMN PRINCE!!!
RAARGH!!
WHOA!
WHAT ARE YOU TALKING ABOUT, PRESIDENT!!!?

MIKOSHIBA THE RIVAL

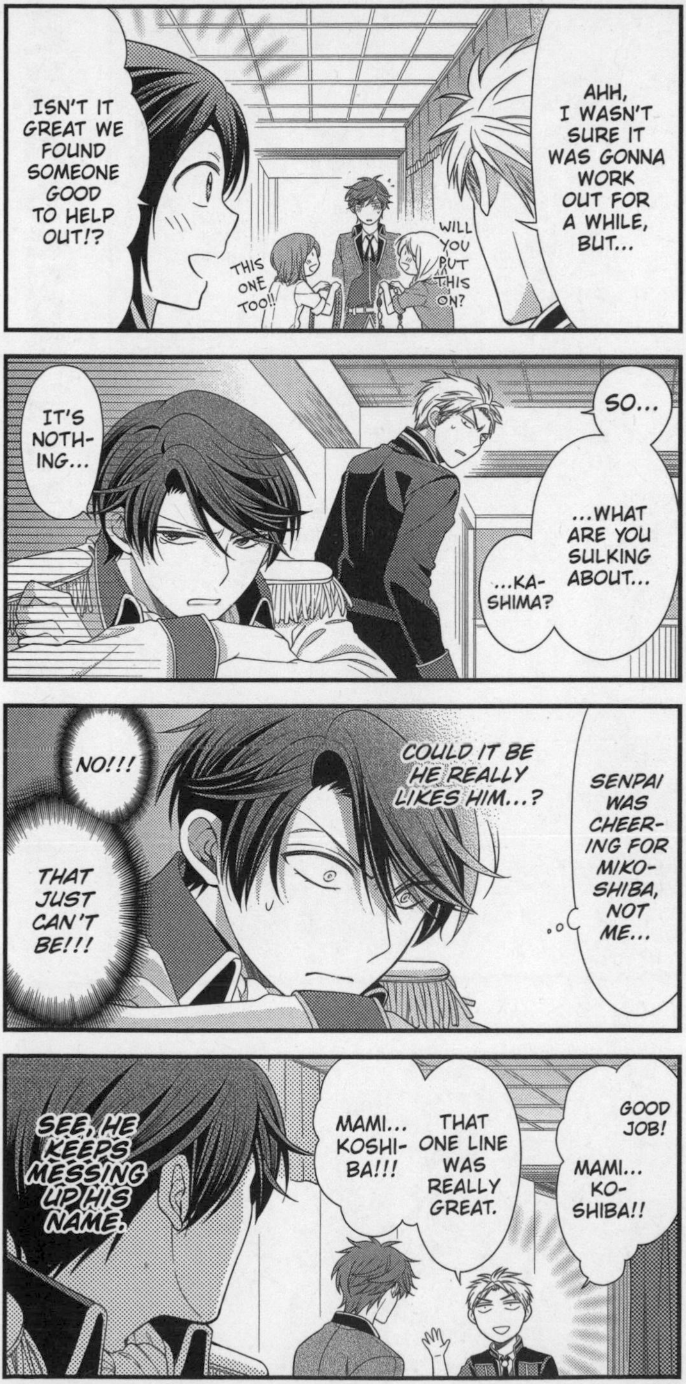
AHH, I WASN'T SURE IT WAS GONNA WORK OUT FOR A WHILE, BUT...
WILL YOU PUT THIS ON?
THIS ONE TOO!!
ISN'T IT GREAT WE FOUND SOMEONE GOOD TO HELP OUT!?
SO...
...WHAT ARE YOU SULKING ABOUT...
...KA-SHIMA?
IT'S NOTH-ING...
SENPAI WAS CHEER-ING FOR MIKO-SHIBA, NOT ME...
COULD IT BE HE REALLY LIKES HIM...?
NO!!!
THAT JUST CAN'T BE!!!
GOOD JOB!
MAMI... KO-SHIBA!!
THAT ONE LINE WAS REALLY GREAT.
MAMI... KOSHI-BA!!!
SEE, HE KEEPS MESSING UP HIS NAME.

BACK TO SQUARE ONE

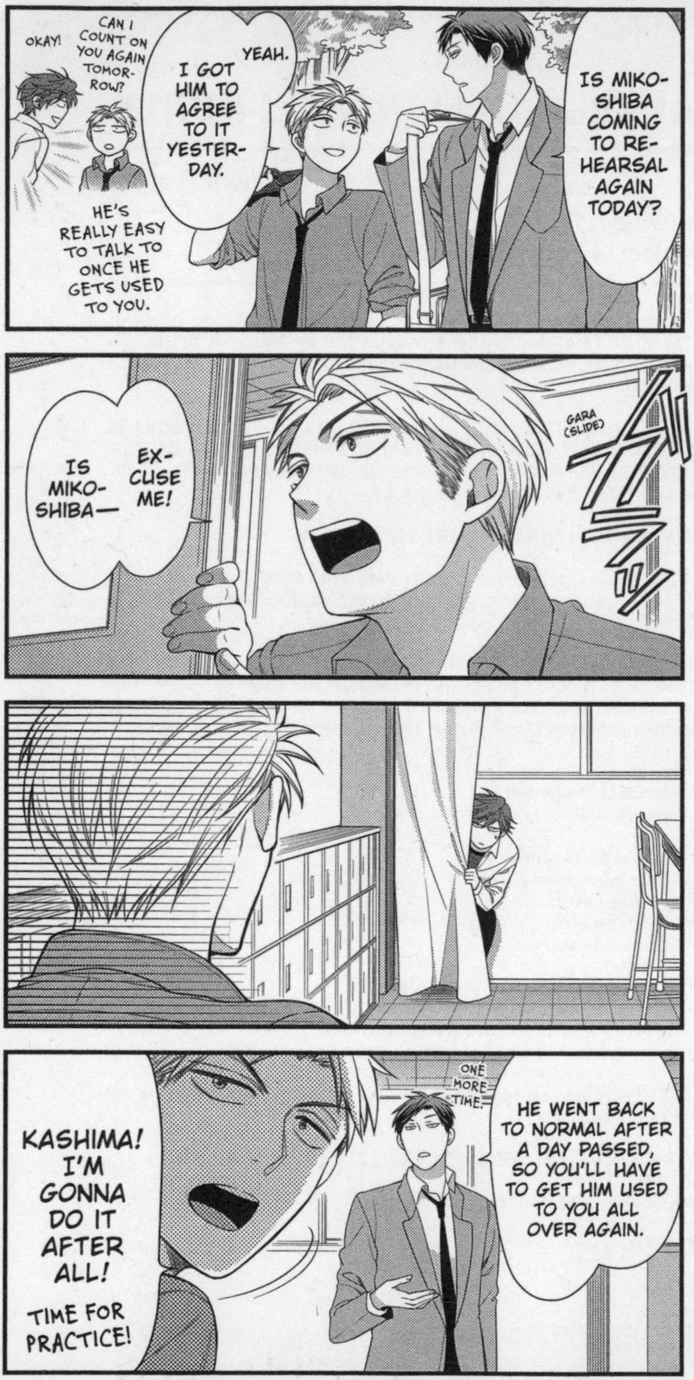
IS MIKO-SHIBA COMING TO RE-HEARSAL AGAIN TODAY?
YEAH.
I GOT HIM TO AGREE TO IT YESTER-DAY.
HE'S REALLY EASY TO TALK TO ONCE HE GETS USED TO YOU.
CAN I COUNT ON YOU AGAIN TOMOR-ROW?
OKAY!
GARA (SLIDE)
EX-CUSE ME!
IS MIKO-SHIBA—
ONE MORE TIME.
HE WENT BACK TO NORMAL AFTER A DAY PASSED, SO YOU'LL HAVE TO GET HIM USED TO YOU ALL OVER AGAIN.
KASHIMA! I'M GONNA DO IT AFTER ALL!
TIME FOR PRACTICE!

MONTHLY GIRLS' NOZAKI-KUN 3 END

MONTHLY GIRLS' NOZAKI-KUN 3

Izumi Tsubaki

Translation: Leighann Harvey
Lettering: Lys Blakeslee

GEKKAN SHOJO NOZAKI KUN Volume 3 © 2013 Izumi Tsubaki / SQUARE ENIX CO., LTD. First published in Japan in 2013 by SQUARE ENIX CO., LTD. English translation rights arranged with SQUARE ENIX CO., LTD. and Yen Press, LLC through Tuttle-Mori Agency, Inc.

English translation © 2016 SQUARE ENIX CO., LTD.

Yen Press
1290 Avenue of the Americas
New York, NY 10104

Visit us at yenpress.com
facebook.com/yenpress
twitter.com/yenpress
yenpress.tumblr.com
instagram.com/yenpress

First Yen Press Print Edition: May 2016

Yen Press is an imprint of Yen Press, LLC.
The Yen Press name and logo are trademarks of Yen Press, LLC.

The publisher is not responsible for websites (or their content) that are not owned by the publisher.

Library of Congress Control Number: 2015952610

ISBN: 978-0-316-39158-0 (paperback)

10 9 8 7 6 5 4

BVG

Printed in the United States of America

[Extra]

THE GUY I LIKE'S PROUD MOMENT

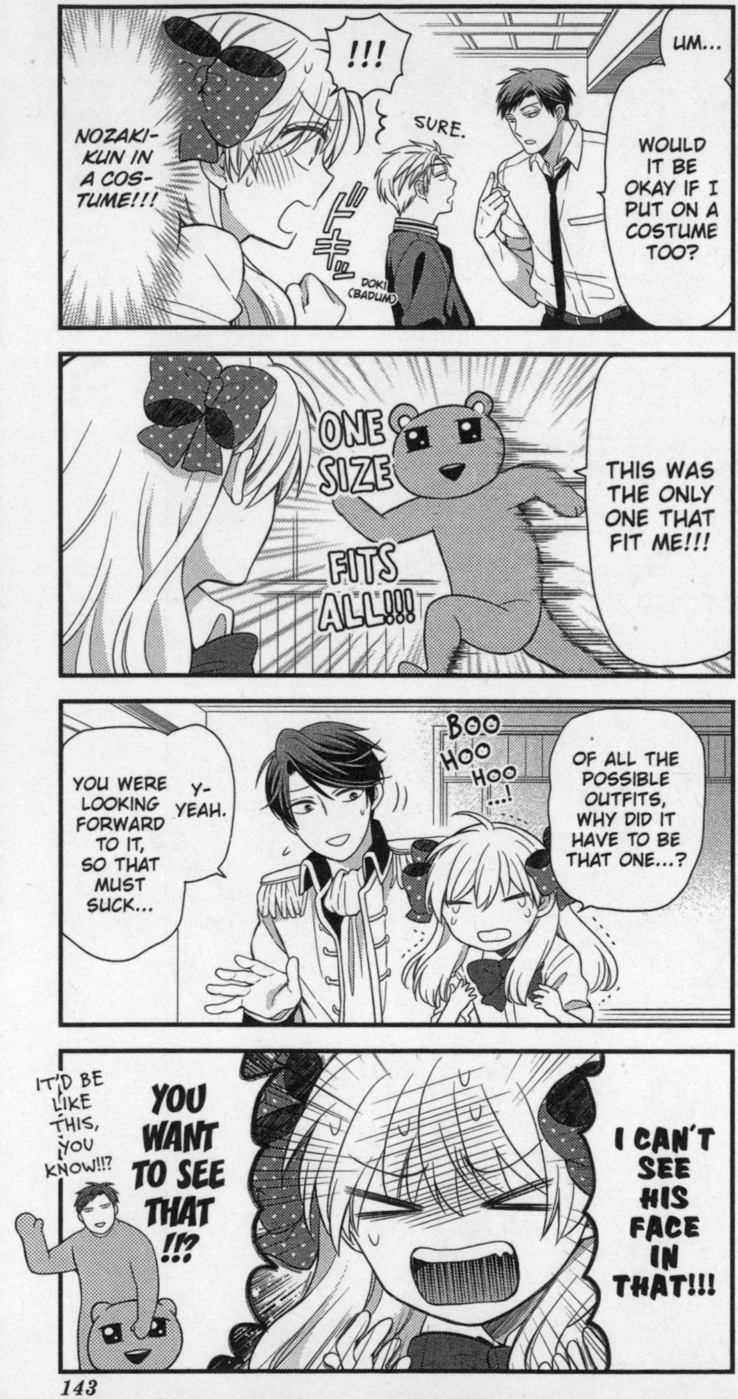
UM...
WOULD IT BE OKAY IF I PUT ON A COSTUME TOO?
SURE.
!!!
DOKI (BADUM)
NOZAKI-KUN IN A COSTUME!!!
THIS WAS THE ONLY ONE THAT FIT ME!!!
ONE SIZE FITS ALL!!!
OF ALL THE POSSIBLE OUTFITS, WHY DID IT HAVE TO BE THAT ONE...?
BOO HOO HOO...!
Y-YEAH.
YOU WERE LOOKING FORWARD TO IT, SO THAT MUST SUCK...
I CAN'T SEE HIS FACE IN THAT!!!
YOU WANT TO SEE THAT!!?
IT'D BE LIKE THIS, YOU KNOW!!?

[Extra]

GYM ELECTIVE

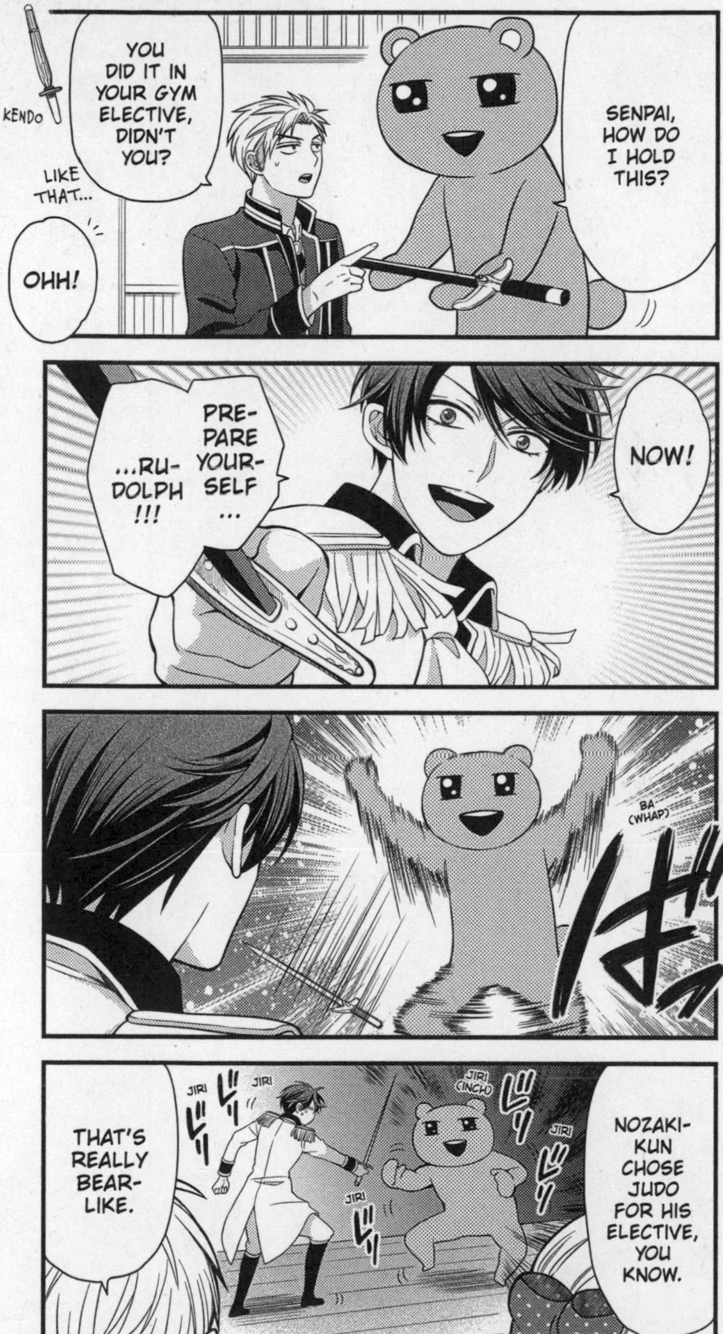
SENPAI, HOW DO I HOLD THIS?
YOU DID IT IN YOUR GYM ELECTIVE, DIDN'T YOU?
KENDO
LIKE THAT...
OHH!
NOW!
PREPARE YOURSELF ...
...RUDOLPH !!!
BA (WHAP)
NOZAKI-KUN CHOSE JUDO FOR HIS ELECTIVE, YOU KNOW.
JIRI
JIRI (INCH)
JIRI
JIRI
JIRI
THAT'S REALLY BEAR-LIKE.

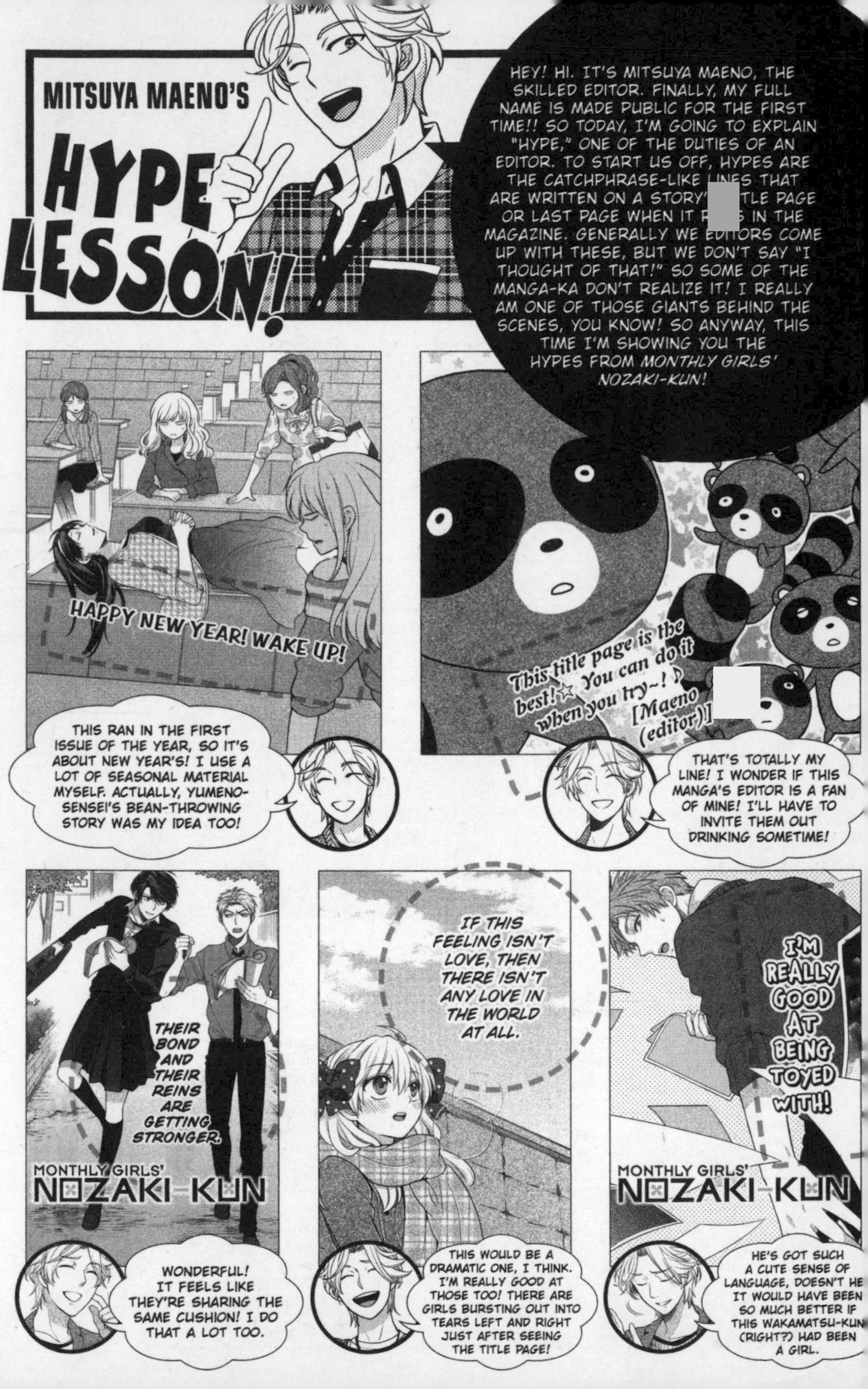
HEY! HI. IT'S MITSUYA MAENO, THE SKILLED EDITOR. FINALLY, MY FULL NAME IS MADE PUBLIC FOR THE FIRST TIME!! SO TODAY, I'M GOING TO EXPLAIN "HYPE," ONE OF THE DUTIES OF AN EDITOR. TO START US OFF, HYPES ARE THE CATCHPHRASE-LIKE LINES THAT ARE WRITTEN ON A STORY' TLE PAGE OR LAST PAGE WHEN IT P S IN THE MAGAZINE. GENERALLY WE EDITORS COME UP WITH THESE, BUT WE DON'T SAY "I THOUGHT OF THAT!" SO SOME OF THE MANGA-KA DON'T REALIZE IT! I REALLY AM ONE OF THOSE GIANTS BEHIND THE SCENES, YOU KNOW! SO ANYWAY, THIS TIME I'M SHOWING YOU THE HYPES FROM *MONTHLY GIRLS' NOZAKI-KUN*!
MITSUYA MAENO'S
HYPE LESSON!
This title page is the best!☆ You can do it when you try~!♪ [Maeno (editor)]
THAT'S TOTALLY MY LINE! I WONDER IF THIS MANGA'S EDITOR IS A FAN OF MINE! I'LL HAVE TO INVITE THEM OUT DRINKING SOMETIME!
HAPPY NEW YEAR! WAKE UP!
THIS RAN IN THE FIRST ISSUE OF THE YEAR, SO IT'S ABOUT NEW YEAR'S! I USE A LOT OF SEASONAL MATERIAL MYSELF. ACTUALLY, YUMENO-SENSEI'S BEAN-THROWING STORY WAS MY IDEA TOO!
I'M REALLY GOOD AT BEING TOYED WITH!
MONTHLY GIRLS' NOZAKI-KUN
HE'S GOT SUCH A CUTE SENSE OF LANGUAGE, DOESN'T HE! IT WOULD HAVE BEEN SO MUCH BETTER IF THIS WAKAMATSU-KUN (RIGHT?) HAD BEEN A GIRL.
IF THIS FEELING ISN'T LOVE, THEN THERE ISN'T ANY LOVE IN THE WORLD AT ALL.
THIS WOULD BE A DRAMATIC ONE, I THINK. I'M REALLY GOOD AT THOSE TOO! THERE ARE GIRLS BURSTING OUT INTO TEARS LEFT AND RIGHT JUST AFTER SEEING THE TITLE PAGE!
THEIR BOND AND THEIR REINS ARE GETTING STRONGER.
MONTHLY GIRLS' NOZAKI-KUN
WONDERFUL! IT FEELS LIKE THEY'RE SHARING THE SAME CUSHION! I DO THAT A LOT TOO.

MITSUYA MAENO'S HYPE LESSON!

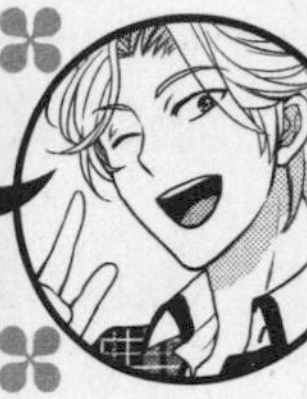

NOW I'LL INTRODUCE YOU TO THE HYPES AT THE END (CALLED "ENDLINES")! THESE SOMETIMES END UP AS THE PUNCH LINES TO THE ENTIRE STORY, SO LET ME SHOW YOU WHAT I CAN DO! AND TO START US OFF, WE HAVE TO HAVE A TANUKI!

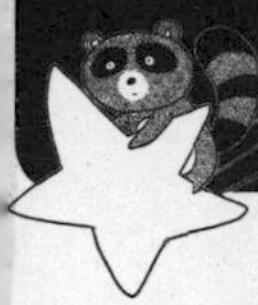

[ISSUE 2]

RIDING THE BIKE TOGETHER

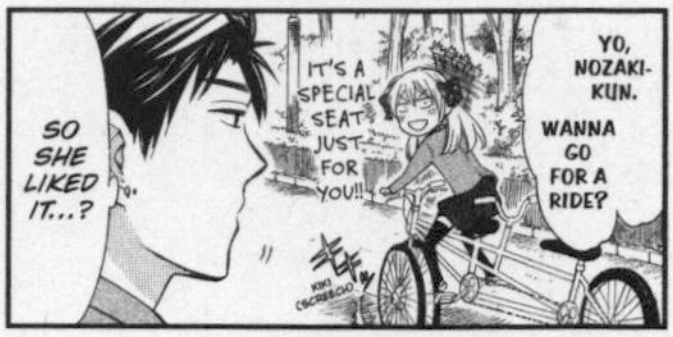
YO, NOZAKI-KUN.
WANNA GO FOR A RIDE?
IT'S A SPECIAL SEAT JUST FOR YOU!!
KIKI (SCREECH)
SO SHE LIKED IT...?

THERE'S A STRANGE DISTANCE BETWEEN THEM, BUT IT GOT SMALLER ON THE WAY HOME FROM SCHOOL.

[ISSUE 6]

THE APPEARANCE OF HORI-SENPAI, THE BACKGROUND ARTIST

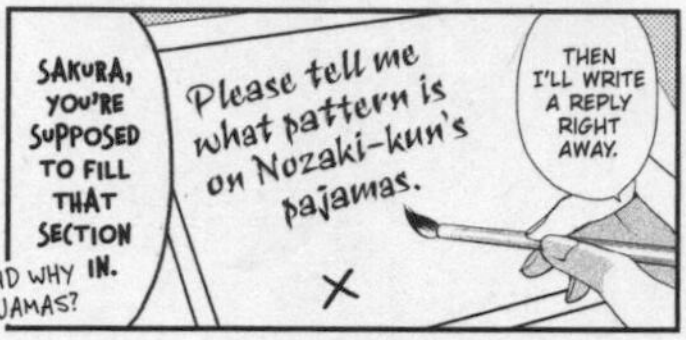
THEN I'LL WRITE A REPLY RIGHT AWAY.
Please tell me what pattern is on Nozaki-kun's pajamas.
SAKURA, YOU'RE SUPPOSED TO FILL THAT SECTION IN.
AND WHY PAJAMAS?

HER WORRIES GOT ALL COVERED UP FOR NOW.

[ISSUE 4]

THE APPEARANCE OF YUZUKI

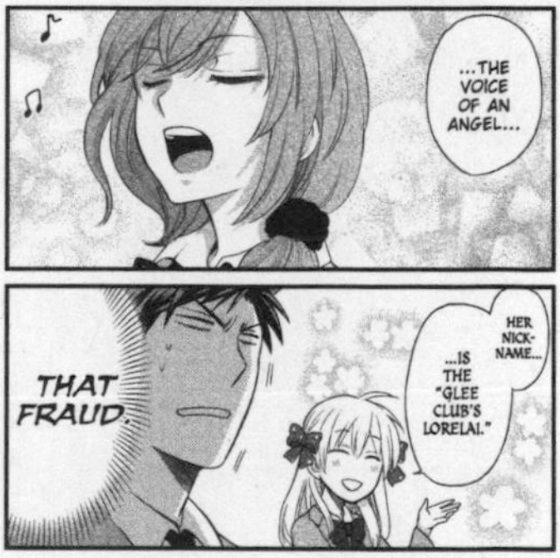
...THE VOICE OF AN ANGEL...
HER NICK-NAME...
...IS THE "GLEE CLUB'S LORELAI."
THAT FRAUD.

THE BEASTLY, DEVILISH ANGEL WITH THE BEAUTIFUL VOICE...

[ISSUE 19]

MIKOSHIBA MODELING FOR THE ART CLUB

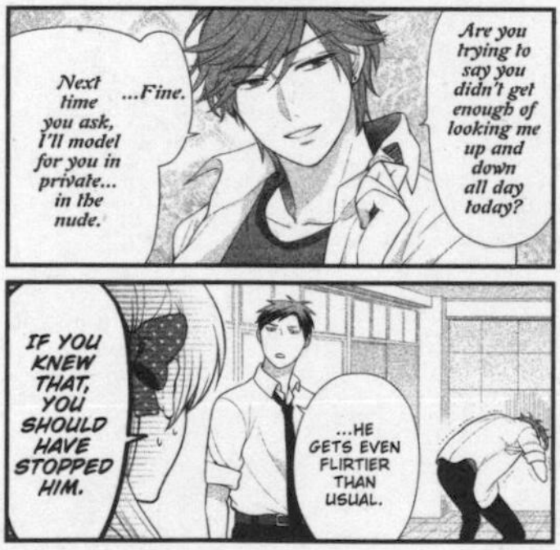
Are you trying to say you didn't get enough of looking me up and down all day today?
...Fine.
Next time you ask, I'll model for you in private... in the nude.
...HE GETS EVEN FLIRTIER THAN USUAL.
IF YOU KNEW THAT, YOU SHOULD HAVE STOPPED HIM.

THE MOUTH IS THE ROOT OF ALL SHAME...

[ISSUE 25]

LORELAI'S TRUE IDENTITY IS...!?

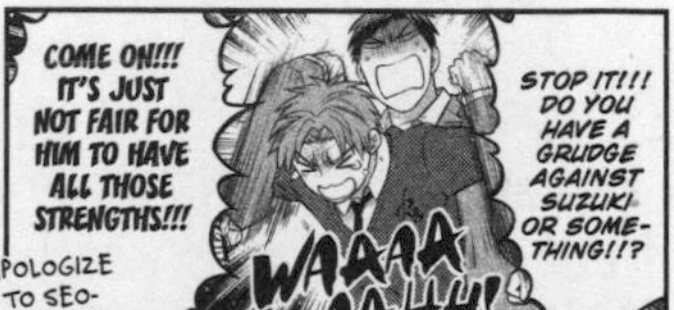
STOP IT!!! DO YOU HAVE A GRUDGE AGAINST SUZUKI OR SOME-THING!!?
COME ON!!! IT'S JUST NOT FAIR FOR HIM TO HAVE ALL THOSE STRENGTHS!!!
WAAAA AAHH!
APOLOGIZE TO SEO-SENPAI!!!

WAKAMATSU'S STRONG POINT → HIS INNOCENCE. HIS WEAK POINT → HE'S TOO INNOCENT.

[ISSUE 27]

MIKOSHIBA AND YUZUKI'S FIRST MEETING

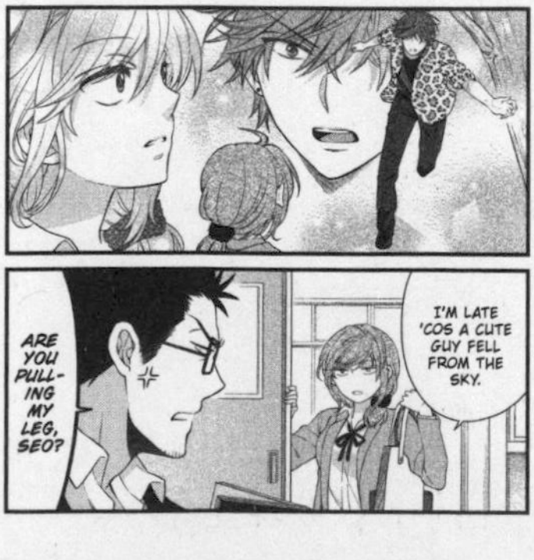
I'M LATE 'COS A CUTE GUY FELL FROM THE SKY.
ARE YOU PULL-ING MY LEG, SEO?

FATED ENCOUNTER.

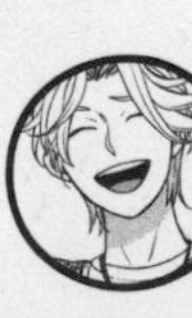

WELL? HAVE YOU GOTTEN A GOOD IDEA OF WHAT I DO? WE HERE AT *GIRLS' ROMANCE* ARE WAITING FOR YOUR SUBMISSIONS! IF YOU BRING IT IN YOURSELF, YOU MIGHT GET LUCKY AND MEET ME. ANYWAY, SEE YOU NEXT TIME!